THINKING
ABOUT THINKING

THINKING
ABOUT
THINKING

BY

JOAN

WYNN

REEVES

GEORGE BRAZILLER · NEW YORK

Printed in Great Britain

SIMON, CAMILLA AND ELIZABETH
PIETER, BARBARA, DUK
AND
ATHOS

CONTENTS

ACKNOWLEDGEMENTS

I WOULD like to thank the following: Professor D. W. Harding for suggesting inquiry into Binet's work and for allowing use of his own ideas in Chapters Ten and Eleven; Dr. W. E. Delp for her interest, and her invaluable help in translating German; Miss M. T. Slocombe for skilled and timely aid in translating Binet and in checking the proofs; Miss G. Blunt and Miss Penelope Brown for help with the typing. None of these are responsible for misunderstandings or mistakes that remain. Other colleagues and friends have assisted in various ways; they include Professor H. B. Acton, Miss M. E. Atkinson and Mrs. B. E. Laycock. My father, in his eighties, read the section on chess players and provided the illustration on p. 207. The publishers have been patient during the author's struggles with intractably difficult material.

The publishers join me in thanking the following for their permission to use certain extracts in this text:

George Allen & Unwin Ltd. for quotations from R. S. Peters' edition of G. S. Brett's *History of Psychology* and James Strachey's edition of Sigmund Freud's *The Interpretation of Dreams*; The Hutchinson Publishing Group and Professor H. H. Price for extracts from *Thinking and Experience*; Chatto & Windus Ltd. and Professor D. W. Harding for extracts from *Experience into Words*; J. M. Dent & Sons Ltd. for extracts from their Everyman Library Editions of *John Locke* and of Sir Francis Galton's *Inquiries into Human Faculty*; The Hogarth Press for extracts from the Standard Edition of Freud's Complete Psychological Works, revised and edited by James Strachey; Oxford University Press for extracts from C. E. Osgood's *Method and Theory in Experimental Psychology*; Macmillan and Co. Ltd. for extracts from C. Spearman's *The Abilities of Man*.

CHAPTER ONE

INTRODUCTION

THIS IS a book of exploratory essays on approaches to thinking. The central topic is the relation of processes of an associative kind (sometimes irrational, in so far as they are not enmeshed with a world of shared experience) to those involving some degree of reference to a common world and hence forming the basis of constructive, critical and logical thought.

This theme runs through a good deal of current psychological controversy. It is a very old theme that has been dealt with many times and in many ways in the course of its history. One might have chosen to discuss approaches to it other than those considered in the present volume. These, however, have been selected for their bearing on one another, and because they form an interesting part of the background to contemporary psychological theory.

Most people are well aware that during the past fifty or sixty years there have been moves, on the part of varied disciplines, away from a 'picture' and towards a 'process' conception of thinking. And in some cases thinking has come to be treated as analogous to action.

In the last quarter of the nineteenth century it was still possible to approach thinking from a standpoint characterized by one or more of the following five assumptions. First, thinking should be studied by seeking the 'elements' into which its content might be analysed. Secondly, these elements were mainly ideas and images. The latter, if one belonged to the empirical tradition, were treated either as copies of sensations, as originally suggested by Hobbes, or they were derived fairly directly from sensations. They might indeed be revived sensations. Thirdly, these sensations, ideas and images were 'presented' to the mind or treated as passing before the mind's eye, somewhat as in a species of internal theatre. Fourthly, the constituents of such thinking obeyed the laws of association by similarity, contrast and contiguity in time and place, or variants of these laws. All this implied, fifthly, that in some respects the thinker, in some cases passively and in others actively, scrutinized that which was 'before his mind'. Few authors, in fact, lost sight altogether of activity in thinking, those in the continental rationalist tradition least of all. But active thinking was sometimes treated almost casually in terms of focusing on or selecting ingredients germane to a purpose, — either without very much consideration of what constituted such relevance, or such 'rational' thought was hammered, if possible, into a framework of associationist assumptions. Witness to this last are parts of the curious argument between Spencer and John Stuart Mill on the relational thinking involved in the syllogism.

In short, in the empirical tradition at any rate, and in this tradition much early systematic psychologizing was rooted, interest tended to be focused on the content of thinking, sensation was considered a fundamental source of that content, and thinking, so far as it was an activity, approximated to some form of internal visual inspection. Ideas, images, their permutations and combinations constituted that which came under this conscious scrutiny.

This broad approach to thinking was the product of the English empirical tradition originating before John Locke, but given special impetus by his writing. As soon as one turns back to Locke himself, however, one begins to appreciate how much tradition omitted. So in discussing Locke in Chapter Two, I have followed scholars, such as R. I. Aaron,[1] in emphasizing the amount of 'rationality' Locke slipped in. Much of Locke's rationalism, together with his interest in language, was lost in the process of transmission and modification of his original outlook.

To the breakdown of an associationist approach at the turn of the last century and the beginning of our own, many complex causes contributed. In the background one can detect the influence of continental rationalism, to which, historically, Descartes in the seventeenth century (and Kant in the eighteenth) were probably the most influential contributors. But apart from his insistence on clear and distinct ideas, an insistence whose historical importance is hard to overestimate, Descartes' treatment of thinking is less interesting to a modern psychologist than that of Spinoza. So, Chapter Three has been devoted to Spinoza's views, considered in the context of modern controversies about conditioning and insight.

Aside from this and other general factors in the background, we can discern four mainly psychological trends contributing to the rejection of a simple associationist treatment of thought. First, are the complex interrelated factors, psychological and otherwise, that led eventually to the notion of unconscious functioning and thought. About this I have tried to say something historically in Chapter Four, following this in Chapter Five with a critical appreciation of certain aspects of Freud's approach in the light of its historical background and of later developments.

Secondly, is the emphasis on *active* perception, apperception and organization that is to be found in some nineteenth-century English writers, such as Ward and Stout, and to a certain extent in their continental contemporary Franz Brentano. From his work, it is possible to trace a historical link, as Professor Boring[2] has briefly shown, with writers such as Ehrenfels, Meinong and Cornelius, the early defenders of *Gestaltqualität*, who emphasized active perception of relation and form. Also in this tradition, though differing in some respects, are Wertheimer, Koffka and Köhler, the founders of modern Gestalt psychology, who stressed the active nature of perception and challenged the whole procedure of analysing thought into elements. Professor Hearnshaw[4] has considered the English work in his recent book *A Short History of British Psychology*. The development of Gestalt treatments of thinking can be traced in Ellis[3] and also in Henle.[5] Only brief comment has therefore been made in Chapter Nine on the much-debated issue of insight and learning on which Gestalt and behaviouristically-oriented psychologists have opposing views.

Only passing comment has also been made on the third important source of the downfall of associationism. This is the work of the Würzburg experimenters. Their studies of thinking, at the beginning of this century, produced evidence of selectivity in imaging, and of the effect, on the development of a train of thought, of the problem set, and of 'determining tendencies', which did not fall within an associationist framework. Their findings also suggested that much thinking was imageless, a viewpoint that became extremely controversial. Professor Humphrey,[6] in his invaluable survey of experimental studies of thinking, has dealt in detail with this work, but he mentions only in passing that of Binet and his colleagues in France.

Binet's work on closer scrutiny seems significant enough to constitute a fourth line of attack on simple associationism. It is particularly interesting in so far as Binet himself started as a loyal associationist and changed to something very different in the course of his own development. This aspect of his work has, moreover, been masked by his better-known contribution to intelligence testing. As many of his books are hard to obtain, and most of his articles untranslated, the long Chapter Seven has been devoted to restoring Binet to his historical position as an important and interesting contributor to studies of thinking, and the forerunner of Piaget. The bearing of studies of intelligence upon those of thinking has been sketched in the process.

Out of all this emerges the suggestion that in assimilating thinking to action and moving away from the inspectionist viewpoint, we must be careful not to throw away key processes such as recognition, without which it seems impossible to derive constructive, realistic and logical thinking from that which is governed by immediate stimulus and motive. In Chapter Ten, therefore, the move towards a dispositional treatment of conceptual thinking (which is involved in the move away from an inspectionist viewpoint) is discussed in the light of Professor Price's treatment of concepts and recognition in his *Thinking and Experience*. Since many current psychological studies of thinking adopt a dispositional view, Price's reflective study is of prime importance in grasping the theoretical issues in the background of such an approach. Chapter Eleven underlines the extent to which psychological treatments of thinking imply that it is the whole man who thinks when thinking is constructive. This involves us in speculation on the social psychological presuppositions of intelligibly formulated constructive thought.

REFERENCES

1. Aaron, R. I., *John Locke*, Oxford: Clarendon Press, 2nd edition, 1955.
2. Boring, E. G., *History of Experimental Psychology*, New York and London: Appleton Century, 2nd edition, 1950.
3. Ellis, W. D., *A Source Book of Gestalt Psychology*, New York: Harcourt Brace, 1939.
4. Hearnshaw, L. S., *A Short History of British Psychology*, London: Methuen, 1964.
5. Henle, M., *Documents of Gestalt Psychology*, Berkeley: University of California Press, 1961.
6. Humphrey, George, *Thinking: An Introduction to its Experimental Psychology*, London: Methuen, 1951.
7. Price, H. H., *Thinking and Experience*, London: Hutchinson, 1953.

CHAPTER TWO

JOHN LOCKE'S EMPIRICISM
AND ITS RATIONALITY

And all our yesterdays have lighted fools
The way to dusty death. Out, out, brief candle!
MACBETH

How far that little candle throws his beams!
So shines a good deed in a naughty world.
PORTIA

THE ENGLISH empirical tradition is usually traced back to Hobbes, who made the first systematic attempt to derive the content of knowledge from sense experience and who hazarded a physical basis for this on lines suggested by Galileo. To many people in the twentieth century, the fact that knowledge is acquired from sense experience, and is in no sense inborn, seems so obvious a proposition as to be hardly worth stating. Not so in the seventeenth, or, for that matter, in the first half of the eighteenth century, when support existed not only for some innate concepts, such as Descartes' idea of God, but also for innate foundations to logical and moral principles. Locke, profoundly liberal both politically and ethically, presented a challenge to the authoritarianism often latent in such a position. Largely on common-sense grounds, he was defending the rôle of the senses and learning in providing the *content* of psychological life, part of that content also being derived from reflection on our own psychological responses and activities. Since the context of Locke's discussion was epistemological, his emphasis was indeed on cognitive processes. To say that the content of knowledge is derived from experience, however, is not to deny that human beings are born with various capacities, e.g. to perceive, retain, discern, or compare. So Locke's empirical standpoint is not equivalent to accounting for the whole of psychological life in terms of the imprinting of sensations upon a receptive wax and their compounding in accordance with the laws of association. With this general statement about Locke's position let us look at his views in slightly more detail.

Having spent a whole book of the *Essay concerning Human Understanding* refuting the notion of innate ideas, Locke turns in Book 2 to his alternative account of the way in which the mind is furnished.

> Let us then suppose the mind to be, as we say, white paper, void of all characters, without any ideas: how comes it to be furnished? Whence comes it by that vast store, which the busy and boundless fancy of man has painted on it with an almost endless variety? Whence has it all the materials of reason and knowledge? To this I answer in one word, from experience; in that all our knowledge is founded, and from it ultimately derives itself.[4a]

According to Locke there are two main sources of experience, namely: sensation, and perception of the operation of our own minds, i.e. internal sense or reflection. External objects furnish the mind with ideas of sensible qualities, which are all those different perceptions these objects produce in us; the mind furnishes the understanding with ideas of its own operations. By sensation Locke understands: 'Such an impression or motion made in some part of the body, as produces some perception in the understanding.' In other words, under sensation he is not including the condition in which a stimulus impinges but is unnoticed. Simple ideas are the units both of sensation and reflection: the understanding once stored with these simple ideas has the power to repeat, compare and unite them to an almost infinite variety and so can make at pleasure new complex ideas. But it is 'not in the power of the most exalted wit or enlarged understanding, by any quickness or variety of thought', to invent or frame one new simple idea in the mind, not taken in by the ways already mentioned. As R. I. Aaron[1] has pointed out, Locke sometimes means by a 'simple idea' that which is primary in presentation, or in the face of which the mind's rôle is passive, and sometimes those units of sensation or reflection which are incapable of further analysis.

Simple ideas may come from one sense only. For example, colours via the sense of sight, and smells by the olfactory senses. Many of these shades and smells, as Locke remarks, have no names. Or they may come from diverse senses; for example, space or extension, figure, rest and motion, make perceivable impressions both visually and tactually. Or they may be derived by reflection upon the two principal actions of the mind, i.e. perception or thinking and volition or willing. Finally, simple ideas may be suggested both by sensation and reflection. Locke offers existence, unity, power and succession as examples of this last class. It is by no means clear how he thought that sensation and reflection co-operated in their production. But that one must leave.

Ideas, in the case of sensations, represent external objects and are neither identical with the properties of external objects nor in many cases do they resemble these properties; the latter are, in fact, powers in external objects to produce ideas in us. In the case of the primary qualities of objects—Locke gives varied lists of these, but solidity, extension, figure, mobility and occasionally number, are the main candidates—the ideas aroused in us resemble inherent properties of the objects that produce the ideas. In other cases, those of sensory or imputed qualities, ideas are produced in us by means of powers due to the insensible primary qualities of the external objects. Such powers are themselves derivative, so what we experience bears no resemblance to any inherent property of the object in question. To use Galileo's example, from which Locke's view is in part derived, motion would be a primary quality of external objects and what we experience both represents and is in principle similar to that which is going on in the object. In certain circumstances, however, motion in the object produces the sensation or sensory quality which we describe as heat. The power to produce that sensation in us is regarded by Locke as a secondary or imputed quality of the object. Locke has confused a good many people by using the words 'quality' and 'power' interchangeably when talking of the external objects, and then using the word 'quality' all over again to designate the character of what is sensed. It remains true that whether a so-called secondary quality designates what is sensed, e.g. warmth, or whether it designates, in effect, a derived relational property of the external object, it neither is nor resembles an inherent property of that object. Locke also refers to a third category of powers, namely 'barely powers', which seem to be causal properties of objects, such that in new relations to each other new sensations are produced in us. Firing something, for example, may alter its primary qualities and result in its producing in us different experiences of colour or consistency. But as Locke does not develop this suggestion very much, we can for the moment regard it as a side line which he did not follow in detail.

Now let us turn to the simple ideas of reflection. The mind in Locke's view is capable of operating on ideas received from sensation. And all these operations of the mind are, when reflected on, another set of ideas derived from that 'other source of our knowledge which I call reflection'. As we noted on p. 18, Locke, when first expounding this, mentions two 'great principal actions of the mind' namely 'perception or thinking, and volition or willing'. Whether he seriously wished to maintain that all the operations of the mind that he subsequently mentions in the *Essay* are modes of these two is not really clear. One supposes so. It is doubtful, however, if this matters very much as long as we remain quite clear that Locke thought the mind capable of quite a lot of operations. As usual he has varying lists. The following are the five basic cognitive operations he discusses in any detail.

First there is perception. Here Locke seems to be using the word in its modern sense (or if the historically-minded reader prefers, we still use the word in Locke's sense) to exclude cases wherein there is a 'sufficient impulse' but no observation by the mind. On the other hand, Locke expressly includes situations in which the interpretation of raw sensations has been learned. In this connexion there arises what is known to philosophers as Molyneux's problem. Molyneux, Locke's personal friend and correspondent, asked whether a man born blind, and later having his sight restored, would be able to differentiate visually the circle and the square that he had learned to differentiate by touch. Locke's answer, so far supported by von Senden's[7] and by other twentieth-century empirical findings, was 'no'. Such differentiation would have to be learned. The blind man, however, would come to *perceive* the difference after sighted experience.

Retention is the second of the mind's operations. Locke subdivides this into (*a*) contemplation, or the keeping of something actually in view for some time, and (*b*) memory, by which he means recall and retention in their modern senses. To the latter he tries to give a surprisingly 'operational' twist by arguing that, since ideas are *actual* perceptions, to say that they are laid up in memory means only that perception of them can be revived, with the additional perception that the mind 'has had them before'. Locke has been criticized, justly, for an inadequate treatment of memory; he has little to say on the sustained process of contemplation. But, reflecting on degrees of attention, on reverie and dreaming, and on sound sleep 'closing the scene', Locke inferred that thinking was probably 'the action, not essence of the soul'. This and allied comments were anti-Cartesian. Locke's reference to contemplation appears natural when sustained meditation was still a part of living tradition. This interesting activity seems to have slipped from the main line of psychological interest with the passing of the religious outlook to which it was integral; that is, with the rise of the 'natural' and 'reasonable' attitude to religion, to which Locke's writing, whether intentionally or not, contributed much. But to justify this bit of historical speculation is outside my competence and the scope of this chapter. The fact remains, as we shall realize more fully in Chapters Seven and Ten, the capacity to 'think' in a rewarding sense seems to require not a little skill in keeping data, and several lines of thought, actively in mind long enough for their mutual implications to be developed associatively, logically, or both. This capacity, characteristic of contemplation or meditation in its literary and religious context, has tended to be neglected by psychologists.

Locke's third operation of the mind is discerning or distinguishing, which he refers to as 'this clear discerning faculty of the mind, whereby it perceives two ideas to be the same or different'.[4a] With his usual casualness, he adds the absolutely fundamental point that this capacity is basic to reason and judgment. He makes use of it at the perceptual level, and again when, in the process of discussing reasoning, he points out quite correctly that the much-vaunted validity of deductive reasoning depends on each link in the chain of reasoning being clearly discerned. The more one reads Locke, the more one endorses the opinion of Aaron that to treat Locke as maintaining a narrowly sensationalistic epistemology is a profound mistake.

The remaining 'operations' recognized by Locke are 'comparison', i.e. the capacity to compare one idea with another in respect of extent, degree, time, place or any other circumstances, and, lastly, 'composition' whereby simple ideas from sensation or reflection are put together into complex ones. Again, Locke does not amplify or adequately illustrate what he means, so he lays himself open, irrevocably, to the charge of an atomistic and additive conception of at least some mental functioning.

The five capacities, thus listed, are introduced by Locke in discussing ideas of reflection. Though *qua* operations they are active, he thought that the mind was 'passive' in relation to them, in that it could not invent such operations itself. Nor, in Locke's view, could it have any idea which did not wholly consist of the simple ideas of sensation and reflection hitherto mentioned. Elsewhere in the *Essay*, Locke proceeds, however, to talk about acts of the mind and he leaves one perplexed about the relation of these 'acts' to the operations just discussed. The first-mentioned 'act' appears to coincide with the operation called composition, except that it is now called combining. The second 'act' doesn't get a name but is described as: '. . . bringing two ideas, whether simple or complex, together, and setting them one by another, so as to take a view of them at once, without uniting them into one'.[4a] It leads, Locke believes, to ideas of relations. It looks remarkably like contemplation and comparison operating together. But, equally, it could be sustained perception with a bit of comparison thrown in. It could well involve the recognition included under 'discerning'. Psychologically, it is by no means easy, again, to be sure what

Locke intended. The third 'act' is called by Locke 'abstraction' and involves 'separating them [ideas] from all other ideas that accompany them in their real existence' (*loc. cit.*). For Locke, this is the means whereby all general ideas are made.

It is time to pause for a moment and scrutinize Locke's usage of the terms 'mind' and 'idea'. Aaron has drawn the only possible conclusion when he treats Locke's usage of 'mind' as irretrievably ambiguous. Sometimes it means the container in which ideas are to be found succeeding each other, at a speed which, Locke conjectures, must be relatively constant for perception to take place at all:

> I leave it to others to judge, whether it be not probable that all our ideas do, whilst we are awake, succeed one another in our minds at certain distances, not much unlike the images in the inside of a lantern, turned round by the heat of a candle. This appearance of theirs in train, though perhaps it may be sometimes faster and sometimes slower, yet, I guess, varies not very much in a waking man: there seem to be certain bounds to the quickness and slowness of the succession of those ideas one to another in our minds, beyond which they can neither delay nor hasten.[4a]

On the other hand, sometimes the mind, for Locke, takes on the rôle of the candle rather than the lantern, a candle which, as we have just seen, is capable of various kinds of illumination, and, moreover, of reflecting its own lighting methods. Candles crop up more than once in the *Essay*. Locke must have often written by their light and one is tempted at times to compare his vision of the mind to that of a Georges de la Tour, symbolic candle and all. But though Locke, as a doctor, will have handled plenty of skulls in his day, temperamentally he is extremely matter-of-fact; one cannot quite imagine him meditating on the skull, also characteristic of seventeenth-century contemplative painting, except as an empirical scientist inescapably aware of the limitations of human knowledge.

What of 'ideas'? Ryle[6] in his Tercentenary Address on Locke, in 1932, distinguished five main senses of the word: (1) sense data or sensible qualities as experienced in the mind, (2) images, (3) acts of thinking, (4) as a paraphrase for 'notions' or 'conceptions', e.g. 'considering x as being an elephant' or even the 'character of being something' such as an elephant, (5) obscure 'contents' or entities which are in the mind as if it were a container. There seems to be no doubt that all these five senses of the word 'idea' are to be found in Locke. All one can say, in defence of him, is that the context or the argument usually makes reasonably clear which sense was intended, and Locke had started off with apparent intention to use this term as widely as he could: 'It being that term which, I think, serves best to stand for whatsoever is the object of the understanding when a man thinks, I have used it to express whatever is meant by *phantasm, notion, species*, or whatever it is which the mind can be employed about in thinking.' As Aaron points out, 'thinking' is here 'used widely to cover all possible cognitive activities'.

For understanding both Locke himself and his position in the history of treatments of thinking, his assimilation of thought to perception is fundamental. It has three important aspects. The first is that Locke, taking for granted representative perception, often wrote as though ideas eked out a 'twilight existence' between the things they represent and the mind that thinks about them. This intermediate status of ideas has coloured modern objections to them. Secondly, given a wholly 'passive' account of perception, in terms of mere registration of stimuli, thinking could come to be viewed as an equally mechanical response, albeit of an indirect or mediating kind. Locke's insistence on 'acts' or 'operations' absolves him, but not some of his successors, from holding this view. Thirdly, however, given more emphasis on perceptual *activity*, then not only would a 'passive' account of thinking make little sense, but the way would open to treating thought, in a narrower usage than Locke's, as latent in perceptual processes from which it is gradually developed. Such a fully evolutionary view is not to be found in Locke; it is fundamental, however, to current writers such as Piaget. With this let us turn to Locke's famous and very relevant discussion of generalization.

Now that representatives of so many different disciplines are asking themselves questions about the nature and function of language, it is a matter of interest that, on his own confession, when Locke embarked on considering 'understanding' he had not expected problems of language to arise. By the end of Book 2 of the *Essay* he found himself immersed in these. Let us look at the important introduction he gives to the whole topic at the opening of Book 3.

1. God, having designed man for a sociable creature, made him not only with an inclination and under a necessity to have fellowship with those of his own kind, but furnished him also with language, which was to be the great instrument and common tie of society. Man therefore had by nature his organs so fashioned, as to be fit to frame articulate sounds, which we call words. But this was not enough to produce language; for parrots and several other birds, will be taught to make articulate sounds distinct enough, which yet by no means are capable of language.

2. Besides articulate sounds, therefore, it was further necessary that he should be able to use these sounds as signs of internal conceptions; and to make them stand as marks for the ideas within his own mind, whereby they might be made known to others, and the thoughts of men's minds be conveyed from one to another.

3. But neither was this sufficient to make words so useful as they ought to be. It is not enough for the perfection of language, that sounds can be made signs of ideas, unless those signs can be so made use of as to comprehend several particular things: for the multiplication of words would have perplexed their use, had every particular thing need of a distinct name to be signified by. To remedy this inconvenience, language had yet a further improvement in the use of *general terms*, whereby one word was made to mark a multitude of particular existences: which advantageous use of sounds was obtained only by the difference of the ideas they were made signs of: those names becoming general, which are made to stand for *general ideas*, and those remaining particular, where the *ideas* they are used for are *particular*.*[4b]

* This quotation is from Wilburn's *Everyman* edition of the *Essay*, as Pringle-Pattison omitted the reference to parrots, which makes Locke so much more interesting in the light of modern animal ethology and psychology.

Three points in this passage are worth special attention. First, the primary social rôle Locke gives to language. Secondly, his assumption that it fulfils that rôle by trafficking in ideas. Thirdly, his recognition that to do so it must involve an element of generality. Now what is Locke's account of how that generality is achieved? To answer this question let us start by summarizing Locke's own arguments.

All things that exist being particular, it would be reasonable to suppose that words are particular in their signification, i.e. that each word denotes a particular thing. But in fact the highest proportion of words in all languages are general in their reference, not by chance but for three main reasons:

(1) It is impossible that every particular thing should have a distinct peculiar name, because such denoting depends on a connexion being established between a distinct idea of a thing and a specific sign for it. Moreover, it is required that both this sign and its specific denotation are retained. But it is beyond the power of human capacity either to frame or to retain such distinct ideas and signs of all the particular things that exist. There are just too many of them.

(2) Even if such linguistic particularity had been possible, it would be useless for purposes of communication of thoughts, for, strictly, the sounds used by me apply to particular things falling under my notice. So unless someone else were acquainted with those same particular things, and the ideas thereof (which is impossible), he could not understand the signs I use.

(3) A distinct name for every particular thing would not be much use for extending knowledge, which depends on reducing things to sorts, which do not multiply every moment 'beyond what the mind can contain or use requires'.

It will be noted that in this argument, so far, Locke is extremely down-to-earth and practical, and at the root of his argument lies a psychological premise of an empirical nature about the limitations of discernment and retention. There is no good reason to query this premise. Now to return to Locke's main argument.

In fact, he asks, if all things that exist are particulars how do we come by general terms, or where do we find those general natures for which they are supposed to stand? His answer amounts to the following:

(1) Words become general by being made the signs of general ideas.

(2) Ideas become general by two main processes. The first is by subtracting from a particular idea the circumstances of time and place and any other ideas that may determine it to this or that particular existence. Locke does not elaborate on the phrase 'any other ideas' in this context, but in view of what he says about the particularity of names of individual people, ownership by a specific person would seem to be a likely example. Secondly, by this process of subtraction, called by Locke abstraction, an idea is made capable of representing more individuals than one, that is to say those of the same *sort*, i.e. individuals each 'having in it a conformity' to the original idea, stripped of its particularity.

Locke numbered children among his close personal friends, and it was natural for him to turn to account the day-to-day examples of particularity in the use of words, of different usages from those of adults, and of fresh and humble generalization, that little children obligingly offer for scrutiny. All of these, in the context of Locke's insistence that, to have meaning, words must be able to be cashed in some sort of sense experience, can be seen in the following, together with Locke's somewhat 'additive' approach to verbal meaning.

A child having taken notice of nothing in the metal he hears called *gold*, but the bright shining yellow colour, he applies the word gold only to his own idea of that colour, and nothing else; and therefore calls the same colour in a peacock's tail gold. Another that hath better observed, adds to shining yellow great weight: and then the sound gold, when he uses it, stands for a complex idea of a shining yellow and very weighty substance. Another adds to those qualities fusibility: and then the word gold signifies to him a body, bright, yellow, fusible and very heavy. Another adds malleability. Each of these uses equally the word gold, when they have occasion to express the idea which they have applied it to: but it is evident that each can apply it only to his own idea; nor can he make it stand as a sign of such a complex idea as he has not.[4b]

Commenting again on the particularity in the reference of initial word usage, Locke says that children's

. . . ideas of the nurse and the mother are well framed in their minds; and, like pictures of them there, represent only those individuals. The names they first gave to them are confined to these individuals. . . . Afterwards, when time and a larger acquaintance have made them observe that there are a great many other things in the world, that in some common agreements of shape and several other qualities, resemble their father and mother, and those persons they have been used to, they frame an idea, which they find those many particulars do partake in; and to that they give, with others, the name *man* for example. And thus they come to have a general name and a general idea. Wherein they make nothing new; but only leave out of the complex idea they had of Peter and James, Mary and Jane, that which is peculiar to each, and retain only what is common to them all.[4b]

This passage of the *Essay*, and others related to it, have given rise to endless controversy; for it is by no means clear what the children are doing when 'they frame an *idea* [my italics] which they find those many particulars do partake in'. The presence of a single, even if complex, image will not fill the bill. Berkeley,[3] in criticizing Locke, restricted Locke's usage of 'idea' to meaning image, and then pointed out that a general image is impossible to conceive. We may agree with Berkeley in this respect, while realizing the irrelevance of his main contention. In Chapter Seven we shall find the comments of actual children on this point. Meanwhile, it is not impossible that they might have a fluctuating series or network of images of people, and of people functioning. In the given example, auditory, tactile, kinaesthetic and olfactory as well as visual images, together with incipient and actual motor and emotional responses, might well constitute the core of what the children have in mind. The modern psychologist would be tempted to

designate that to which the children's use of the term 'man'
refers as a 'concept'. But this by itself goes only a little way
towards explaining how generality creeps in. It can go a little
way if a particular term, linked with fluctuating series of
images, is used to refer to 'this or that or that'. This leaves us
with the question of the limits of the series. In other words, how
and why does this particular collection of images and responses
of various kinds get grouped together?

Now although Locke sometimes used the word 'idea' for a
quite specific sensation or image, e.g. of a shade of yellow, he
never restricted his usage to this. So considering his insistence
on the fact that 'universality belongs not to things themselves
which are all of them particular in their existence, even those
words and ideas which in their significance are general', it was
unfair of Berkeley to accuse him of believing in such oddities as
'general images'. 'Words', writes Locke, 'are general when used
for signs of general ideas, and so are applicable indifferently to
many particular things; and ideas are general when they are
set up as the representatives of many particular things. . . .'[4b]
That is to say, any given word or idea is existentially particular
and may have generality of reference; much as though a given
function of a variable could in certain circumstances act as a
representative of others. Locke is quite emphatic on the point
that the general nature of what remains when we quit particulars 'is nothing but the capacity they are put into, by the
understanding of signifying or representing many particulars.
For the signification they have is nothing but a relation that,
by the mind of man, is added to them.'[4b] In short, generality
lies not in ideas or words as such but in their use. Moreover, to
return momentarily to the little child and 'gold', it is clear
that the word may be used with varying complexity of reference, e.g. to the child's shining yellow or to 'a body bright,
yellow, fusible and very heavy'. Locke is emphatic that, in
either case, the usage, though referring to what *the user* has in
mind, is coloured by his assuming that the words evoke similar
meaning for others and that the '*words stand for the reality of
things*' (Locke's italics).

It is at this point that we stumble upon one of the most
original arguments in the whole *Essay* (Bk. III. 3). This shows

Locke struggling, three hundred years ahead of his time, with the notion that, although the ingredients of the world, by virtue of varying degrees of similarity, lend themselves to various kinds of classification, the actual classification imposed upon them is man-made and, particularly obvious in border-line cases, it has an element of the arbitrary and the con-venient. This represented a direct revolt on Locke's part against the doctrine of fixed essences, current at the time and, in the hands of Cuvier, still making a profound nuisance of itself to biology more than a hundred years later.

That Locke was struggling towards the conception of a word or an image functioning as the signpost of a variable, the other values of which were determined not by the existence of fixed 'essences' and 'species', but by mankind finding it convenient to group particular things with varying degrees of similarity into 'sorts', seems to be clear from the succeeding paragraphs.

That then which general words signify is a *sort* of things; and each of them [i.e. general words] does that, by being a sign of an abstract idea in the mind; to which idea, as things existing are found to agree, so they come to be ranked under that name, or, which is all one, be of that sort. Whereby it is evident that the *essences* of the sorts, or, if the Latin word pleases better, *species* of things, are nothing but these abstract ideas. . . . the abstract idea for which the name stands, and the essence of the species is one, and the same. From whence it is easy to observe, that the essences of the sorts of things, and, consequently, the sort-ing of things, is the workmanship of the understanding that abstracts and makes those general ideas.

I would not here be thought to forget, much less to deny, that nature, in the production of things, makes several of them alike: there is nothing more obvious, especially in the races of animals, and all things propagated by seed. But yet I think we may say, *the sorting of them under names is the workmanship of the understanding, taking occasion, from the similitude it observes amongst them, to make abstract general ideas.*[4b]

Now by 'abstract idea', in the phrase 'to which idea as things

existing in themselves are found to agree', Locke could mean,
possibly, an image used as an exemplar of a sort. By the end
of the paragraph it is harder to interpret 'idea' in this way;
particularly as the wider context of his discussion makes clear
that Locke is thinking in biological terms, even if the factual
content of his biology rings queerly in our ears.

> . . . in all the visible and corporeal world, we see no
> chasms or gaps. All quite down from us the descent is by
> easy steps, and a continued series of things, that in each
> remove differ very little one from the other. There are
> fishes that have wings, and are not strangers to the airy
> region: and there are some birds that are inhabitants of
> the water, whose blood is cold as fishes, and their flesh is
> so like in taste that the scrupulous are allowed them on
> fish-days. There are animals so near of kin both to birds
> and beasts, that they are in the middle between both:
> amphibious animals link the terrestrial and aquatic to-
> gether; seals live at land and at sea, and porpoises have
> the warm blood and entrails of a hog, not to mention what
> is confidently reported of mermaids, or sea-men. There
> are some brutes that seem to have as much knowledge and
> reason as some that are called men: and the animal and
> vegetable kingdoms are so nearly joined, that if you will
> take the lowest of one and the highest of the other, there
> will scarce be perceived any great difference between
> them; and so on, till we come to the lowest and most
> inorganical parts of matter, we shall find everywhere that
> the several species are linked together, and differ but in
> almost insensible degrees.[4a]

In fairness to Locke, we must note that his mermaids and
sea-men are only 'confidently reported' and he has a threefold
purpose in the discussion from which this passage comes. He
wishes, first, to consign the notion of fixed real essences to
limbo, and, second, to stress how little is known of these supposed 'real essences'.

> Nor indeed can we rank and sort things, and consequently
> (which is the end of sorting) denominate them, by their
> real essences, because we know them not. Our faculties

carry us no further towards the knowledge and distinction of substances than a collection of those sensible ideas which we observe in them; which however made with the greatest diligence and exactness we are capable of, yet is more remote from the true internal constitution from which these qualities flow, than . . . a countryman's idea is from the inward contrivance of that famous clock at Strasbourg, whereof he only sees the outward figure and motions.[4a]

Locke's third purpose, in this context, is to argue that although the doctrine (fundamentally of Platonic origin) of real and fixed essences is not acceptable, nevertheless things do have properties by virtue of which they lend themselves to being sorted. The criteria we use for sorting are sometimes such that in effect we create a species or a concept in the process. In this case, the 'real essence' and the 'nominal essence', i.e. the constituents used by mankind for justifying this designation rather than that, coincide. But because of our ignorance and of the probabilistic status of empirical scientific knowledge on the one hand, and, on the other, of the undoubted resemblances of things, there is a discrepancy, in some cases, between the 'nominal' and 'real' essence. So that things that really go together are often not so classed by us and we make a class of things that are 'really' different.

Though it has caused considerable difficulty, this position of Locke's does not strike the modern scientific reader as particularly obscure, so far as it goes, but there are profoundly difficult questions underlying the surface, to which we shall draw attention in Chapter Ten. Locke is open to the obvious criticism that having (with reason) thrown away the classical doctrine of fixed essences, he does not go on to discuss the criteria he would use for deciding that a man-made classification should be changed to conform better with nature's division. He can, however, be completely absolved from supposing that there are no natural 'sorts' to be discovered. To talk of essences of species as 'the workmanship of the understanding taking occasion from the similitude it observes among things to sort them under names', does not deny but presupposes, according to Locke, that 'nature in the production of things makes several of them alike'. Moreover, 'it is past doubt that there must be some real constitution on which any collection of simple ideas coexisting must depend'. But for Locke it is possible to have two views about the nature of this constitution. The one, that of fixed essences or species, he cannot accept, primarily, in fact, on biological grounds. The other is that things have a 'genuine but unknown constitution of their insensible parts'. There he stops, not inconsistently in view of his doctrine of representative perception. Modern science has proceeded on the assumption that by experimental methods, mathematics and refined aids to observation from electron microscopes onwards, a vast amount could be inferred, with reasonable probability, about that which Locke was right to consider as largely unknown.

From this long but necessary digression into 'essences', let us return to the problem of how words become general. By standing, it is said, for 'general ideas'. After this discussion we can surely dismiss the travesty of Locke which suggests that a general idea was a 'general image' of simple ideas at their simplest, spectres, as it were, of flashes, clashes and pin-pricks, or images corresponding to sensations, in turn supposedly simple because too transitory to analyse. Without knowledge of Locke's own imagery we cannot admit or deny the possibility that he may have conceived a general idea as a fluctuating series of images, of varying degrees of similarity either in one respect or to one image taken as an exemplar. Aaron suggested long ago and rightly, so it seems, that Locke oscillated between a common element, or common internal relation treatment of the basis of generalization, and that which takes the notion of a class, constituted by similarity to an exemplar, as fundamental.* For example, if Locke had been asked to fill in a Galtonian questionnaire about breakfast (see Chapter Six), would he have recognized the class of feasts to be considered as that having the common element of being the first meal of the day? Or would he have visualized a breakfast table, complete with a beautiful seventeenth-century coffee pot on the right, blue and white cups and saucers, steaming home-made bread, farmhouse butter in a blue dish, silver cutlery and a mackerel?

* For further consideration of what this involves see Chapter Ten.

And would he then have treated this complex image as one representative of the class breakfasts, to which other breakfasts approximate—in various degrees of remoteness? He would not, we can be sure, have built up the class through the common element derived from fleeting gustatory images of marmalade. But this is for historical not logical reasons. In either case, though Locke avoids the pitfall, into which so many modern writers fall, of not letting in the universal designated by 'similarity', his account of generalization leaves us wondering just what we have got to admit in order to make the notion of x standing for 'this or that or that' work. Degrees of similarity, and the power to recognize and respond to them, seem essential presuppositions of generalization.

As many people know full well, Locke's viewpoint, particularly his stress on experiential roots to the content of knowledge, was fundamental to the empirical tradition that has lasted in one form or another till now. Locke's thinking directly affected the approach of those following him in the eighteenth century, such as Berkeley, Hume and Hartley, whether or not they agreed on other major or minor aspects of his position as a whole. His views gained currency in France, due in part to Voltaire, and are again reflected in eighteenth-century writers such as Helvétius and Condillac.

In the process of historical transmission, the sensory elementarism implicit in Locke's treatment of simple ideas of sensation was sharpened, in the sense in which Bartlett,[2] and other psychologists after him, apply this term to disproportionate emphasis in remembering, and to the comparable accentuation of items in the content of rumours in the course of their transmission. Similarly, the active cognitive processes, sometimes called by Locke 'acts of the mind', were levelled, by the temptation to treat thinking in terms of ingredients of sensory origin, presented to or passing before the mind's eye, and ordered and re-ordered in accordance with the laws of association. To this temptation, James Mill and Taine seem to have fallen. Writers in the empirical tradition varied, however, in their insistence on similarity, contrast and contiguity in time and place as affecting association. Some, for example Hartley, tried to reduce all kinds of association to contiguity, and invoked

Newtonian vibrations, translated into physiological terms, as a basis for them. Others, as Herbert Spencer, gave much more weight to the assimilation of feelings and relations to those *like* them and, in addition, discussed the whole topic from an evolutionary standpoint. Those retaining similarity tended to retain recognition and relational thought. There was variation, too, in stress on feeling and emotion and on the thinker's active structuring of his empirically-derived ideas. Bain, for example, stressed the rôle of interest and emotion and invoked 'constructive imagination' as of importance in thought. Though, as Price has argued, it is false, historically, to suppose that writers in the empirical tradition nurtured a wholly passive and mechanical conception of thought, it remains broadly true that those in the continental rationalist tradition that assumed the existence, in some form, of innate ideas laid more stress on the structuring and relating processes in thinking. In both traditions, thought was often assimilated to vision, which is hardly surprising, in so far as 'idea' comes from the Greek ἰδεῖν, to see.

During the late nineteenth and early twentieth centuries, as we have already suggested, this inspectionist approach to thinking came under attack. Locke's almost casual assumption that recognition underlay thinking was often lost sight of; as, for example, in Freud's early insistence on unconscious functioning and motivation. By contrast, in Binet's work, to which French and English empiricism, continental rationalism and empirical inquiry all contributed, this active recognizing process was retained. There, as we shall see in Chapter Seven, it formed part of an active, selective and developmental approach to thinking which made its own contribution to reversing the *relatively* passive, sensory, associationist trend, already mentioned. Indeed Piaget's, the one sustained attempt to give, on the basis of empirical inquiry, a systematic account of thought development from primitive assimilation and accommodation to high logicality, is historically related to Binet's work, via that of Claparède. It belongs in this fused empirical/rational tradition, supported by observation and experiment.

With this broad indication of those of Locke's views that were retained, rejected, or ultimately woven into a new continental psychological tradition, let us look at one representative seventeenth-century rationalist, Spinoza, to see if any of his concepts also help us to grasp more clearly what underlies our thinking about thinking now.

REFERENCES

Numbers in brackets indicate the pages in this book where
given references occur

1. Aaron, R. I., *John Locke*, Oxford: Clarendon Press, 2nd edition, 1955.

2. Bartlett, F. C., *Remembering*, London: Cambridge University Press, 1932.

3. Berkeley, George, *The Principles of Human Knowledge*, edited by T. E. Jessop, London: Nelson, 1942.

4. Locke, John, *An Essay Concerning Human Understanding*, edited (a) by Pringle-Pattison, Oxford: Clarendon Press, 1934, pp. 42 (17), 85 (21), 93 (21), 108–9 (22), 246 (31), 247–8 (30).
   (*b*) by Raymond Wilburn, London: J. M. Dent, Everyman Library, 1947, pp. 201–2 (24), 205 (26), 208–9 (27), 210 (28), 211 (29).

5. Ryle, Gilbert, *The Concept of Mind*, London: Hutchinson, 1949.

6. ——*Locke on the Human Understanding*, Tercentenary Addresses, London: Oxford University Press, 1933.

7. Senden, N. von, *Space and Sight: the perception of space and shape in the congenitally blind before and after operation*, translated by P. Heath, with Appendices by A. H. Riesen, G. J. Warnock and J. Z. Young, London: Methuen, 1960.

CHAPTER THREE

SPINOZA'S TREATMENT OF THINKING IN RELATION TO MODERN APPROACHES

Vivere est cogitare
CICERO

SPINOZA'S TREATMENT of thinking is based on a distinction of more than historical interest. On the one hand, there is understanding or knowledge which may indeed be valid but which is fundamentally 'inadequate' because derived from a process of association or conditioning. On the other, there is understanding or knowledge at the roots of which lie either deductive inference or insight. Underlying this main distinction there is, I believe, an attempt on Spinoza's part to suggest that, whereas from the point of view of its content no thought process can have unquestionable validity, there are yet some thought processes (irrespective of content) beyond whose presumptive validity we cannot go—because we are face to face with intelligence in action and this is presupposed in any further argument. That Spinoza found difficulty in either exemplifying or stating the criteria by which processes of inherent validity could be recognized, goes without question. The fact remains that the possibility of there being at least two types of thought process, one of which obeys the general rules roughly designated as those of association or conditioning, and one of which does not, remains a burning question at the core not only of experimental and genetic psychology but of current speculation in many fields. It is extremely interesting to look at the greatest of the seventeenth-century attempts to come to grips with this topic.

Spinoza's account of thinking is embedded in his metaphysics and certain aspects of this must be recalled to mind before we can appreciate why his treatment of thinking is so important. While, however, some grasp of his general position is needed for understanding Spinoza's views on thinking, the latter, in my opinion, do not stand or fall with his metaphysics, against which a good deal of criticism can be levelled. For example, it rests on a subject-predicate logic, and although Spinoza is profoundly interested, psychologically, in the causes of erroneous judgment, it is hard to see how, in his system as a whole, errors could arise. We need, therefore, to concentrate on the psychological interest of what he says.

Spinoza sees the universe as a system, self-determined and determining according to rationally-conceived natural laws. Viewed in terms of extension, or its spatial attributes, it may be regarded as matter. Viewed in terms of the rational thinking he believes inherent in such a system, it may be regarded as mind. Mind and matter are then, in effect, two great frames of reference applicable in understanding a universe which, for Spinoza, is identified with God and is divine. Individuals, broadly, sub-systems of varying degrees of complexity, can be treated in relative (never complete) isolation from the system as a whole. Such individuals can also be viewed from the physical or the mental frame of reference. Part of what is meant by calling such a sub-system an individual is that it tends to persist as such as long as it can. The core of this effort of self-preservation is designated *conatus*. Man is one among other individual entities all of which are animate in differing degrees. He is, in fact, a system of a level of complexity that can undergo considerable modification in response to external or internal changes without disintegrating. Writing of *conatus* in man, Spinoza says in *Ethics* 3, ix, Scholium:

This effort, when it is related to the mind alone, is called *will*, but when it is related at the same time both to the mind and the body, is called *appetite*, which is therefore nothing but the very essence of man, from the nature of which necessarily follow those things which promote his preservation, and thus he is determined to do those things. Hence there is no difference between appetite and desire, unless in this particular, that desire is generally related to men in so far as they are conscious of their appetites, and it may therefore be defined as appetite of which we are conscious. From what has been said it is plain, therefore, that we neither strive for, wish, seek, nor desire anything because we think it to be good, but, on the contrary, we adjudge a thing to be good because we strive for, wish, seek or desire it.[3]

Though it may be obvious, perhaps one should emphasize that for Spinoza this is not equivalent to supposing man to be an altogether passively-driven entity, whose actions (physical aspect) and thoughts (mental aspect) are determined by desires wholly divorced from thought processes of any kind. Nor is man determined *in toto* by external circumstances outside his control. It is of the essence of man to be partly active and partly passive. Complete self-determination is predictable only of the universe in its entirety. Man's capacity for self-determination is limited to the extent to which his actions, by following logically from clear ideas as to himself and his situation at any given moment, in fact partake in the overall rational activity of the universe. Of necessity, most of men's ideas are not adequate, i.e. clear in the sense just indicated, and their corresponding actions not self-determined. But implied in Spinoza's whole attitude and purpose in writing is the belief that while men believe themselves to be wholly 'free', they are in fact more influenced by inadequate ideas, and are therefore more at the mercy of internal and external circumstances, than they need be. In our own age, which all too readily accepts the rather muddle-headed version of determinism that leaves out the individual's own contribution to affairs, it is this last implication of Spinoza's view that needs stress.

For Spinoza, man's 'blessedness' increases in proportion to his increasing appreciation, emotionally and intellectually, of his humble, not entirely inactive, position in a universe self-determined according to rational natural law. In so far as his actions follow logically from a grasp of the situation as it is, he can play a more active rôle in this universe. The process of increasing vitality, thus involved, constitutes joy; sorrow consists of the process of reversion to the passive. Spinoza, unlike

Freud, whose general position resembles his in many subtle ways, saw the desire that springs from joy as stronger (other things being equal) than that which springs from sorrow. Austere as is the stoical tradition to which it belongs, Spinoza's version of determinism offers to man no facile rationalization for avoiding responsibility for what he does. For Spinoza, it is man's true nature to endeavour to think clearly and act accordingly. So much for the broad context. Now let us look a little more closely at Spinoza's discussion of thought processes, adequate and inadequate.

Spinoza's main accounts of understanding (it is convenient for the moment to use this rather general term) are to be found in the treatise *On the Improvement of Understanding* and in the *Ethics*. Both accounts attempt to distinguish degrees of understanding (or perception) in terms of inherent validity or susceptibility to error. In the *Improvement of Understanding* Spinoza distinguishes four grades. They are:

First degree. 'Perception arising from hearsay or from some sign which everyone may name as he pleases.' It is exemplified here by knowing the date of one's birth or one's parentage. The example seems more convincing, superficially, if one remembers that in seventeenth-century Holland such matters will not have been registered.

Second degree. 'Perception arising from mere experience—that is, from experience not yet classified by the intellect, and only so called because the given event has happened to take place, and we have no contradictory fact to set against it, so that it therefore remains unassailed in our mind.' For example: 'By mere experience I know that I shall die, for this I can affirm from having seen that others like myself have died, though all did not live for the same period or die by the same disease. I know by mere experience that oil has the property of feeding fire, and water of extinguishing it.' The example may be puzzling unless it is understood that Spinoza is not saying anything about the actual truth or falsity of these beliefs, nor whether the facts in question could be known in another way. He is interested in the level of understanding implied. One could substitute the modern example of a cook who knows by mere experience that marinading a steak is likely to make it more tender. In so far as she has tried it out, and found it to work, her grasp is not at the hearsay level; but she has no inkling of how the effect is brought about.

Third degree. 'Perception arising when the essence of one thing is inferred from another, but not adequately; this comes when from some effect we gather its cause, or when it is inferred from some general proposition that some property is always present.' For example, 'after I have become acquainted with the nature of vision, and know that it has the property of making one and the same thing appear smaller when far off than when near, I can infer that the sun is larger than it appears, and draw other conclusions of the same kind'.

Fourth degree. 'Lastly, there is the perception arising when a thing is perceived solely through its essence, or through the knowledge of its proximate cause.' For example, 'we know that two and three make five, or that two lines each parallel to a third are parallel to one another'.

'In order', says Spinoza, 'that the whole matter may be put in a clearer light, I will make use of a single illustration as follows: Three numbers are given, it is required to find a fourth which shall be to the third as the second is to the first.' His exemplification of the four different ways of approaching this problem is stated very concisely. If I have understood him correctly, however, it amounts to the following: Perception of the first kind is illustrated by tradesmen who 'will at once tell us that they know what is required to find the fourth number, for they have not yet forgotten the rule which was given to them arbitrarily without proof by their masters'. Perception of the second kind is shown by those who 'construct a universal axiom from their experience with simple numbers, where the fourth number is self-evident, as in the case of 2, 4, 3, 6; here it is evident that if the second number be multiplied by the third, and the product divided by the first, the quotient is 6; when they see by this process the number is produced which they knew beforehand to be the proportional, they infer that the process always holds good for finding a fourth number proportionally'. According to Spinoza, however, mathematicians may approach the problem in two other ways exemplifying, respectively, the third and fourth levels of understanding.

They may 'know by the proof of the nineteenth proposition of the seventh book of Euclid, what numbers are proportionals, namely, from the nature and property of proportion it follows that the product of the first and fourth will be equal to the product of the second and third, still they do not see the adequate proportionality of the given numbers'. The implication is that 'if they do see it, they see it not by virtue of Euclid's proposition, but intuitively' without going through a process of inference. In which case, the level of understanding exemplifies Spinoza's fourth degree.

Once more, the point Spinoza is trying to make is rendered in some ways easier to grasp, but in others more difficult, through his choice of an example in which the problem is solved satisfactorily at all levels. The example focuses interest, usefully, on the level of understanding involved, rather than the content of the answer. But Spinoza's reasons for regarding understanding at the first two levels as 'inadequate', are masked by the success of the processes in each case, and by his quiet acknowledgement, elsewhere, that most of our time we function at these inadequate levels. To grasp the nature of the inadequacy that he nevertheless deplored, we must look at Spinoza's treatment of degrees of understanding in the *Ethics*, which was written much later.

In *Ethics* 2, xl–xlii, Spinoza distinguishes three, not four, levels of understanding. The context is consideration of concept formation. What he says can be summarized thus:

First '. . . it clearly appears that we perceive many things and form universal ideas:

(*a*) from individual things, represented by the senses to us in a mutilated and confused manner, and without order to the intellect; (*b*) from signs; as, for example, when we hear or read certain words, we recollect things and form certain ideas of them similar to them, through which ideas we imagine things.' These two ways constitute 'knowledge of the first kind, opinion or imagination'. In principle, Spinoza seems to have in mind the same levels of functioning as those classified as first and second in the earlier *Treatise*, but between which he no longer wants to make a hard and fast distinction. This supposition is supported by his use of the same illustration.

Exemplifying the first degree of knowledge, as now explained, is the merchant who multiplies the second and third numbers together and divides the product by the first, 'either because he has not yet forgotten the things which he heard without any demonstration from his schoolmaster or because he has seen the truth of the rule with the more simple numbers'. Presumably, he is thought to be generalizing from a rule of thumb, found to work, as expounded on p. 40.

Second 'From our possessing common notions and adequate ideas of the properties of things.'

Here we run into problems of interpretation, for Spinoza appears to be exemplifying this level not merely by correct inference from the 19th proposition in the 7th book of Euclid. He is also allowing for the possibility of *adequate* ideas of the notion of proportion being involved at this level. The context of the discussion suggests that this is intentional; in which case the new second degree of knowledge differs subtly from the former third degree, in so far as at least some 'adequate' ideas are not excluded. It is not implausible, psychologically, to suppose that inference at this level does involve straightforward insight into at least some of the mathematical concepts involved. The point is interesting, for it suggests that Spinoza is allowing the conclusion to emerge from a combination of insight and learning.

Third From intuitive insight.* 'This kind of knowing advances from an adequate idea of the formal essence of certain attributes of God to the adequate knowledge of the essence of things.' In other words, the whole situation is grasped 'adequately'. To exemplify the process, Spinoza returns to the simple intuitive understanding of ratio; for he says, by way of explanation, that given 1, 2, and 3 we can see that 6 must be the fourth proportional 'much more clearly than by any demonstration'.

Again we must stress that the content of the proposition is of little or no importance. It is true that in the seventeenth century mathematics was the paradigm of clear thought. But it would be false to Spinoza to restrict his third level of understanding to intuitive grasp of a relatively simple mathematical relation or indeed to mathematics. Though it can operate at a

---

* This seems the most acceptable translation of *scientia intuitiva*.

simple level, such intuitive insight into a *complex* mathematical sequence would, it seems, be a rare occurrence. Possibly, Spinoza has in mind, at a high level, the functioning that we half recognize in the twentieth century when we hesitate wholly to rule out the possibility of an intuitive insight that distinguishes those of exceptional from those of very great mathematical ability. But it is important that the context, which is, after all, the *Ethics* as a whole, clearly indicates that Spinoza not only extended the possibility of such insight outside mathematics but made no strict antithesis between thought and emotion, when this last is integral to thinking that is lucid. Hence, when he is considering man's progression towards an ideal of insight into his own position in the universe (an ideal impossible of attainment), Spinoza perfectly consistently suggests overtones of empathic satisfaction and of emotional acceptance of a state of affairs rewarding in its impersonal intelligibility. Intuitive understanding into matters of this complexity is, for him, a limiting case of something which psychologically he starts to explain at an unpretentious level. It is not unjustified to imagine Spinoza quite at home with the Einstein who would help a little girl to understand her sums. He might have agreed that her delighted grasping of a clear, if limited, issue is on a continuum with profound insight into the most complex considerations, even if the latter is something she will never attain. But this is to speculate.

Abandoning this excursion into the upper regions, we must attend to Spinoza's conception of inadequate ideas and the uncertain validity of the opinion that embodies them. As we have seen, such opinion is exemplified in the first and second degrees of understanding in the *Treatise*, and in the first level in the *Ethics*. The question we have to answer is: why did Spinoza consider this level inadequate? The answer, I believe, lies in Spinoza's assumption that such understanding involves unscrutinized imagery and in the account he gives of the way in which images and emotions come to be formed and associated.

The first general indication we have of the nature of *inadequate* understanding occurs in the appendix to *Ethics* i.

Spinoza is commenting on differences in brains and differences in taste and arguing that 'men decide upon matters according to the constitution of their brains, and imagine rather than understand things'. He adds 'If men understood things, they would, as mathematics prove, at least be all alike convinced if they were not all alike attracted.' And he continues: 'We see, therefore, that all those methods by which the common people are in the habit of explaining nature are only different sorts of imaginations, and do not reveal the nature of anything in itself, but only the constitution of the imagination.' He implies that the concepts involved in this level of understanding 'have names as if they were entities existing apart from the imagination' but that they should be seen for what they are, i.e. 'entities not of reason but of the imagination'. How do we come to acquire such concepts? Basically by conditioning. Here is the gist of the argument in which, surprising as it may be for the seventeenth century, this answer seems to be clearly involved.

First the physiological aspect. Fairly early in *Ethics* 2, xiii, Lemma 7, Spinoza puts forward the following propositions as postulates:

(1) The human body is composed of a number of individuals of diverse nature, each of which is composite to a high degree.

(2) Of the individuals of which the human body is composed, some are fluid, some soft, and some hard.

(3) The individuals composing the human body, and consequently the human body itself, are affected by external bodies in many ways.

(4) The human body needs for its preservation many other bodies by which it is, as it were, continually regenerated.

(5) When a fluid part of the human body is determined by an external body, so that it often strikes upon another which is soft, the fluid part changes the plane of the soft part, and leaves upon it, as it were, some traces of the impelling external body.

(6) The human body can make and arrange external bodies in many ways.

All of these postulates are useful for a general understanding of Spinoza's view, though it is numbers 1, 2, 3, and 5 whose relevance to imagery becomes apparent as soon as we add Spinoza's next proposition, viz.: 'the human mind is adapted to the perception of many things, and its aptitude increases in proportion to the number of ways in which its body can be disposed'. In the demonstration of this he reminds us of the axiomatic nature of both mental and physical reflection of what is happening. In effect, if an external body impinging on us leaves a 'trace', as implied in postulate 5, this can be treated as mental or physical indifferently. The next two stages of the argument follow rapidly in Propositions XIV to XXXIII which I will here attempt to summarize.

'The idea of every way in which the human body is affected by external bodies must involve the nature of the human body, and at the same time the nature of the external body.' But the ideas we have of external bodies in fact indicate the constitution of our own. Spinoza has in mind here the familiar argument, originating from Galileo, that, for example, smells, tastes, tactile impressions and sounds as experienced are not inherent in the objects perceived. 'If the human body is affected in a way which involves the nature of an external body, the human mind will contemplate that external body as actually existing or present, until the human body be affected by an affect which excludes the existence or presence of the external body.' But, and here comes the nub of the argument, 'the mind is able to contemplate external things by which the human body was once affected as if they were present, although they are not present and do not exist'.

Though he allows, in principle, that there might be other causes than those he specifies, Spinoza hazards a physiological explanation of this conclusion. This is what he says:

When external bodies so determine the fluid parts of the human body that they often strike upon the softer parts, the fluid parts change the plane of the soft parts; and thence it happens that the fluid parts are reflected from the new planes in a direction different from that in which they used to be reflected, and that also afterwards when they strike against these new planes by their spontaneous motion, they are reflected in the same way as when they were impelled towards those planes by external bodies. Consequently those fluid bodies produce an affection in the human body while they keep up this reflex motion similar to that produced by an external body. The mind, therefore, will think as before, that is to say, it will again contemplate the external body as present. This will happen as often as the fluid parts of the human body strike against those planes by their spontaneous motion. . . . We see, therefore, how it is possible for us to contemplate things which do not exist as if they were actually present. . . . We will give to those affections of the human body, the ideas of which represent to us external bodies as if they were present, the name *images of things* [Spinoza's italics], although they do not actually reproduce the forms of things. When the mind contemplates bodies in this way, we will say that it imagines. Here I wish it to be observed, in order that I may begin to show what *error* is, that these imaginations of the mind, regarded by themselves, contain no error, and that the mind is not in error because it imagines, but only in so far as it is considered as wanting in an idea which excludes the existence of those things which it imagines as present.

In current terminology, this could mean that repeated stimulation of a nerve (or cell body) by an external source changes the state of the nerve and modifies the corresponding sensation. But similar stimulation of the nerve (or cell body) by internal electro-chemical impulses may give rise to a conditioned sensation, i.e. image, which in the absence of contradictory observation is projected outwards as if an external source of stimulation were present. We shall meet a far more detailed version of this view when we discuss Taine, writing in the second half of the nineteenth century. As for the notion that images are conditioned sensations, it returned across the Atlantic in 1960 as the key hypothesis presented by Professor Mowrer[1] to enrich the 'mediation processes' required to integrate the experimental findings of behaviouristic learning theory. A question of moment is whether physiology can establish the existence of sustained modifications in the modern equivalent of what Spinoza designated as 'soft parts', i.e. nerve endings, 'cell assemblies' and the like.

Spinoza, as one would expect, develops his position with logical elegance. 'If the human body has at any time been simultaneously affected by two or more bodies, whenever the mind afterwards imagines one of them, it will also remember the others.' Memory thus emerges as a 'concatenation of ideas' about things outside the body. The arrangement of these ideas corresponds not to the way in which they might be ordered intellectually (by implication objectively, or, 'in the same way by all men') but to the 'order and concatenation of the affections of the human body'. This argument he rounds off as follows in *Ethics* 2, xviii:

Hence we can clearly understand how it is that the mind from the thought of one thing at once turns to the thought of another thing which is not in any way like the first. For example, from the thought of the word *pomum* a Roman immediately turned to the thought of fruit, which has no resemblance to the articulate sound *pomum*, nor anything in common with it, excepting this, that the body of that man was often affected by the thing and the sound; that is to say, he often heard the word *pomum* when he saw the fruit. In this manner each person will turn from one thought to another according to the manner in which the habit of each has arranged the images of things in the body. The soldier, for instance, if he sees the footsteps of a horse in the sand, will immediately turn from the thought of a horse to the thought of a horseman, and so to the thought of war. The countryman, on the other hand, from the thought of a horse will turn to the thought of his plough, his field, etc.; and thus each person will turn from one thought to this or that thought, according to the manner in which he has been accustomed to connect and bind together the images of things in his mind.

Spinoza is not out to criticize the soldier or the countryman because their associations to the imprint of a horse's hoof are

different. He is only saying, by implication, that given the
way in which their knowledge had been acquired—in effect
by contiguous association or conditioning—there would be no
particular reason for supposing that either of their trains of
thought, were they taken as interpretations of the sign in
question, would be correct. Nor indeed would there be more
(or less) reason to trust any rival interpretation similarly rooted
in individual conditioning.

Spinoza does not hesitate to cast doubts, similar in principle,
on the functioning of high-order abstractions, such as 'trans-
cendental', 'being', 'thing', 'something', which, in his eyes, are
no more than high-order confusions arising from the empirical
fact that physiologically, and hence psychologically, we just
cannot hold distinctly in mind the vast collection of discrete
images that supposedly have gone towards their making. He
grants utility to some general ideas such as 'genus' and 'species'
in facilitating remembering and imagining. Other 'modes of
thought', e.g. time, measure and number, have explanatory
value. G. H. R. Parkinson's[2]* useful discussion of these suggests,
however, that Spinoza came near to treating these as concepts
which we use in our efforts to bring some sort of manageable
order into the universe in which we find ourselves, but which
it would be a mistake to treat as having absolute, in contrast to
utilitarian, validity. To the twentieth-century social psychologist, such a viewpoint, if not wholly acceptable, is at least very
familiar from discussions of the extent to which language
structure may be responsible for some of the categories we seek
to impose on experience. (See Chapter Eleven.)

Before leaving Spinoza's conception of thinking, we must look
at what he had to say on the relation of thought and emotion.
It is particularly important to realize that he was not a faculty
psychologist. On the contrary, he tended to take for granted
emotional overtones, either positive, negative or mixed, to any
human response. In the twentieth century many psychologists
have returned to this viewpoint. Thus it is a misunderstanding

* *Spinoza's Theory of Knowledge*. This book came into my hands when most
of this chapter was already written and I left what I had to say on 'conditioning' unchanged. In discussing the 'modes of thought', however, Dr.
Parkinson has had access to writings by Spinoza not readily available to me.
For further points the reader is therefore referred to this volume.

of Spinoza to suppose him an 'intellectual' in the usual narrow derogatory sense of this term. Moreover, it would be un-imaginative to leave out of account the depth and intensity of feeling betrayed in his references to man's possible progression towards insight into himself and his position, in his treatment of this notion of insight, and in his profound deploring of unnecessary misery. The fundamental distinction for Spinoza is not between intellect, and emotion, but between whatever *active* emotion and intellectual understanding is involved in progress towards insight, and the state of *passive* understanding and emotion suffered much of our time. This last is debited by Spinoza either to unavoidable ignorance of the true nature of occurrences affecting us, or to the hazards of the way in which images and emotional responses become conditioned to irrelevancies. Hence we can be all too easily at the mercy of 'affects', both emotional and imaginal, about whose sources we are wholly mistaken.

Spinoza's full treatment of the emotions is too long and too subtle to summarize. The most we can do here is to outline it in principle, so that its bearing on his conception of thinking is apparent.

As already mentioned on p. 37, *conatus*, the individual's defining characteristic of maintaining itself as such, is Spinoza's basic conception. Taken together with Spinoza's view that man is by nature partly 'active' and partly 'passive', joy and sorrow fit into the total picture as reflections of increased or diminished 'adequacy' as the individual that one happens to be. We may say that it was of Spinoza's true nature to gaze straight at all the phenomena associated with egotistical, misinformed, mean-spirited muddle-headedness and to consider dispassionately that some could and should be avoided. While this is a value judgment with which Spinoza was identified, it is not equiva-lent to a programme for how other people should live, except in one respect: he was implying that scrutiny of the sources of misery and misunderstanding might lead to some of these vanishing under the scrutinizing gaze. Some sources of misery, external to the person and beyond his control, would un-questionably remain. What of the internal sources? Here we must look at Spinoza's attempt to derive other emotions from his primary conception of *conatus*, together with joy and sorrow, in the rather special sense already indicated.

Spinoza's key principle is clear from the discussion of emotion that follows immediately after his general enunciation of the conditioning principle in *Ethics* 3, Proposition XIV. This Proposition runs: 'If the mind at any time has been simultaneously affected by two affects, whenever it is afterwards affected by one of them, it will also be affected by the other'.

The context shows 'affect' to be a very general term for which we could substitute the result of an externally or internally originating stimulus.* In Proposition XV and its demonstration, Spinoza immediately envisages the possible transfer of the emotional tone of an exciting or depressing stimulus to a neutral stimulus, if the latter happened to occur at the same time. Hence, when the neutral stimulus subsequently affects the person it will take on emotional colouring that does not belong to it in its own right. His argument runs as follows:

Proposition XV. Anything may be accidentally the cause of joy, sorrow or desire.

Demonstration. Let the mind be supposed to be affected at the same time by two affects, its power of action not being increased or diminished by one, while it is increased or diminished by the other. From the preceding proposition it is plain that when the mind is afterwards affected by the first affect through its true cause, which (by hypothesis) of itself neither increases nor diminishes the mind's power of thinking, it will at the same time be affected by the other affect, which does increase or diminish that power, that is to say it will be affected with joy or sorrow; and thus the thing itself will be the cause of joy or of sorrow, not of itself, but accidentally. In the same way it can easily be shown that the same thing may accidentally be the cause of desire.

In the corollary and its demonstration Spinoza extends the argument to imagery; so that, in effect, the image of the

* In the sense of something that makes an impact. I have used the word 'stimulus' to sharpen the point I am trying to make clear.

stimulus, originally neutral but now emotionally toned, may arouse joy or sorrow, desire or aversion. He adds:

> We now understand why we love or hate certain things from no cause which is known to us, but merely from sympathy or antipathy, as they say. To this class, too . . . are to be referred those objects which affect us with joy or sorrow solely because they are somewhat like objects which usually affect us with those affects. I know indeed that the writers who first introduced the words 'Sympathy' and 'Antipathy' desired thereby to signify certain hidden qualities of things, but nevertheless I believe that we shall be permitted to understand by those names qualities which are plain and well known.

In Proposition XVII, Spinoza develops his position to allow for ambivalent emotions, in something remarkably like its twentieth-century meaning of fused positive and negative feeling towards the same thing; as distinct from merely liking parts of something, if it is complex, and disliking others, though this too can occur. In Proposition XVIII, he implies that the emotional impact of an image may be the same whether it be of a past, present or future thing. For, inasmuch as something is imagined, it is taken to exist, unless there is evidence to the contrary, 'so the body is affected by the image of the thing in the same way as if the thing itself were present'. Temporal judgment is secondary. Experience leads to hesitation when past or future things are considered, so the emotional impact of a given image becomes less constant, and will usually be disturbed by the images of other things until the person is more sure of the issue. From the varying degrees of constancy of imagery and of positive or negative feeling, Spinoza derives: hope as 'unsteady joy arising from the image of a future or past thing about whose issue we are in doubt', fear as 'unsteady sorrow, arising from the image of a doubtful thing'. If the doubts are removed, hope becomes confidence and fear becomes despair. With this basic theoretical equipment, Spinoza finds it possible to say straightforward illuminating things about, for example, the functioning both of individual emotions, such as jealousy, and the operation of prejudice on an international scale.

The detailed consideration of Spinoza's treatment of emotion, with its astonishing strengths, and its weaknesses, is beyond the scope of this chapter. It suffices if we have shown how, in principle, his account of emotion, which because of association or conditioning can become misplaced, supplements Spinoza's basic criticism of functioning at the level of the first degrees of understanding. We must reiterate that it is wholly mistaken to attribute to Spinoza any disapproval of emotion as such. He states perfectly clearly that: 'Besides the joys and sorrows which are passions, there are other affects of joy and sorrow which are related to us in so far as we act.' (*Ethics* 3, Proposition LVIII.)

To our disillusioned, relativistic twentieth century, the impersonal analysis of at least one source of mankind's misery that shocked the seventeenth century takes on a visionary quality at times. Spinoza believed that built into man there was at least the potentiality of insightful action. And he believed that the joy that was part and parcel of this was 'altogether different from the joy by which the drunkard is enslaved'. A vast amount of modern psychotherapy, Freudian and otherwise, proceeds in practice on similar assumptions. But it states them less clearly. It also entangles the whole procedure in the theoretical belief that pleasure arises only in restoration of equilibrium; in effect, removal of tension due to deficit. This is stressed without assuming, as did Spinoza (following Aristotle), that the equilibrium is one of maximum integrated activity, progress towards which is delightful in itself. All the Freudian pleasures are those Aristotle would have designated 'accidental'. For the pure enjoyment associated by Aristotle and Spinoza with effective functioning as such, there is little room either in modern Freudian or, for that matter, modern Behaviouristic systems. If, therefore, we leave Spinoza for the moment, admitting that his statement of positive aims may be less readily intelligible or convincing than his diagnosis of the causes of much misunderstanding, we must also stress that the modern restriction of happiness to the remedy of deficit is only half the story. There seems no good evidence, or theoretical justification, for losing the other half.

So far as 'thinking' is concerned, Spinoza presents us with a key problem which is still unsolved: Granted that much of our so-called 'knowledge' is but opinion acquired by association or conditioning, and much 'thinking' is mulling over the ingredients of such opinion (complete with appropriately associated or displaced emotions), is there or is there not as well a lucid sifting or insight on which common understanding and objectivity depend? And what is the nature of this insight?

So far as I know, Spinoza dropped only one hint that the third level of thinking might be reached through the second. He coupled this with firm belief that the third could never be derived from the first. Born in 1632, the same year as Spinoza, but first publishing his *Essay* in 1690, thirteen years after Spinoza's death, Locke hinted that an intelligent animal could sometimes make a better job of problem-solving than a very limited human being. But Locke and Spinoza were a century ahead of the first formulations of an evolutionary viewpoint, and nearly 200 years ahead of its full development by Darwin. Leibniz, Spinoza's immediate successor in the continental rationalist tradition, *perhaps* moved one step nearer to an evolutionary view of perception and thought, by positing an infinite series of 'monads' capable of reflecting the state of the universe in varying degrees. But like Spinoza, and unlike Locke, Leibniz approached perception and apperception as a mathematically-minded philosopher, and not as a doctor sympathetic to biology. This leads us on to consider the more immediate historical background of various degrees of awareness and, ultimately, of unconscious motivation and thought.

REFERENCES

1. Mowrer, O. H., *Learning Theory and the Symbolic Processes*, New York: Wiley, 1960.
2. Parkinson, G. H. R., *Spinoza's Theory of Knowledge*, London: Oxford University Press, 1954.
3. Spinoza, Benedict de, *The Chief Works of Benedict de Spinoza*, translated by R. H. M. Elwes, London: Bell, 1884. (*Improvement of Understanding*, pp. 7 ff., and *Ethics*.)

CHAPTER FOUR

UNCONSCIOUS THINKING IN ITS HISTORICAL SETTING

> The teaching of most modern psychologists is that Consciousness forms but a small item in the total of psychical processes. Unconscious sensations, ideas and judgments are made to play a great part in their explanations.
>
> G. H. LEWES, 1877

FREUD'S TREATMENT of unconscious thinking was a milestone, significant, if for no other reason, for arousing enormous interest in the passers-by. Serious study of Freud shows repeatedly that its true significance was far greater than this capacity to attract attention and controversy. On the other hand, its importance may lie in a somewhat different direction from what is popularly supposed.

Milestones and cairns are usually found *en route* from one place to another. Mountaineers will know that they sometimes give confusing directions or mark off a route into a mist. The vast cairn of unconscious processes constructed by Freud is no exception. In strange and sometimes terrifying country any cairn can be a comfort; some human being has been there before and the later traveller, even if the map-making is found to be only approximate, may remain grateful for those who started to humanize an unknown route.

Freud's milestone, however, is apt to be treated popularly as a cairn constructed in isolation by one man alone. Those who admire him somewhat uncritically, place Freud and the cairn on a peak, on which no comment is allowed and from which no further progress seems possible. The hostile consign them both to a dark ravine, in the depths of which is a confusing network of dismal streams. In this ravine, analysts of all persuasions are seen to dredge eternally, when not throwing boulders at each other. Jungians, wandering hopefully in swirling shadows, attempt to survey an underground lake (a bog to the really unsympathetic), the alleged common source of individual outpourings. Adlerians cluster round submerged power-houses. Rogerians camp contentedly by individual streams and make non-committal cluckings as they watch them flow.

One question often left unasked is whether there were other cairns on the route before Freud's, and some other directions which explorers might have followed. Those already familiar with pre-Freudian thought will know that the answer to the first half of this question is certainly, and to the second half, probably, yes. But it is a bold historian who tries to deal briefly with Freud's predecessors, let alone Freud himself. The picture is so complex that awareness of one's own ignorance increases the more one delves into what happened. These two chapters must therefore be taken as the sketchy summaries that they are. The first points to some treatments of unconscious functioning prior to Freud's. Scrutiny of Freud's great cairn in its context then suggests that some of its foundation stones now have merely historical not functional significance. Hence instead of crediting (or debiting) Freud with 'discovering the unconscious', one is led to stress his importance in recognizing the affinities between thought and action, even though we must avoid using these terms as co-extensive. With this brief indication of where we are going, let us now get down to history.

As we have seen, there were hints of the notion of unconscious functioning, in a wide sense, in Spinoza's distinction between *conatus*, as the striving to be itself which is the defining characteristic of an individual thing, and *cupiditus*, which Spinoza used to indicate such striving when it is conscious. Another, and different, aspect of unconscious functioning is to be found in the varying degrees of awareness, and the varying degrees of reflection of facts in the external world, with which Leibniz credited his monads. Spinoza's implied view is the ancestor of the modern distinction of conscious and unconscious striving. Leibniz posited degrees of awareness, from that of fully focused attention, through the peripheral and subliminal, presumably to a level much lower than this. Psychologically, it is not at all clear what sort of functioning the *petites perceptions* of Leibniz's simple monads was supposed to be. But it is certain that Leibniz thought these monads capable, in *some* degree, of reflecting happenings external to them. This perception at a very low level was, as it were, the limit to which full conscious awareness might diminish.

The implications of these seventeenth- and early eighteenth-century foreshadowings of a modern viewpoint were not, however, developed in detail by their originators. This remains true even though, as suggested in Chapter Three, the re-reading of Spinoza in the light of modern controversies shows how deeply he had appreciated a key source of human confusion and misery. For Spinoza, this lay in emotionally-toned opinion, rooted in an associative or conditioning process, not necessarily unveridical but in reality often false to objective fact, and of whose roots we are unaware. That men's actions may arise from misguided opinion is, of course, a view much older than Spinoza's. His account of the genesis of such opinion, however, drawing attention to the way in which, in principle, men may come to act from motives of which they have no understanding, seems unique for its period. For insight in this respect, no modern writer with whom I am acquainted can compete with Spinoza in originality or terse economy of statement. Nevertheless, it would be anachronistic to attribute to him the full notion of unconscious thought as this was conceived some 200 years later.

The anticipations of unconscious functioning, to be found in Spinoza and Leibniz, have to be enriched by later eighteenth- and early nineteenth-century contributions, before the concept as it came to be treated by Freud can be seen to be forming. To its evolution, the literature of dissociated states, pseudo-science (as represented by Mesmer), psychotherapy, physiology and neurology, evolutionary biology, educational psychology, philosophy and experimental psychology all contributed their quota. Let us look at these in turn.

The notion of another side of our nature operating outside normal awareness, for example in dreaming, is at least as old as Plato, who argued that the man who in waking life had not come to terms with strong emotions could be rent in sleep by all sorts of desires, incest not excluded. There are plenty of examples in literature of people who reveal in dissociated states, of which sleep-walking can be counted as a mild example, emotional outlooks running counter to those of their conscious waking life. Lady Macbeth's revelation of unacknowledged horror of her actual deed is a famous instance. But in Western Europe, interest in this, *die Nachtseite des Lebens*, as it was designated by German romanticism, seems to have achieved a special intensity in the last quarter of the eighteenth and the early years of the nineteenth century. Against this background of German romanticism must be set both the notorious activities of Anton Mesmer himself, in producing dissociated states supposedly by magnetism, and the predilections of individual doctors and writers whom he influenced, either directly or indirectly.

Mesmer was born at Iznang near Lake Constance in 1734. He qualified as a doctor and had strong mystical leanings. In particular, he was impressed by the views of the sixteenth-century alchemist (and scientist) Paracelsus, who believed that the stars influence the health and general condition of human beings by way of a subtle and invisible fluid. Mesmer became convinced of the healing power in his own hands and, in 1775, first called this force, supposedly emanating from his body, animal magnetism. In Vienna, where he had worked since about 1766,* he was accused by medical colleagues of practising magic and was ordered to leave Austria in 1778. He settled in Paris, and, in the years just prior to the French Revolution, became for a while enormously popular, but, in due season, equally suspect in the eyes of the French Government. If one reads Binet's account of Mesmer's activities at their height, supplemented as it is by that of an eye-witness, it is not at all difficult to understand why.

All the world wished to be magnetized, and the crowd was so great that Mesmer employed a *valet toucheur* to magnetize in his place. This did not suffice; he invented the famous *baquet*, or trough, round which more than thirty persons

* Mesmer arrived at the University of Vienna in 1759 as a Law student. He shifted to Medicine. The date 1766 is that of the public reading of the *Disputatio de Planetarium Influxu*, for which the faculty awarded him a diploma.

could be magnetized simultaneously. A circular oaken case, about a foot high, was placed in the middle of a large hall, hung with thick curtains, through which only a soft and subdued light was allowed to penetrate; this was the *baquet*. At the bottom of the case, on a layer of powdered glass and iron filings, there lay full bottles, symmetrically arranged, so that the necks of all converged towards the centre; other bottles were arranged in the opposite direction with their necks towards the circumference. All these objects were immersed in water, but this condition was not absolutely necessary, and the *baquet* might be dry. The lid was pierced with a certain number of holes, whence there issued jointed and movable iron branches, which were to be held by the patients. Absolute silence was maintained. The patients were ranged in several rows round the *baquet*, connected with each other by cords passed round their bodies, and by a second chain, formed by joining hands. As they waited a melodious air was heard, proceeding from a pianoforte, or harmonicon, placed in the adjoining room, and to this the human voice was sometimes added. Then, influenced by the magnetic effluvia issuing from the *baquet*, curious phenomena were produced. These are well described by an eye-witness named Bailly: 'Some patients remain calm, and experience nothing; others cough, spit, feel slight pain, a local or general heat, and fall into sweats; others are agitated and tormented by convulsions. These convulsions are remarkable for their number, duration, and force, and have been known to persist for more than three hours. They are characterized by involuntary, jerking movements in all the limbs, and in the whole body, by contraction of the throat, by twitchings in the hypochondriac and epigastric regions, by dimness and rolling of the eyes, by piercing cries, tears, hiccough, and immoderate laughter. They are preceded or followed by a state of languor or dreaminess, by a species of depression, and even by stupor.

'The slightest sudden noise causes the patient to start, and it has been observed that he is affected by a change of time or tune in the airs performed on the pianoforte; that his agitation is increased by a more lively movement, and that his convulsions then become more violent. Patients are seen to be absorbed in the search for one another, rushing together, smiling, talking affectionately and endeavouring to modify their crises. They are all so submissive to the magnetizer that even when they appear to be in a stupor, his voice, a glance, or sign will rouse them from it. It is impossible not to admit, from all these results, that some great force acts upon and masters the patients, and that this force appears to reside in the magnetizer. This convulsive state is termed the *crisis*. It has been observed that many women and few men are subject to such crises; that they are only established after the lapse of two or three hours, and that when one is established, others soon and successively begin.

'When the agitation exceeds certain limits, the patients are transported into a padded room; the women's corsets are unlaced, and they may then strike their heads against the padded walls without doing themselves any injury.'

Mesmer, wearing a coat of lilac silk, walked up and down amid this palpitating crowd, together with Deslon and his associates, whom he chose for their youth and comeliness. Mesmer carried a long iron wand, with which he touched the bodies of the patients, and especially those parts which were diseased; often, laying aside the wand, he magnetized them with his eyes, fixing his gaze on theirs, or applying his hands to the hypochondriac region and to the lower part of the abdomen. This application was often continued for hours, and at other times the master made use of *passes*. He began by placing himself *en rapport* with his subject. Seated opposite to him, foot against foot, knee against knee, he laid his fingers on the hypochondriac region, and moved them to and fro, lightly touching the ribs. Magnetization with strong currents was substituted for these manipulations when more energetic results were to be produced. 'The master, erecting his fingers in a pyramid, passed his hands all over the patient's body, beginning with the head, and going down over the shoulders to the feet. He then returned again, to the head,

both back and front, to the belly and the back; he renewed
the process again and again, until the magnetized person
was saturated with the healing fluid, and was transported
with pain or pleasure, both sensations being equally salutary.'
Young women were so much gratified by the crisis, that
they begged to be thrown into it anew; they followed Mesmer
through the hall, and confessed that it was impossible not to
be warmly attached to the magnetizer's person.

Binet comments with dry detachment:

> It must have been curious to witness such scenes. So far
> as we are now able to judge, Mesmer excited in his patients
> nervous crises in which we may trace the principal signs of
> the severe hysteric attacks which may be observed daily.[6]

It is to the credit of the then French Government that, faced
with this sensational assault on susceptibilities, whether
diseased or fashionably foolish, it set up a series of committees
of inquiry, on one of which Lavoisier and Benjamin Franklin
consented among others to serve. The reports were sufficiently
sceptical of Mesmer's claim that this and allied procedures
were either curative or scientifically founded on 'animal magnetism', to ensure that Mesmer had to leave Paris. That some
at least of the phenomena produced by Mesmer were genuine
and in need of explanation was not denied. It was even
admitted in principle that some cures might ensue. Nevertheless this fandango was not to be allowed. Posterity, having
blackened Mesmer as an out-and-out charlatan, has moved for
the moment into the mood for whitewashing him. Very dark
grey seems the more appropriate hue. The judgment of the
committees would seem to have good sense on its side, in
questioning the professed explanation of the facts observed and
in trying to stop their exploitation. At all events, Mesmer was
disgraced, he retired to private life in Versailles and then found
refuge in Switzerland. He died in 1815 at Meersburg, on the
north side of Lake Constance, where he is claimed as the
originator of psychotherapy—though his astrological grave-
stone is thought a little strange.

Mesmer's activities were sufficiently well known for various
individual doctors, and no doubt quacks as well, to experiment

in inducing Mesmeric trances. Plenty of evidence suggests that characteristic of the trance state was the occurrence of behaviour outside the patient's usual repertoire, and of which he had no recollection on return to normal conditions. Such phenomena are enthralling to the romantically inclined, and between 1796, when Jean Paul Richter coined the word *Doppelgänger*, and the early 1820's, a swarm of dissociating, alternating, doubling and otherwise multiplying personalities invaded German romantic writing. Dissociation in one form or another was treated by Jean Paul himself, by Chamisso, whose haunting and beautifully written *Pieter Schlemihl* symbolically handled the subtlest problems of identification, by Kleist in his dramas, by E. T. A. Hoffmann in tales populated by Janus-faced oddities. There were also satirical treatments both of Mesmer and of the phenomena he had popularized; witness, in 1789, Mozart's quack doctor in *Cosi fan Tutte*, complete with a magnet and an enchanting orchestral equivalent to quivering animal spirits. And in 1817 Brentano satirized his contemporaries' fascination with all these phenomena.

In fact, dissociation in varying degrees interested some of the best German writers of their day, not excluding Heine who, about 1823, produced the *Doppelgänger* that is probably most familiar to English readers:

> Still ist die Nacht, es ruhen die Gassen,
> In diesem Hause wohnte mein Schatz;
> Sie hat schon längst die Stadt verlassen,
> Doch steht noch das Haus auf dem selben Platz.
>
> Da steht auch ein Mensch und starrt in die Höhe,
> Und ringt die Hände vor Schmerzensgewalt;
> Mir graust es, wenn ich sein Antlitz sehe—
> Der Mond zeigt mir meine eig'ne Gestalt.
>
> Du Doppelgänger! du bleicher Geselle!
> Was äffst du nach mein Liebesleid,
> Das mich gequält auf dieser Stelle,
> So manche Nacht in alter Zeit?[22]*

* Literal translation:

> Still is the night, and hushed are the roadways,
> Within this house there lived my love,

In this instance, the (romantically) tragic *alter ego* of the main character is projected rather than wholly dissociated. But some degree of dissociation is implied in the man's initial failure to recognize himself in the apparition he sees. It is also reflected in the emotional force of the recognition when it occurs in the second stanza and in the implied rejection of full recognition in the last. It seems as if Heine caught the traumatic state wherein attitudes hitherto kept apart are almost at the point of fusing with the conscious personality. Franz Schubert, who belonged to a reading circle in Vienna specially studying Kleist, set Heine's poem in 1828. It was Schubert's penultimate song and the music accentuates the eeriness of Heine's divided character, deepening its emotional impact in the process.

Heine's and Schubert's *Der Doppelgänger* belongs to the end of the literary heyday of divided personalities. Marked literary interest in dissociation seems then to have subsided, to be revived later in the century in writers such as Poe, Stevenson and Dostoevsky, though other brilliant literary treatments of related states are to be found. Of these Conrad Ferdinand Meyer's[29] *Die Richterin*, completed in 1885, is probably the most interesting here, since we know that it attracted considerable attention from Freud.* Meyer, with superb skill, leaves the reader guessing whether the main character, a woman with a murderous past, but now honourably responsible for the law of her territory, is at one point seeing ghosts or

---

Long, long ago she deserted the city,
Yet still stands the house in the self-same place.

There stands too a man gazing up numbly,
And wringing his hands from the force of grief;
I shudder when I perceive his countenance,
The moon points out to me my own person.

You second self! You wan associate!
What mean you apeing the pain of love
That tormented me in this same spot
So many nights, so long ago?

* Freud's correspondence with Fliess[12] shows the extent to which Freud was reading and reflecting on Meyer at the time of evolving *The Interpretation of Dreams*.

experiencing in a dream state events and emotions dissociated or repressed because of the overwhelming threat they offer to her present rôle. By the time that Meyer was writing, the phenomena of dissociation were again in the forefront of psychiatric attention. Here we must pause to collect up the threads of such medical interest.

According to Professor Tymms,[34]* Kleist and E. T. A. Hoffmann, at any rate, had derived indirectly from Mesmer some of the knowledge of trance states that they reveal in their writings. This knowledge came via two doctors, Kluge and more particularly G. H. von Schubert.† The close association between literature and medicine at this period, and in this respect, is emphasized by Schubert, in his turn, quoting Jean Paul. Schubert's lectures in Dresden were attended by Kleist and his books were read by Hoffmann. Through medical friends Hoffmann appears to have supplemented reading with first-hand observation, as a layman, of induced trance states. One is tempted to surmise that Kleist, who was severely neurotic and finally committed suicide, may have experienced dissociated states in himself. Whatever may be the truth here, it is worth pausing to look at Schubert in order to appreciate the odd fusion of insight and fantastic speculation characterizing a then eminent doctor who took mesmeric trances seriously.

G. H. von Schubert[31] was born in 1780, practised as a doctor in Altenburg and then went to Freiburg and Dresden. From 1809-16 he was Director of the Realinstitut in Nuremberg. In 1819 he moved to Erlangen as Professor of Natural Science and thence in 1827, in the same capacity, to Munich, where he stayed till his death in 1860. He was influenced initially by Schelling's *Naturphilosophie* and later gave himself up to mysticism. Schelling was a devotee of Spinoza. It is unlikely that Schubert is worth resuscitating *in toto*. His short book *Die Symbolik des Traumes* is, however, of historical interest, for it contains the germs of many ideas later woven into twentieth-century psychotherapy. And it contains them in their original, strange, speculative setting. The book was first published in 1814 when the author was evidently a rising young

* This section owes a lot to his *Doubles in Literary Psychology*.
† No relation of the more famous Franz.

man of thirty-four. The fourth edition, published posthumously, appeared in 1862. It is possible that Schubert was read by Ludwig Feuerbach, who went to Erlangen as a student of Natural Science in 1828 and who appears to have been the first person to treat organized religion as a complex projection system. 'The fundamental dogmas of Christianity', he wrote, 'are realized wishes of the heart.'[1] While Schubert would have been appalled at such an idea, the notion could easily occur to someone aware of his writings and trying out a simple inversion of what Schubert said. Whether or not Feuerbach read Schubert, it is quite certain that Freud read *Die Symbolik des Traumes* and we have Ernest Jones'[26] authority for saying that Freud continually quoted Schubert. Now what sort of thing did Schubert say?

As a mystically-inclined doctor, he was immensely impressed with the '*Zweideutigkeit*', the double significance, ambiguity, ambivalence, and Janus-faced quality which he saw in nature, in some religious practices, in myth, oracular sayings, prophecies and in the lives of prophets, in poetry, in the behaviour revealed in somnambulism and in dreams. His general explanation of this *Zweideutigkeit* betrays elements of gnosticism, cabbalistic doctrine and neo-platonism which support Professor Tymms in designating Schubert as a Rosicrucian. Schubert's broad theory amounts to the belief that the sensorily experienced world is *per se* a largely rigidified form of an image language in which God originally spoke to man. Schubert appears to follow Jewish cabbalism in treating the beings of the original world as androgynous. Such rigidity as is reflected by fossils of earlier species, and by the relatively stable divisibility of the familiar external world into species and sexes, came about, he seems to think, by a catastrophe;* through which the world as we know it ceased to function in phase with the spiritual activity of the world that lies behind the visible. Only faint echoes of that world penetrate to us and hence the

* This reference is open to rival interpretations. Schubert may possibly have in mind 'the fall' of conventional Biblical history. He may, however, be referring to the then current theory of a series of catastrophes by which Cuvier sought to reconcile the theological account of creation in a short time with the evolutionary evidence suggested by fossils.

contradictory quality of visible nature itself and all those representations of it which still show some trace of contact with the Beyond. Among them Schubert considers those, from religious practices to dreams, already listed above.

Now this general theory falls fairly comfortably into the class of speculations which nothing can prove or disprove, but in which it is virtually impossible to believe. One would dismiss it as irrelevant, but for the fact that when Schubert writes of the examples of double significance that struck him so forcibly he is most suggestive psychologically.

Schubert thinks of man as composed of spirit, soul (*die Seele*) and body. The first functions as conscious perception and thought and is associated by him with the workings of the cerebral nervous system. *Die Seele*, whose essence is nearer the emotional core of man, but which is capable of awareness, is associated with the operation of the ganglia. As *Die Symbolik* first appeared only a few years after Bichat had distinguished the functioning of the central and autonomic nervous systems, it is no great discredit to Schubert that he should think in terms of two poles of nervous functioning, one cerebral and one 'ganglionic'. When, however, he maintains that in trance, and allied states, *die Seele* can be influenced by the world soul operating on the ganglia, he is heading for mesmeric perdition.

Animals are possessed of body and *Seele*. Man alone, in a standard Christianized Platonic fashion, has a spirit. The essence of spirit and *Seele* for Schubert is striving or desire, and he remarks in passing that only those things which appeal directly or indirectly to such desires arouse our interest. Herein lies the source of possible personality change. Desire of the spirit is oriented loftily towards the world beyond the senses, the desires of the *Seele* are naturally directed to the satisfaction of bodily needs, such as hunger and sex. In this respect, *die Seele* operates largely on a pleasure-pain principle. On the other hand, it is open directly, if obscurely, to intimations from the world beyond and these intimations may be good or evil in effect.

Presumably, as a Rosicrucian, Schubert held a Manichean version of the spiritual world, but in this book he is more interested in the ethical and psychological implications of his

C

general position than in expounding his theology as such. So his theological view is here uncertain. It is clear, however, that, for Schubert, when *Seele* and spirit operate in the same direction, i.e. upwards and outwards beyond the limited sphere of sensation and biological drive, all augurs well. He is apt to rhapsodize on this rare state wherein conflict, which is more usual, has been overcome. He tries to describe the condition of abnegation necessary before such radiant integration can be attained; in this context he writes with intense seriousness almost as though he had grasped the process of relinquishing narcissism. When, on the contrary, the operation and the desires of the spirit are entangled in the more restricted sphere of the *Seele* and biology, the result is a disastrous narrowing of total psychological outlook and an intensification of attachment to a limited object of which the reverse side is destruction. In other words, intense attachment and aggressive destruction go hand in hand.

When, moreover, *die Seele* has been influenced not by good but by evil spirits, often in the disguise of good, one may get pathological guilt. Schubert is very firm on the point that the voice of conscience as heard is by no means infallible. Conscience, originally the voice of God, has also become Janusfaced; so some of its grim admonitions may be listened to only at peril. This can include denial of the saner and sunnier desires of the spirit and even personal suicide. Malevolent distortion may also contribute to such morbid manifestations of ecstasy as are found in religious mania and fanaticism. Schubert seems to have had few illusions about the sensual element manifest in many states of distorted enthusiasm. He remarks, also, that those who most powerfully and most often experience a spiritual happiness (that he treats as genuine in contrast to 'pythic enthusiasm'*) are often those who have contended successfully with the strongest sensual desires. Intense attachment, however, and destructive impulses lie very close together in the natural, the biological and the social world as he sees it.

* This is a reference to the legend of the Pythian oracle at Delphi, whose priestess Pythia served a snake, offspring of earth. This snake God was eventually overcome by Apollo, the sun God, worshipped in the form of a Dolphin. Hence the shrine became Apollo's, and the oracle the Delphic.

This returns us to the '*Zweideutigkeit*' that so impressed
Schubert. He was aware of the process of dissociation and of
the fact that, in states then designated somnambulistic, a
person would emerge from a trance with no recollection of the
events taking place during it. On returning to the trance state,
however, she would remember everything said and done in the
earlier condition and even pick up a conversation where it had
been interrupted. Moreover, during the trance state she might
have a greatly enlarged awareness of occurrences in her life
and remember happenings in her remote past:

> But in the genuine out and out somnambulism there is at
> the same time a clear general view of the sphere of waking
> life. Although the somnambulist on awakening no longer
> retains any memory of all that befell her in and during the
> crisis; yet, conversely, she knows very well whatever has
> happened to her when awake and she remembers very
> exactly events of a remote past which in ordinary waking
> circumstances she is not in the least able to recall.*

A key concept of which Schubert also makes use, both
physiologically and psychologically, is metastasis, the process
whereby an organ designed to function in one way takes over
the function of another to which it is not suited; or, desire and
emotion aptly aroused by one object may be extended or
transferred to something associated with that object but not
in itself an appropriate recipient. This may occur at an obvious
and superficial level, as when a lover dotes on some trivial
possession of the beloved. More profoundly, as we have seen,
things may go wrong 'metastatically' when the spirit designed
to operate at a cerebral and wide-ranging (for Schubert, otherworldly) level, in fact functions at a 'ganglionic' level, in the
narrow illusion-dominated world of sensuous desire. The

* 'Aber der eigentliche, vollkommene Somnambulismus hat zugleich
einen hellen Überblick über das Gebiet des wachen Zustandes. Obgleich
die Somnambule beim Erwachen keine Erinnerung mehr an alles das
behält, was in und mit ihr während der Krise vorgegangen: so weiß
sie doch umgekehrt alles sehr wohl, was während des Wachens jemals
geschehen, und sie erinnert sich sehr bestimmt an Vorgänge einer
fernen Vergangenheit, auf die sie sich, während des gewöhnlichen wachen
Zustandes auf keine Weise mehr zu besinnen vermag.'[31]

double significance, characteristic, in Schubert's view, of the practices of cults and the language of myth, prophecy, poetry and dreams, is due in part to a species of metastatic linguistic confusion of reference. The language of daily life, for example, incorporates a relatively fossilized version of a world which in itself, as we have seen, is a partly rigidified image-language in its own right. In the symbolic image-language of myth, prophecy and poetry, both references may be present—to the world of restricted observation and to that beyond. Schubert maintains that in dreams, similarly *zweideutig*, we may see, at the humblest level, comparable traces of veridical communication with the active world beyond that of waking life, intermingled with distortions similar in principle to those through which conventional language mis-reflects true 'Reality'.

For Schubert, the symbolic condensation whereby one hieroglyphic image does duty as symbol for something more complex, betrays the existence of such duality of reference in all the forms of image language already mentioned, including dreams. A prophet in this sense may symbolize the conscience of his people. A dream hieroglyph, when unpacked, may reveal the solution to a problem over which someone has troubled for years. Though Schubert is not quite clear on this point, dream reference to another world may also be implied in the stress he lays on the speed whereby, in dreaming, the events of a lifetime may be reviewed in a few moments. He clearly wishes to explain premonitory dreams by the same principle of otherworldly reference, which operates also in the common cross-cultural significance he believes some dream imagery to have.

Above all, however, dual reference is shown in the ironic reversal of the evaluation of waking life that may occur in dreams, when 'the poet within us is not wholly at ease in the circumstances in which we find ourselves'. The close conjunction, in one outlook, of opposites, such as happiness and sorrow, intense attraction and destructive hate, together with the ironic reversal of evaluation already mentioned, e.g. great riches presented as poverty, power as helplessness, constitute *eine Art von Witz**. Schubert sees this as characteristic of

---

* This may be translated as 'a species of wit', though the German 'Witz' has more ironical overtones than the related English word.

dream imagery, poetry, prophecy (often based on dreams) and nature itself, in ascending order of their possible contact with the unseen world. He gives numerous examples of such ironically penetrating and quizzical inversion of the usual waking evaluation of events.

One may be highly sceptical of Schubert's ontology and highly critical of the ponderous, repetitive and often rhapsodic quality of his style. But it is not easy in a small space to do justice to the quirkishly acute observation entangled in this metaphysical mishmash. The *Zweideutigkeit* that he noticed is often important and interesting, however one chooses to explain it. Occasionally, also, the lyrical quality of the imagery he uses (sometimes borrowed from his contemporaries) is evocative. The mind dreaming ordinarily is likened to a little boat riding at anchor. The pilot of daily life, never able to do more than trim the sails in adjustment to external pressures of wind and water and the danger of rocks, has relinquished his task in rest. There float before the mind, left alone with an inner creation over which it has no control, windpuffs of action, experience, desire, reminiscent of the previous day or long ago, recurrent forms of the past that appear to develop but in fact gyrate in a circle. Or the notion of the *alter ego*, who perpetually reminds us of the possible opposite evaluation of what we say and do, is presented with the aid of Jean Paul's armless itinerant preacher Schmelzle, whose cassock was 'possessed' by one whose gestures reversed the meaning of the preacher's words.

In deep sleep, says Schubert, *die Seele* talks in an inborn image language, emanating from emotion and largely directed by it, and which follows a different law of association from the acquired language of daily life. The latter in fact becomes 'blocked', much as it is sometimes in ordinary life. Awake, it worries us that we say the opposite of what we intend or slip into using a word superficially similar to one we seek but with an alien meaning, such as *Messer* instead of *Wasser*. In deep sleep such blocking of usual speech is of no concern, for *die Seele* is at ease, creating in its own image language. There seems, for Schubert, however, to be an intermediate stage wherein the two different languages run parallel, in so far as they do not mix together or only in a very disconnected fashion. So, for example, when we are thinking of the word 'write', we have at the same time the image of two people before us, one of whom carries the other on his back. In the process of falling asleep, the dream condition allows the waking understanding to go on prating for a little while in its word language, but already makes strange gesticulations behind it. In due season, the disguise of the word language fades and the hidden dream world steps out freely from behind.

The contribution of such German medical and literary writing to the notion of unconscious functioning and thought cannot possibly be disregarded. For later medical developments let us now turn to the French and in particular to Bernheim, for whom suggestion and suggestibility were genuine processes while mysticism and magic were anathema.

Bernheim,[5] in the historical chapter of his book on suggestion, confirms that mesmerism had spread in spite of Mesmer's being discredited. Numerous societies had been founded in the principal cities of France, and that of Strasbourg, La Société de l'Harmonie, composed of more than five hundred members, published results of its work for some years. The French Revolution and the wars of the Empire turned attention to other matters; when order was restored, the official world and learned societies showed rather less hostility. Dupotet, for example, experimented in 1820 at the Salpêtrière and l'Hôtel-Dieu, two important Paris hospitals. In 1825 the Academies of Science and Medicine were persuaded to review the evidence on mesmerism again; a guarded, not unsympathetic report was made, it seems, by Husson in 1831. The Academy did not risk printing this and some reputation for credulity was attached to Husson, though in Bernheim's view his honesty was unimpeachable. Various other attempts were made to disentangle fact from fiction without success. In 1840 the Academy decided it would hear no further reports on animal magnetism.

The notion of magnetic fluid, considered either as a universal fluid or as an emanation from the human organism (warmth or animal electricity), gained, in fact, no scientific credence· Interpretations with a different emphasis arose, and Bernheim sketches the history of these.

The influence of the imagination on the production of the

phenomena observed had struck the representatives of learned societies and even Deslon, Mesmer's first pupil. About 1815, the Abbé Faria, a Portuguese Indian, had produced 'magnetic' phenomena on this hypothesis and a certain General Noizet, a disciple of Faria, convinced Bertrand, an orthodox magnetizer of the 'fluid' variety, of the power of imagination. But writes Bernheim:

> Extraordinary situation! While able to win over Bertrand to his original way of thinking, it was not long before General Noizet himself, under the influence of his own spiritualistic notions, in an effort to reconcile the divergent opinions, fluidism and anti-fluidism, lapsed into the fluidist doctrine. It is by the hypothesis of a vital fluid that the author explains these interesting phenomena.*

Thus, according to Bernheim, although there were precursors of the doctrine of suggestion, this was not accepted as an alternative hypothesis until the advent of James Braid. This Scots doctor in Manchester succeeded in disposing of the magnetic fluid theory by producing hypnotic phenomena by suggestion—with or without the presence of his portmanteau key. His account of this was first published in 1846, about the time that Elliotson in London and Esdaile in India (whom Bernheim doesn't mention) were producing hypnotic sleep, presumably on the older hypotheses. Esdaile, like some of his London colleagues, used it for surgical purposes. It is generally supposed that the advent of chloroform as an anaesthetic in 1847 contributed to diminishing interest in these findings. Braid's work, it seems, made little stir in England and was almost unknown in France at this time.

The next move came in 1848 from the U.S.A. in the guise of 'electrical psychology'. This notion was propounded by Grimes (in ignorance of Braid) and expounded by a Dr. Dods in 1850. It penetrated immediately to England. Here all sorts of respectable doctors, as well as Duguld Stewart, are said to

* 'Chose singulière! Le Général Noizet, tandis qu'il ralliait Bertrand à ses premières conceptions, ne tarda pas lui-même, dominé par ses idées spiritualistes, cherchant à concilier les deux opinions divergentes, fluidiste et antifluidiste, à retomber dans la doctrine fluidiste. C'est par l'hypothèse d'un fluide vital que l'auteur explique les phénomènes intéressants . . .'[5]

have confirmed the 'observations'. In France these studies left the public indifferent; only one doctor, Durand de Gros (under the pseudonym of Philipps), called the attention of doctors and the learned to the findings in 1853, 1855 and 1860. He did not succeed in removing from them the discredit attaching to magnetism. Braid's views were not revived until 1859, when his experiments were repeated successfully by Azam, one of whose colleagues had read an article by Carpenter entitled 'Sleep' in Todd's *Encyclopaedia*. Azam's publication of his results in the *Archives de Medicine* in 1860 gave ephemeral renown to Braid and suggestion. About the same time, various French doctors published interesting observations, including those on renewed attempts (by Broca among others) to use hypnotism instead of chloroform in surgery. These attempts, according to Bernheim, were soon abandoned as unsatisfactory. Suggestion as a method, seeming of no immediate practical application, was left aside again until its most important revival in psychotherapy by Liébeault. In 1866 he described its use in *Du Sommeil et des états analogues considérés surtout au point de vue de l'action du moral sur le physique*.

In the eyes of Bernheim, this work by Liébeault was the most important book then published on the lines of Braid, but taking his ideas further. Nevertheless it also remained uninfluential for the time being. In 1875, however, Richet repeated on men hypnotic experiments that had been carried out on animals. This aroused the interest of the medical world in the psychological aspects of somnambulism. From this it is but a short historical step to Charcot's influential studies of dissociation produced in hysterical patients in 1878 at the Salpêtrière. Bernheim mentions a host of physiological, neurological, chemical and other explanations, mainly German and French, over which there was now controversy. He includes, as specially interesting, the suggestion published in 1880 by Despine of Marseilles which he summarizes as follows:

There exists, says the author, an automatic cerebral activity which manifests itself without the participation of the self [le moi]; for all the nervous centres have, through the laws which regulate their activity, power of intelligence without any self, without personality. The psychological faculties can, in certain pathological cerebral states, manifest themselves in the absence of the self, of the intellect, of consciousness [du moi, de l'esprit, de la conscience] and produce actions resembling those which are manifested normally by the initiative of the self. This is automatic cerebral activity: that, by contrast, which manifests the self, is conscious cerebral activity. In the normal state, these two activities are intimately linked with each other, they form but one and show themselves always conjointly; in certain pathological nervous states, they may separate from each other and function in isolation.

Somnambulism is characterized, physiologically, by the exercise of the brain's automatic activity alone, during the paralysis of its conscious activity. The ignorance, on the part of the somnambulist, of all that he has done in somnambulism, is due therefore not to forgetting, but to the non-participation of the self in his actions.[5]

Despine linked this explanation with a physiological doctrine, propounded by Luys, of the different functioning of different layers of cortical grey matter. About this period many writers, including Huxley and Maudsley, appear to have invoked some form of 'unconscious cerebration' to account for the phenomena observed in dissociated states. Bernheim himself, though interested, came in fact to reject Despine's general theory, on the grounds that, in most of his (and Liébeault's) extensive experience of patients influenced by suggestion and hypnosis, there was still evidence of the operation of 'le moi', in the sense that traces of the patient's personal style remained. Moreover, some of the relevant behaviour of somnambulists would, Bernheim thought, be better explained in terms of increased speed of translation of suggested image into action. Writing in 1891, Binet also came to argue that, as it stood, 'unconscious cerebration' was inadequate to account for all the phenomena involved. It would be out of place here to explore any further this hornet's nest of difficult problems. Enough has been said to indicate the kind of controversy that Freud will have encountered when he arrived at the Salpêtrière to work with Charcot in 1885. Perhaps it is worth reminding the reader that Freud translated Bernheim and visited Liébeault, still working as an old man at Nancy. This school held, in opposition to others, that the phenomena found in somnambulism were not restricted to hysterical personalities and were to be explained on psycho-physiological lines, with particular emphasis on suggestion. Freud summarized the main points at issue in his introduction to his German translation of Bernheim, produced in 1888-9.

In what we have already said, some relevant nineteenth-century physiological views have been implied. It is important, however, to collect together those whose bearing on the modern notion of unconscious functioning seems to have been most direct. First, there is the distinction drawn by Bichat, at the turn of the eighteenth century, between central and autonomic nervous functioning (mentioned in passing on p. 65). There derived from it a whole host of investigations and speculations centred upon the amount of functioning possible without cerebral co-operation or control. Secondly, there are the studies, to which Du Bois Reymond and Helmholtz contributed so much, of the speed of transmission of nervous impulse. That the impact of a stimulus and its registration are not instantaneous events (a time interval being needed between the first and the second) still startles the unwary into realizing the complexities of their make-up. Thirdly, there are the nineteenth-century studies of reflexes, again reinforcing awareness of what we may do unawares.

Fourthly, there is the recognition by Claude Bernard[4] of the processes, later designated homeostatic by W. B. Cannon, whereby the body regulates maintenance, e.g. of temperature, and the mechanisms whereby an imbalance is corrected. The *biological* principle of an equilibrium, maintained by the balance of input and output of energy, seems to be partly traceable historically to the conservation of energy principle in physics. This principle is associated particularly with Helmholtz, who lectured on it in 1847, and with Du Bois Reymond, his close contemporary. It had an enormous influence on Brücke, whose physiology (in the words of Ernst Kris[27]) was 'firmly based on ideas taken from the world of physics' and who was regarded by Helmholtz and Du Bois Reymond as their 'ambassador in Vienna'. The influence of Brücke on Freud was, of course, profound. Breuer in 1895, quoting from Janet in 1894, cites a comment of Cabanis in 1824 which is also interesting and relevant. 'Sensibility seems to behave like a fluid whose total quantity is fixed and which, whenever it pours into one of its channels in greater abundance, becomes proportionately less in others.'[9] To Breuer's use of this principle, subtly but significantly different from Freud's, we shall return later.

Flügel[15] has drawn attention, in his brilliant essay on the concept of the death wish, to Fechner's and Spencer's use of the notion of equilibrium. Fechner enumerated four states of stability, namely: (1) 'absolute', where there is neither change nor motion; (2) 'complete', in which such movements as occur lead back to the original configuration in more or less equal periods of time; (3) 'approximate', in which return to the previous condition is less perfect; (4) 'absolute instability', in which there is constant change. In Flügel's view, Spencer's psychology was based on a principle of this kind, in so far as 'adaptation of inner relations to outer relations' aims at a state of equilibrium. Freud[13] explicitly refers to Fechner in *Beyond the Pleasure Principle* and the phrase 'the stability principle' derives from him.

From all this we get a glimpse of the widespread use of this conception. It is a short step from this 'conservation', or equilibrium, principle to thinking of stimuli as disturbers of the peace and of responses as attempts to restore equilibrium. This is particularly true if one's attention is focused (as was that of the current French psychiatry represented by Janet) on states of nervous excitability, which are then seen as an imbalance needing correction.

Finally, but worthy of separate mention under this heading of physiology, are the studies of aphasia carried out by Hughlings Jackson[25] and published in 1879. Consciously borrowing the term 'dissolution', coined by Herbert Spencer as the reverse of 'evolution', Hughlings Jackson hypothesized two levels of neural and verbal functioning in the understanding and use of language and drew a distinction between, as it were, the automatic emission of sounds and words and 'pro-positionizing'. He envisaged the possibility of reversion from the later and more highly developed form to the more primitive, both neurologically and psychologically; this paved the way for Freud's concept of 'regression'. Hughlings Jackson both implied the emotional significance of relatively primitive verbalization and generalized, apropos of the oaths and other ejaculations of which some aphasics are capable, in the following way:

> They are all parts of emotional language; their utterance by healthy people is on the physical side a process during which the equilibrium of a *greatly** disturbed nervous system is restored, as are also ordinary emotional mani-festations (all actions are in one sense restorations of nervous equilibrium by expenditure of energy).[25]

In the same series of articles, he extended the use of the 'dissolution' principle as a possible explanation of phenomena observed in pathological states, such as the furious mania of epilepsy or the hallucinations of the insane. He also made abundantly clear that he saw symptoms, such as recurrent utterances or hallucinations, as 'positive', not as, in themselves, disordered functions. He writes:

> These positive mental symptoms arise during activity of lower centres or lower nervous arrangements which have escaped injury, and are only to be thought of as symptoms in the sense of being the fittest psychical states arising during slightly hyper-normal discharge of lower more organized nervous arrangements which are *then* highest, the normally highest having lost functions.[25]

In developing an explanation of the hyper-normal discharge of the lower, more organized nervous arrangements (and also

* Hughlings Jackson was of course perfectly well aware of the habitual nature of some interjections. He was also at pains to avoid confusing the neurological and psychological viewpoints, though he was interested in both. This, however, is not the place for a more detailed account of his work. That Hughlings Jackson influenced both Pavlov and Freud is also another story. For a useful review of Hughlings Jackson's influence in psychiatry, see Stengel.[32]

of those activated immediately prior to a lesion occurring) Hughlings Jackson came to argue that 'destruction of function of a higher centre is removal of inhibition over a lower centre'.

From 1859 onwards, these developments in physiology and neurology have to be seen in the light of the changing outlook engendered within biology, and outside it, by Darwin's theory of evolution, published that year. Nine or so years be fore Hughlings Jackson's studies, for example, this evolutionary slant was clearly shown in Hering's[24] treatment of memory. In 1870 Hering, as Professor of Physiology, delivered in Vienna a lecture on this subject that has gone down in history. It was natural to him to think in physiological terms of the unconscious recording of experience and, with a Lamarckian slant, of change induced by the impact of events on such unconscious registration. Hering saw psychology and physiology as essential complementaries, and stressed the need to extend the word memory beyond voluntary recall to cover 'unvoluntary reproductions of sensations, ideas, perceptions and efforts'. He treated memory, however, as 'a faculty of our unconscious states', organically, not psychologically, conceived.

The bond of union, therefore, which connects the individual phenomena of our consciousness lies in an unconscious world; and as we know nothing of this but what investigation into the laws of matter teach us—as, in fact, for purely experimental purposes, 'matter' and the 'unconscious' must be one and the same thing—so the physiologist has a full right to denote memory as, in the wider sense of the word, a function of brain substance, whose results, it is true, fall, as regards one part of them, into the domain of consciousness, while another and not less essential part escapes unperceived as purely material processes.[24]

The evolutionary and the Lamarckian element are perfectly clear in Hering's peroration, so also is some of the charm with which he was capable of endowing these ingredients.

The brain processes and phenomena of consciousness which ennoble man in the eyes of his fellows, have had a less ancient history than those connected with his physical needs. Hunger and the reproductive instinct affected the oldest and simplest forms of the organic world. It is in respect of these instincts, therefore, and of the means to gratify them, that the memory of organized substance is strongest—the impulses and instincts that arise hence having still paramount power over the minds of men. The spiritual life has been superadded slowly; its most splendid outcome belongs to the latest epoch in the history of organized matter, nor has any very great length of time elapsed since the nervous system was first crowned with the glory of a large and well-developed brain.

Oral tradition and written history have been called the memory of man, and this is not without its truth. But there is another and a living memory in the innate reproductive power of brain substance, and without this both writings and oral tradition would be without significance to posterity. The most sublime ideas, though never so immortalized in speech or letters, are yet nothing for heads that are out of harmony with them; they must be not only heard, but reproduced; and both speech and writing would be in vain were there not an inheritance of inward and outward brain development, growing in correspondence with the inheritance of ideas that are handed down from age to age, and did not an enhanced capacity for their reproduction on the part of each succeeding generation accompany the thoughts that have been preserved in writing. Man's conscious memory comes to an end at death, but the unconscious memory of Nature is true and ineradicable; whoever succeeds in stamping upon her the impress of his work, she will remember him to the end of time.[24]

Freud will have been a boy of fourteen when this lecture was given. There is no evidence that he encountered it at that stage, though later in life he was personally acquainted with Hering and was asked to be his assistant. In commenting on this address, Freud attributes to Hering a clearer suggestion of an unconscious *mind* than the text in German appears wholly to justify. One is left wondering whether Freud read into Hering implications that are not there, or whether he rightly interpreted Hering in the light of conversations of which we have no record. What we do know is that Freud, as a student under Brücke in Vienna and later as an excellent neurologist himself, will have been familiar with the main neuro-physiological findings and speculations of his day. From Ernest Jones we also know that Freud will have approached them equipped from his schooldays with Herbartian psychology. This brings us to the elements of then current psychology and philosophy that were also earlier cairns on the route to Freud's concept of unconscious functioning.

Until the middle of the nineteenth century British orthodox psychological treatment of thinking was largely associationist: interest was focused on the contents of the mind, as derived originally from sensory experience (conceived atomistically), with overtones of pleasure and pain. Such initially simple ingredients combined, of course, into a mental experience whose complexity no serious writer wished to deny. But such complexity depended theoretically on variants of the Aristotelian laws of association, by which the integration of elements is due to similarity, contrast or contiguity in space and time.

Between the 1850's and 1890's, the standard English texts were those of Alexander Bain[2] who, remaining largely associationist in approach, reinforced British psychological theory with up-to-date physiology and expounded a form of associationism that credited brain and mind alike with spontaneous activity. As we have seen in Chapter Two, John Locke is not open to the criticism of reducing people to impotent bundles whose only rôle is to register changes in the experiences that befall them. But the degenerate associationism of a century or more later than Locke, exemplified by the elder Mill, was much criticized by Bain and others on this score. Bain's spontaneous activity was criticized in its turn by those who liked to see the world as a closed determinist system in which everything is pushed around passively in accordance with immutable laws.

In continental psychological thought, stress on activity was noticeable earlier than in England. This is specially true in Germany, where there was a direct tradition stretching from

Leibniz, and of course Kant, to those whom they influenced. In nineteenth-century France, markedly influenced in the eighteenth century by British associationism, physiological approaches to psychology were strong, while emphasis on mental activity was sporadic. Sometimes, as in the case of Maine de Biran, it too can be traced back in part to Leibniz.

So far as unconscious psychic processes are concerned, the most important psychological theorist of the late eighteenth and early nineteenth century was Herbart[23] (1776-1841). From him there filtered into German psychological textbooks (and educational theory) the following key notions, well summarized by Brett.[8] First, he believed in a limited fund of mental energy available for the maintenance of psychological experience. Secondly, Herbart's account of the ingredients of this experience was largely associationist, except that *die Seele* (unknowable in the best Kantian tradition) was invoked as a unifying principle and endowed with an active effort of self-preservation. Thirdly, the so-called faculties, attention, memory and the like, plus the ingredients of psychological life, i.e. 'presentations', were seen as indirect products of this self-preservative activity of the *Seele*.

Fourthly (in Brett's words), 'A certain amount of energy is expended in every act of self-preservation. It is this energy that carries the presentation up to the summit; that is to say, makes it a conscious presentation. If a second disturbance follows, the total amount of energy is divided, what the second gains the first loses, and therefore as the second rises into consciousness the first dies away. . . . No presentation ever disappears completely; it only becomes infinitesimal in respect of its energy, which is equivalent to becoming a negligible factor until some access of energy raises it again into consciousness.' Hence: 'The whole state of mind is determined at any given time by the degrees of activity belonging to each element or presentation. Thus the elements a, b, c, d, . . ., according to their respective qualities, will be either clear or obscure, and they will stand to one another in different relations which can be measured as degrees of distance from the point at which they become relatively negligible. This point of least activity is called the threshold of consciousness. Below the threshold the contents exist with no measurable activity; they are not annihilated and they continue to affect the whole consciousness.'[8]

Fifthly, and again quoting Brett, 'When the contents of the mind attain equilibrium there is a static condition which would, presumably, continue if no fresh disturbance occurred. But the objects of the outer world continually enter in; they continually disturb the equilibrium which tends to establish itself in consciousness; there is therefore a threshold for static conditions and another for dynamic conditions. If a presentation has been through the process of conflict and succumbed, it is below the static threshold and as good as dead; if, on the other hand, its energy is unexhausted and its obscurity is due to not having excited itself, it is describable as below the threshold in a different sense: it is below the dynamical threshold.'[8]

This argument is hard to understand without reference to the doctrine of apperception, the last and most famous of Herbart's views which it is relevant to extract from him. This doctrine amounts to the view that a newly impinging presentation may tap the available fund of energy monopolized by a consciously active system of presentations only if it is psychologically consonant with that system. If it is not, it is likely to be 'verdrängt', which can be translated as 'pushed aside' or 'repressed', according to whether one interprets Herbart on a 'two dimensional' or a 'three dimensional' (including 'depth') basis. It seems likely that the two-dimensional model is the more correct. In any case, since Freud, the word 'repressed' has taken on such a specialized meaning that it would be fatally easy to read into Herbart even more of the later view than would be justified. As it stands, even without this 'depth' interpretation, however, it is easy to see the historical development of ideas. That Freud encountered Herbartian psychology in a school textbook by Lindner is vouched for by Ernest Jones,[26] from whom we also learn that Lindner was taught by Exner, the father of Freud's tutor at the Brücke Institute.

While Freud was avowedly influenced by Herbart, it is not certain that the stress on unconscious striving and willing found in German philosophical writing, such as that of Schopenhauer and Von Hartmann, affected the early formulation of Freud's notions directly. It is worth realizing the existence of a philosophical trend, however, to which Freud referred as a matter of course in his later writings. There are passages in Schopenhauer reflecting other suggestive speculations; one of the most interesting of these is the notion that madness involves a breakdown in memory, and is the last resort of nature when an individual is faced with a burden of unbearable pain or sorrow.* This is to be found in Schopenhauer's otherwise unconvincing discussion of the relation of madness and genius. Where, elsewhere, he is amplifying this theory of the significance of memory disturbance we find Schopenhauer writing as follows:

> The exposition of the origin of madness will become more comprehensible if it is remembered how unwillingly we think of things which powerfully injure our interests, wound our pride, or interfere with our wishes; with what difficulty do we determine to lay such things before our own intellect for careful and serious investigation; how easily, on the other hand, we unconsciously break away or sneak off from them again; how, on the contrary, agreeable events come into our minds of their own accord, and, if driven away, constantly creep in again, so that we dwell on them for hours together. In that resistance of the will to allowing what is contrary to it to come under the examination of the intellect lies the place at which madness can break in upon the mind. Each new adverse event must be assimilated by the intellect, i.e. it must receive a place in the system of the truths connected with our will and its interests, whatever it may have to displace that is more satisfactory. Whenever this has taken place, it already pains us much less; but this operation itself is often very painful, and also, in general, only takes place slowly and with resistance. However, the health of the mind can only continue so long as this is in each case properly carried out. If, on the contrary, in some particular case, the resistance

* When Otto Rank drew Freud's attention to this discussion by Schopenhauer, Freud was at pains to express approval but disclaimed having read *The World as Will and Idea*. This does not exclude the possibility of indirect influence. It remains an historical fact that Schopenhauer wrote in this vein before Freud was born. Also Meynart was much influenced by him.

and struggles of the will against the apprehension of some knowledge reaches such a degree that the operation is not performed in its integrity, then certain events or circumstances become for the intellect completely suppressed, because the will cannot endure the sight of them, and then, for the sake of the necessary connexion, the gaps that thus arise are filled up at pleasure; thus madness appears. For the intellect has given up its nature to please the will: the man now imagines what does not exist. Yet the madness which has thus arisen is now the lethe of unendurable suffering; it was the last remedy of harassed nature, i.e. of the will.[30]

Directly influencing Freud or not, such ideas will have formed part of the German nineteenth-century climate of opinion within which he lived and worked, and they cannot be disregarded.

It would have been surprising if other philosophers and psychologists of the 1860's to 1880's had not become involved in discussion of conscious and unconscious functioning. And, indeed, in this period we find an immense amount of controversy well before Freud's appearance on the scene. In England this seems to have been precipitated by Hamilton[21] who, in lectures given from 1836 to 1856, went harking back to a fine example of the production of childhood memories in a later, dissociated state which Samuel Taylor Coleridge reported as occurring in Germany about 1797.

A young illiterate woman . . . was seized with a nervous fever; during which, according to the asseverations of all the priests and monks of the neighbourhood, she became possessed, and, as it appeared, by a very learned devil. She continued incessantly talking Latin, Greek, and Hebrew, in very pompous tones and with most distinct enunciation. This possession was rendered more probable by the known fact that she was or had been a heretic. The case had attracted the particular attention of a young physician, and by his statement many physiologists and psychologists visited the town and cross-examined the case on the spot. Sheets full of her ravings were taken down from her own mouth, and were found to consist of sentences, coherent and intelligible each for itself, but with little or no connexion with each other. Of the Hebrew, a small portion only could be traced to the Bible; the remainder seemed to be in the Rabbinical dialect. All trick or conspiracy was out of the question.[10]

As many readers of Coleridge may know, 'the young physician' who was 'determined to trace her past life step by step' succeeded eventually in tracking down the source of the Hebrew, the Rabbinical writings, and the Greek and Latin fathers, in an old protestant pastor. He had charitably taken the girl, as a nine-year-old child, into his house, where she remained till his death. It 'had been the old man's custom, for years, to walk up and down a passage of his house into which the kitchen door opened, and to read to himself with a loud voice, out of his favourite books'.

Hamilton, familiar with much of the German literature we have already mentioned, happily trounced the English, and for that matter the French of his day,* for their unsympathetic attitude to the possibility that 'the mind exerts energies and is the subject of modifications, of neither of which it is conscious'. J. Stuart Mill discussed Hamilton, arguing that unconscious awareness is a contradiction in terms. Bain tried to disentangle different senses of the word 'conscious'. Lewes, writing in 1877, propounded a theory of degrees of 'sentience' of which reflective awareness lay at one extreme. James, entering the lists a little later, i.e. in 1890, saw 'the supposed distinction between the unconscious and the conscious being of a mental state' as 'the sovereign means for believing what one likes in psychology, and of twisting what might become a science into a tumbling ground for whimsies'. James, steeped in the French and German literature, was not, be it noted, querying the vast amount of factual material accumulated by his time on latent knowledge, dissociated states, subliminal awareness and the like. To these

---

* Hamilton is amusingly cross with the French psychologists Cardaillac and Damiron, who have 'marvellously propounded the doctrine, long and generally established in Germany, as something new and unheard of before their own assertion of the paradox'.

he was vastly sympathetic. He was querying a particular hypothesis, while quite willing to assign 'consciousness' a relatively minor rôle in thought. Sully,[33] in 1892, critically summarized much of the earlier discussion, giving the main references which I have followed up.

Eighteen years earlier, i.e. in 1874, we find Franz Brentano[7] citing all the then relevant English writers (Hamilton, Mill, Bain, Maudsley, Lewes and others) together with the Germans (Fechner, Beneke, Lotze et al.), the Italian Ulrici, and St. Thomas Aquinas, thrown in for good measure. Brentano, in a complex and extraordinarily interesting chapter, was busy maintaining, among other things, that though psychic processes were by nature 'object-directed', it does not follow that all object-directed processes are themselves objects of consciousness. Hence the notion of unconscious psychic processes need not be contradictory as the younger Mill supposed. We need, he said, to distinguish two uses of the word 'unconscious'; one active, referring to that which is not conscious of something; the other passive, referring to something of which we are not conscious. In the first sense 'unconscious awareness' would be a contradiction in terms, but it is not so in the second. In the same year that Brentano was publishing in this vein, Freud, as an eighteen-year-old, started to attend Brentano's reading seminar.[26]

It remains to say something of experimental psychology's contribution, in particular that of Sir Francis Galton, initially published in 1879. So far as I have been able to trace, he was the first person to experiment in systematic analysis of associations to given stimuli. The inference Galton drew is best given in his own words, for it shows immediately the relevance of his work to 'unconscious thinking'.

Perhaps the strongest of the impressions left by these experiments regards the multifariousness of the work done by the mind in a state of half unconsciousness, and the valid reason they afford for believing in the existence of still deeper strata of mental operations, sunk wholly below the level of consciousness, which may account for such mental phenomena as cannot otherwise be explained.[18]

How Galton conceived the idea of studying associations systematically we can only surmise. In *Memories of my Life** he relates these inquiries to a period after he had become very much interested in heredity and 'was so harassed with the old question of Determinism, which would leave every human action under the control of Heredity and Environment, that I made a series of observations on the actions of my own mind in relation to Free Will'. Explaining that he is using the phrase 'in the *special* sense of an *uncaused* and *creative* action', he writes that 'whenever I caught myself in an act of what seemed to be 'Free Will' in the above sense, I checked myself and tried hard to recollect what had happened before, made rapid notes, and then wrote a full account of the case'. He found, to his surprise, how much, supposedly performed by a creative act or inspiration, was 'really due to straightforward causation'.

While this concern over free-will and determinism is undoubtedly the immediate context of Galton's psychometric experiments, it is worth recalling three other facts that *may* have contributed indirectly to their existence. First, of course, Galton lived in a milieu wherein 'associationist' accounts of mental processes were dominant and he must have been familiar with some of the controversies just mentioned. Secondly, it was natural to him, whenever something caught his attention, to set about investigating it as objectively and systematically as he could. Thirdly, more interesting and perhaps less familiar to many readers, are the following kinds of experience which he had had in earlier years. When working at Birmingham General Hospital in his teens, Galton had first-hand acquaintance with head injury cases, as well as 'many protean forms of that strange disorder hysteria'. While at Cambridge he himself had a species of breakdown. Another transitory breakdown, partly of a psychological nature, occurred in 1866 round about the time of the studies of heredity. From both illnesses he obviously recovered, but well aware, from the way

* Galton's reference in *Memories of my Life*, p. 295, is to 'Psychometric Experiments, Free Will' (*Brain*, Vol. III). In the title of the article as published in this volume of *Brain*, the phrase 'Free Will' does not occur. On the reason for this omission in *Brain* (or addition in the *Memories*) one can only speculate.

he writes, of the state wherein normal psychological processes border upon the pathological.

It is also true that Galton's[20] past included first-hand knowledge of some studies of dissociation similar in principle to those already discussed in this chapter. During his third long vacation at Cambridge, i.e. in 1843, he went to Germany. In Saxony, where he stayed, the practice of magnetism was forbidden by law. Characteristically, for in Galton's life well-informed friends played an enormous rôle, an Austrian acquaintance in Dresden invited him to his house across the frontier. 'There' (referring in his own words to 'animal magnetism') Galton saw 'an elementary part of its practice', that is to say 'its inducing catalepsy and insensibility to pain'. The true Galton is also reflected in the upshot. He 'practised it at home and magnetized some eighty persons in this way, but it is an unwholesome procedure, and I have never attempted it since'. He had experimented quite long enough, however, to learn something of what was involved. Finding fatiguing the concentrated 'will power', at that time supposedly necessary on the magnetizer's part, Galton experimented in relaxing, though 'looking all the time in the same way as before'. 'At last', he writes, 'I succeeded in letting my mind ramble freely while I maintained the same owl-like demeanour. This acted just as well. The safe conclusion was that the effect is purely subjective on the part of the patient, and that will-power on the part of the operator has nothing to do with it.' Indirectly contributary to his studies of association or not, these facts must return us to the association experiments he reported in the 1870's, first in the *Nineteenth Century*, for March 1879,[17] and second in July 1879 in *Brain*, Vol. II.[18]

What did Galton do in these experiments? From these two articles taken together one gets the following picture. Galton drew a distinction between 'two main categories of thought processes. In the first of these, ideas present themselves by association either with some object newly perceived by the senses or with previous ideas; in the second process, such of the associated ideas are fixed and vivified by the attention, as happen to be germane to the topic on which the mind is set.' Galton makes quite clear that he is concerned in his inquiries with the first process and *not* the second. For him this first process 'is an automatic one; the ideas arise of their own accord, and we cannot, except in indirect and imperfect ways, compel them to come'.

Galton's first experiments in studying this process were, as he was well aware, 'imperfect, but sufficient to inspire . . . keen interest in the matter'. They suggested the more controlled studies with which he continued. This is one of Galton's own accounts of his first experiments:

On several occasions, but notably on one when I felt myself unusually capable of the kind of effort required, I walked leisurely along Pall Mall, a distance of 450 yards, during which time I scrutinized with attention every successive object that caught my eyes, and I allowed my attention to rest on it until one or two thoughts had arisen through direct association with that object; then I took very brief mental note of them, and passed on to the next object. I never allowed my mind to ramble. The number of objects viewed was, I think, about 300, for I have subsequently repeated the same walk under similar conditions and endeavouring to estimate their number, with that result. It was impossible for me to recall in other than the vaguest way the numerous ideas that had passed through my mind; but of this, at least, I was sure, that samples of my whole life had passed before me, that many bygone incidents, which I never suspected to have formed part of my stock of thoughts, had been glanced at as objects too familiar to awaken the attention. I saw at once that the brain was vastly more active than I had previously believed it to be, and I was perfectly amazed at the unexpected width of the field of its everyday operations. After an interval of some days, during which I kept my mind from dwelling on my first experiences, in order that it might retain as much freshness as possible for a second experiment, I repeated the walk, and was struck just as much as before by the variety of the ideas that presented themselves, and the number of events to which they referred, about which I had never consciously occupied

myself of late years. But my admiration at the activity of
the mind was seriously diminished by another observation
which I then made, namely that there had been a very
great deal of repetition of thought. The actors on my mental
stage were indeed very numerous, but by no means so
numerous as I had imagined. They now seemed to be
something like the actors in theatres where large processions are represented, who march off one side of the
stage, and, going round by the back, come on again at the
other. I accordingly cast about for means of laying hold of
these fleeting thoughts, and, submitting them to statistical
analysis, to find out more about their tendency to repetition and other matters.[18]

The method Galton finally adopted is described as follows:

I selected a list of suitable words and wrote them on
different small sheets of paper. Taking care to dismiss them
from my thoughts when not engaged upon them, and
allowing some days to elapse before I began to use them,
I laid one of these sheets with all due precautions under a
book, but not wholly covered by it, so that when I leant
forward I could see one of the words, being previously
quite ignorant of what the word would be. Also I held a
small chronograph, which I started by pressing a spring
the moment the word caught my eye, and which stopped
of itself the instant I released the spring; and this I did so
soon as about a couple of ideas in direct association with
the word had arisen in my mind. I found that I could not
manage to recollect more than two ideas with the needed
precision, at least not in a general way; but sometimes
several ideas occurred so nearly together that I was able
to record three or even four of them, while sometimes I
only managed one. The second ideas were never derived
from the first, but always direct from the word itself, for
I kept my attention firmly fixed on the word, and the
associated ideas were seen only by a half glance. When the
two ideas had occurred, I stopped the chronograph and
wrote them down, and the time they occupied. I soon got

into the way of doing all this in a very methodical and automatic manner, keeping the mind perfectly calm and neutral, but intent and, as it were, at full cock and on hair trigger, before displaying the word. There was no disturbance occasioned by thinking of the imminent revulsion of the mind when the chronograph was stopped. My feeling before stopping it was simply that I had delayed long enough, and this in no way interfered with the free action of the mind. I found no trouble in ensuring the complete fairness of the experiment, by using a number of little precautions, hardly necessary to describe, that practice quickly suggested, but it was a most repugnant and laborious work, and it was only by strong self-control that I went through my schedule according to programme.[18]

In the *Brain* article, Galton refers to a list of seventy-five words that he finally secured, having started with more. The earlier and *Nineteenth Century* version of the story reveals that he started with 100 words 'for the convenience of writing down the percentages', but (in the guiltless age of Victoria!) he admits in print that he mislaid some of them. It seems that it is the seventy-five that he has in mind when, in *Brain*, he refers to going through the list on four separate occasions, 'under very different circumstances, in England and abroad, and at intervals of about a month'.* 'In no case', he adds, 'were the associations governed to any degree worth recording, by remembering what had occurred to me on previous occasions, for I found that the process itself had great influence in discharging the memory of what it had just been engaged in, and I of course took care between the experiments never to let my thoughts revert to the words.'

Throwing the results into a 'common statistical hotchpotch', Galton first examined the rate at which the associated ideas were formed. It had taken a total time of 660 seconds to form 505 ideas. Thus his ideas were formed at the rate of about 50 in a minute or 3,000 in an hour. Galton comments that 'this

* In *Memories of my Life* he refers to the series of observations as 'carried out almost continuously for six weeks, and off and on for many subsequent months'.

would be miserably slow work in reverie, or whenever the thought follows the lead of each association that successively presents itself. In the present case, much time was lost in mentally taking the word in, owing to the quiet unobtrusive way in which I found it necessary to bring it into view, so as not to disturb the thoughts.' 'Moreover,' he adds, 'a substantive by itself is usually the equivalent of too abstract an idea for us to conceive it properly without delay.'

Although the 75 words, gone over 4 times, had given rise to 505 ideas, there were also 13 cases of puzzle, 'in which nothing sufficiently definite to note occurred within the brief maximum period of about 4 seconds that I allowed myself to any single trial.' And of the 505 ideas, only 289 were different. Galton gives a table showing the proportions of the total ideas recurring and the proportion of recurrent ideas which cropped up on one, two, three or four of the occasions on which he experimented.

TABLE I[18]

Proportions of Recurrent Associations

Total number of Associations	quadruplets	triplets	doublets	singles
505	116	108	114	167
per cent ·100	23	21	23	33

Total number of different Associations	four times	three	twice	once
289	29	36	57	167
per cent ·100	10	12	20	58

Galton's comment on this evidence of restriction and recurrence of ideas is illuminating.

I was fully prepared to find much iteration in my ideas, but had little expected that out of every hundred words twenty-three would give rise to exactly the same association in every one of the four trials; twenty-one, to the same association in three out of the four, and so on, the experiments having been purposely conducted under very different conditions of time and local circumstances. This shows much less variety in the mental stock of ideas than I had expected, and makes us feel that the roadways of our minds are worn into very deep ruts. I conclude from the proved number of faint and barely conscious thoughts, and from the proved iteration of them, that the mind is perpetually travelling over familiar ways without our memory retaining any impression of its excursions. Its footsteps are so light and fleeting that it is only by such experiments as I have described that we can learn anything about them. It is apparently always engaged in mumbling over its old stores, and if any one of these is wholly neglected for a while, it is apt to be forgotten, perhaps irrecoverably. It is by no means keen interest and attention when first observing an object, that fixes it in the recollection. We pore over the pages of a 'Bradshaw', and study the trains for some particular journey with the greatest interest; but the event passes by, and the hours and other facts which we once so eagerly considered become absolutely forgotten.

So in games of whist, and in a large number of similar instances. As I understand it, the subject must have a continued living interest in order to retain an abiding-place in the memory. The mind must refer to it frequently, but whether it does so consciously or unconsciously, is not perhaps a matter of much importance.[18]

Galton next determined, 'as far as feasible', the dates at which each of the associated ideas had first become attached to the word now calling it up. This he found possible to do in 124 cases. Table 2 taken from Galton best summarizes his results.

He infers the greater fixity of the earlier associations by noting that a quarter of these occurred in all four trials, whereas only about a sixth of those referring to 'subsequent manhood', and none of those counted as recent, occurred as frequently. Looking through the list of all the associations, Galton adds: 'It was easy to see how they are pervaded by purely English ideas, and especially such as are prevalent in that stratum of English society in which I was born and bred, and have subsequently lived.' He supplements this with anecdotal evidence of how 'narrowly we are bound by the fetters of our early education'.

Finally, Galton attempted a rough classification of the associated ideas in terms of their psychological character. It is evident that he had some difficulty in grouping the ideas and

TABLE 2[18]

Relative Number of Associations Formed at
Different periods of Life

Total number of different Associations		Occurring four times		Occurring three times		Occurring twice		Occurring once		Whose first formation was in
	per cent		per cent		per cent		per cent		per cent	
48	39	12	10	11	9	9	7	16	13	boyhood and youth
57	46	10	8	8	7	6	5	33	26	subsequent manhood
19	15	—	—	4	3	1	1	14	11	quite recent events
124	100	22	18	23	19	16	13	63	50	Totals

the results are not wholly satisfactory.* Nevertheless his description of the grouping is too interesting in its own right, as well as historically, to omit. He found his associated ideas could be divided into three main groups:

First there is the imagined sound of words, as in verbal quotations or names of persons. This was frequently a mere parrot-like memory which acted instantaneously and in a meaningless way, just as a machine might act. In the

* After his experiments were over, Galton also found that the words he used could be divided into three groups; those admitting mental imagery, those admitting 'excellently of histrionic representation' and those of a more abstract nature such as 'afternoon', 'ability' and 'abnormal' which were 'variously and imperfectly dealt with by my mind'. While it is methodologically important that the list of words used by Galton may have affected the results he obtained, this is not a problem we are justified in exploring here, particularly as he never quotes the list in full. So his attempt to relate the analysis of the words to the type of association process elicited is omitted from this account; though its existence should be on record as showing Galton's awareness of its methodological significance.[18]

next group there was every other kind of sense-imagery; the chime of imagined bells, the shiver of remembered cold, the scent of some particular locality, and much more frequently than all the rest put together, visual imagery. The last of the three groups contains what I will venture, for want of a better name, to call 'Histrionic' representations. It includes those cases where I either act a part in imagination, or see in imagination a part acted, or, most commonly by far, where I am both spectator and all the actors at once, in an imaginary mental theatre. Thus I feel a nascent sense of some muscular action while I simultaneously witness a puppet of my brain—a part of myself— perform that action, and I assume a mental attitude appropriate to the occasion. This, in my case, is a very frequent way of generalizing, indeed I rarely feel that I have secure hold of a general idea until I have translated it somehow into this form. Thus the word 'abasement' presented itself to me, in one of my experiments, by my mentally placing myself in a pantomimic attitude of humiliation with half-closed eyes, bowed back, and uplifted palms, while at the same time I was aware of myself as of a mental puppet, in that position. This same word will serve to illustrate the other groups also. It so happened in connexion with 'abasement' that the word 'David' or 'King David' occurred to me on the one occasion in each of three out of the four trials; also that an accidental misreading, or perhaps the merely punning association of the words 'a basement', brought up on all four occasions the image of the foundations of a house that the builders had begun upon.[18]

A further analysis showed that, for Galton at any rate, 'histrionic ideas' definitely tended to occur first; verbal associations occurred first and with great quickness on many occasions but on the whole they were only a little more likely to occur first than second. Imagery was decidedly more likely to be the second than the first of the associations called up by a word. 'In short,' says Galton, 'gesture language appeals the most quickly to our feelings.'

Galton, in spite of difficulties he refers to more than once, was prepared to embark on experimental studies of this sort and thought 'it would be very instructive to print the actual records at length, made by many experimenters, if the records could be clubbed together and thrown into a statistical form'. But he also thought 'it would be too absurd to print one's own singly. They lay bare the foundations of a man's thoughts with curious distinctness, and exhibit his mental anatomy with more vividness and truth than he would probably care to publish to the world.' He uses two main analogies for describing the depth of the processes of which he had become aware. One, that of the basement of a house revealed in the process of repair, occurs in the *Brain* 1879 article. It survives to the third version of these experiments, included in *Inquiries into Human Faculty*,[19] first published in 1883, and which follows the *Brain* article very closely. The following is the version from *Brain*:

> I must add, that I found the experiments to be extremely trying and irksome, and that it required much resolution to go through with them, using the scrupulous care they demanded. Nevertheless the results well repaid the trouble. They gave me an interesting and unexpected view of the number of the operations of the mind, and of the obscure depths in which they took place, of which I had been little conscious before. The general impression they have left upon me is like that which many of us have experienced when the basement of our house happens to be under thorough sanitary repairs, and we realize for the first time the complex system of drains and gas and water pipes, flues, bell-wires, and so forth, upon which our comfort depends, but which are usually hidden well out of sight, and with whose existence so long as they acted well, we had never troubled ourselves.[18]

The second analogy is drawn from the sea. It occurs only in the original article in *The Nineteenth Century*, in which Galton refers explicitly to the importance of unconscious cerebration. He writes:

The more I have examined the workings of my own mind,

whether in the walk along Pall Mall, or in the seventy-five words, or in any other of the numerous ways I have attempted but do not here describe, the less respect I feel for the part played by consciousness. I begin with others to doubt its use altogether as a helpful supervisor, and to think that my best brain work is wholly independent of it. The unconscious operations of the mind frequently far transcend the conscious ones in intellectual importance. Sudden inspirations and those flashings out of results which cost a great deal of conscious effort to ordinary people, but are the natural outcome of what is known as genius, are undoubted products of unconscious cerebration. Conscious actions are motived, and motives can make themselves attended to, whether consciousness be present or not. Consciousness seems to do little more than attest the fact that the various organs of the brain do not work with perfect ease or co-operation. Its position appears to be that of a helpless spectator of but a minute fraction of a huge amount of automatic brain work. The unconscious operations of the mind may be likened to the innumerable waves that travel by night, unseen and in silence, over the broad expanse of an ocean. Consciousness may bear some analogy to the sheen and roar of the breakers, where a single line of the waves is lashed into foam on the shores that obstruct their course.[17]

The article in *Brain* shows Galton aware, not only of processes going on at a level hitherto unsuspected, but also that the sudden recollection of dormant early associations could be traumatic and that some people might suppose, on the evidence presented, that nothing is ever completely forgotten. He was none the less explicit and emphatic in rejecting this hypothesis:

Forgetfulness appears absolute in the vast majority of cases, and one's supposed recollections of a past life are, I believe, no more than that of a large number of episodes in it, to be reckoned in hundreds and thousands, certainly not in tens of hundreds of thousands, which have escaped oblivion.[18]

Galton comments that his associated ideas 'were for the most part due to my own unshared experiences, and the list of them would necessarily differ widely from that which another person would draw up who might repeat my experiments'. The conclusion he drew related to the impossibility of 'two grown-up persons laying their minds together in perfect accord. The same sentence cannot produce precisely the same effect on both, and the first quick impressions that any given word in it may convey, will differ widely in the two minds.' While this social interest in his findings is revealed, his strongest emphasis is on discovering processes hitherto unsuspected and on evolving a method of studying them.

This returns us at long last to Breuer (when Freud was still a student) struggling with the problems of a patient. For however much priority Galton may have had in suggesting the existence of mental processes of which we are unconscious, and which are susceptible of psychological study, there is no hint in Galton's writing of adopting this method for therapeutic purposes. It is in the situation, described by Breuer, of studying and trying to help the brilliant Anna O, that the gradually formulated notions of unconscious functioning appear to have been crystallized therapeutically. Though well known to many readers, Freud's shortened account of the first recorded case of the mitigation of symptoms by the exploration of associations is so interesting and so important that some quotation must be made to round off the story with which this chapter has been concerned. Freud is writing of the years 1880-82, though Breuer's account of this case was not published until 1895.

I was a student, busy with the passing of my last examinations, when another physician of Vienna, Dr. Joseph Breuer [was experimenting with methods of treating hysterical patients] . . . Dr. Breuer's patient was a girl of twenty-one, of a high degree of intelligence. She had developed in the course of her two years' illness a series of physical and mental disturbances which well deserved to be taken seriously. She had a severe paralysis of both right extremities, with anaesthesia, and at times the same affection of the members of the left side of the body; disturbance

D

of eye-movements, and much impairment of vision; difficulty in maintaining the position of the head, an intense *Tussis nervosa*, nausea when she attempted to take nourishment, and at one time for several weeks a loss of the power to drink, in spite of tormenting thirst. Her power of speech was also diminished, and this progressed so far that she could neither speak nor understand her mother tongue; and, finally, she was subject to states of 'absence', of confusion, delirium, alteration of her whole personality. These states will later claim our attention. . . . The illness first appeared while the patient was caring for her father, whom she tenderly loved, during the severe illness which led to his death, a task which she was compelled to abandon because she herself fell ill. . . . [Dr. Breuer] gave his patient sympathy and interest, although at first he did not understand how to help her. . . . His sympathetic observation soon found the means which made the first help possible. It had been noticed that the patient, in her states of 'absence', of psychic alteration, usually mumbled over several words to herself. These seemed to spring from associations with which her thoughts were busy. The doctor, who was able to get these words, put her in a sort of hypnosis and repeated them to her over and over, in order to bring up any associations that they might have. The patient yielded to his suggestion and reproduced for him those psychic creations which controlled her thoughts during her 'absences', and which betrayed themselves in these single spoken words. These were fancies, deeply sad, often poetically beautiful, day dreams we might call them, which commonly took as their starting point the situation of a girl beside the sick bed of her father. Whenever she had related a number of such fancies, she was, as it were, freed and restored to her normal mental life. This state of health would last for several hours, and then give place on the next day to a new 'absence', which was removed in the same way by relating the newly created fancies. It was impossible not to get the impression that the psychic alteration which was expressed in the 'absence' was a consequence of the excitations originating from these intensely emotional fancy-images. The patient herself, who at this time of her illness strangely enough understood and spoke only English, gave this new kind of treatment the name 'talking cure', or jokingly designated it as 'chimney sweeping'.[14]

It is possible and even likely (but unproven) that Freud read Galton's article, from which in the main we have quoted, either at the time or later. It appeared as the opening article of *Brain*, July 1879, in which the second of a series of articles by Hughlings Jackson on aphasia was also published. Freud was one of the few people who took note of Hughlings Jackson's work, to which he refers in his own first book, *On Aphasia*, published in 1891. Both Binswanger and Stengel[32] agree on the immense importance of Hughlings Jackson for under-standing Freud's subsequent thinking. To establish a historical link between Galton's work and the therapeutic use of explor-ing associations, however, it would seem more important to show that Breuer knew of Galton or derived the notion some-how from Wundt's laboratory, whence Galton's ideas seem to have been carried by Cattell in the 1880's. But this bit of detec-tive work would be of doubtful worth, for with Breuer and Anna O we enter a new era. Certainly, Breuer's[9] description of his attention to Anna's phantasies has all the freshness of a situation at first not understood and then, with enormously sympathetic insight, transformed into a cure.

Before moving to discuss what light on 'unconscious thinking' we can now glean from Freud, his predecessors and con-temporaries taken together, let us try to sum up so far. In brief, I have argued that from Freud's predecessors it is possible to extract the following notions, all of which have some signifi-cance for understanding unconscious functioning and, there-after thinking, as Freud conceived it.

In von Schubert's writings are to be found the germs of the following notions: dissociation; the symbolic significance of dreams; condensation and the reversal of conscious evaluation as reflected in some dream and other imagery (e.g. poetic and pro-phetic); the close affinities of love and hate; the basically andro-gynous character of human nature; hierarchies of physiological and psychological functioning, together with the possibility of reversion from one level to a lower, parallel operation at both levels or 'metastatic' confusion of level; belief that functioning at the more primitive (for Schubert 'ganglionic') level is dominated by biological needs, such as hunger and sex, together with pleasure and pain; the possible reflection, in the double significance of some language usage, of confusion of two different levels of functioning; affinities in the sexual overtones to some pathological (somnambulistic) states and those of morbid religious ecstasy; the destructive as well as constructive potentialities of conscience. Ludwig Feuerbach, whether influenced (inversely) by Schubert or not, conceived religion as a species of wish-fulfilment, in effect as a projection system. Nineteenth-century psychiatry added a mass of evidence on what can occur in dissociated states and moved gradually towards attempts at psychological explanation of these. Literature portrayed such states.

Physiology and neurology reinforced belief in hierarchies of neurological functioning, added basically homeostatic concepts, and (via Helmholtz as a physicist who influenced Brücke as a physiologist) encouraged belief in a limited amount of 'energy' underlying individual activity. By implication, these disciplines tended to favour the concept of a person reacting to a stimulus as to something which disturbs equilibrium, in contrast to the concept of a person as initiating action. Darwin shifted biological thinking on to evolutionary lines. Spencer made use of the additional possibility of 'dissolution' or reversion of evolutionary development.

In Hughlings Jackson's extraordinarily suggestive writing, one can see in greater detail how these notions might be adapted in the understanding both of general psychological functioning and of specific disfunction, as in aphasia or psychotic states.

Herbart had used the notion of limited energy as a *psychological* principle and was followed in this by Fechner, who also influenced Brücke and Breuer. Herbart also contributed the notion of ideas being *verdrängt* if not consonant with the 'apperceptive mass' or dominant system of energized ideas. Schopenhauer suggested that the rejection from memory of overwhelmingly painful experience lay at the root of madness.

Associationist psychology, as well as the largely opposed emphasis on dynamic aspects of human nature,* were both part of the nineteenth-century climate of opinion. Galton, writing in the same journal as Hughlings Jackson, explored the possibility of analysing word associations, and inferred the enormous importance of unconscious cerebration and the retention of some early experiences. Galton's procedure for studying associations became known in Wundt's laboratory.

All of these trends seem to have been fused in the clinical work of Breuer and Freud. All of Freud's basic theoretical discussions of unconscious functioning, and of thought, are profoundly coloured by the ideas in question, whether derived directly or indirectly from the sources here mentioned or independently conceived. Whatever conclusion one reaches on this question it remains a fact that, after exploring this literature, turning to Freud means entering an original world of insight into the clinical potentialities of such notions when they are related to each other. This point must be emphasized, for in discussing what we can now usefully extract from Freud, his predecessors and contemporaries, for understanding thinking, one can but agree with some of the obvious criticisms that have been directed to some of the ideas we have so far discussed and to some of the uses Freud (and others) made of them.

REFERENCES

Numbers in brackets indicate the pages in this book where given references occur

1. Acton, H. B., *The Illusion of the Epoch*, London: Cohen & West, 1955, p. 117.
2. Bain, Alexander, *The Senses and the Intellect*, London: Parker, 1855.
3. Bernard, Claude, *An Introduction to the Study of Experimental Medicine*, translated by H. C. Green, New York: Macmillan, 1927.
4. —— See Fulton, J. F., *Selected Readings in the History of*

* This dynamic emphasis was specially characteristic of certain trends in German philosophy and French psychotherapy. 'Voluntarism' in physiology must also not be wholly forgotten.

Physiology, Springfield and Baltimore: Charles C. Thomas, 1930.

5. Bernheim, H., *De la Suggestion et de ses Applications à la Thérapeutique*, Paris: Doin, 2nd edition, 1888, pp. 155 (71), 170-1 (72-3).

6. Binet, Alfred, and Féré, Charles, *Animal Magnetism*, London: Kegan Paul, 3rd edition, 1891, pp. 8-11.

7. Brentano, Franz, *Psychologie vom Empirischen Standpunkte*, Leipzig: Duncker and Humblot, Vol. I, 1874.

8. Brett, G. S., *History of Psychology*, abridged and edited by R. S. Peters, London: Allen & Unwin, 2nd edition, 1962, pp. 549 (80), 550-1 (81).

9. Breuer, Joseph, and Freud, Sigmund, *Studies on Hysteria*, Standard Edition, edited by James Strachey, London: Hogarth Press, 1955, pp. 195-6.

10. Coleridge, Samuel Taylor, *Biographia Literaria*, Bohn's Standard Library, London: George Bell, 1905, pp. 54-5.

11. Feuerbach, Ludwig, see Acton, H. B.

12. Freud, Sigmund, *The Origins of Psycho-analysis*, Letters to Wilhelm Fliess, Drafts and Notes. Edited by Marie Bonaparte, Anna Freud and Ernst Kris, London: Imago, 1954.

13. —— *Beyond the Pleasure Principle*, Standard Edition, edited by James Strachey, Vol. XVIII, London: Hogarth Press, 1955.

14. —— *Five Lectures on Psycho-analysis*, quoted from *Sigmund Freud. A General Selection*, edited by John Rickman, London: Hogarth Press, 1937, pp. 3-6.

15. Flügel, J. C., 'The Death Instinct, Homeostasis and allied Concepts' in *Studies in Feeling and Desire*, London: Duckworth, 1955.

16. —— *A Hundred Years of Psychology*, London: Duckworth, 2nd edition, 1953.

17. Galton, Sir Francis, 'Psychometric Facts', *The Nineteenth Century*, Vol. 5, 1879, pp. 425-33.

18. —— 'Psychometric Experiments', *Brain*, Vol. 2, 1879, pp. 151 (88-9), 152 (89-90), 154 ff. (91-2), 157 (Table 2) (93), 159-61 (93-4), 162 (85, 95).

19. —— *Inquiries into Human Faculty*, London: Macmillan, 1883.

20. —— *Memories of my Life*, London: Methuen, 1908.

21. Hamilton, Sir William, *Lectures on Metaphysics and Logic*, edited by H. L. Mansel and John Veitch, Edinburgh: Blackwood, Lecture VIII, Vol. I, 1869.

22. Heine, Heinrich, *Samtliche Werke*, Leipzig: Tempel Verlag, Vol. I, no date.

23. Herbart, J. F., see Brett.

24. Hering, Ewald, 'On Memory as a Universal Function of Organised Matter', translated by Samuel Butler in *Unconscious Memory*, London: Fifield, 1920, pp. 72 (77), 85-6 (77-8).

25. Jackson, J. Hughlings, 'On Affections of Speech from Disease of the Brain', *Brain*, 1879, Vol. I, pp. 304 ff.; Vol. II, pp. 203 ff. (76), 323 ff. (76).

26. Jones, Ernest, *Sigmund Freud, Life and Work*, London: Hogarth Press, 3 Vols., 1953-7, Vol. I, pp. 41 (85), 410 (81).

27. Kris, Ernst, see Freud, 12 above.

28. Lewes, G. H., 'The Physical Basis of Mind', *Problems of Life and Mind, Second Series*, London: Trübner, 1877. Problem 3, Chapter 4.

29. Meyer, Conrad Ferdinand, 'Die Richterin', *Ausgewählte Werke*, Stuttgart: Europäischer Buchklub, 1953, Vol. 2, pp. 395-460.

30. Schopenhauer, Arthur, *The World as Will and Idea*, translated from the German by R. B. Haldane and J. Kemp, London: Trübner, 3 vols., 1883-6, Vol. III, pp. 168-9.

31. Schubert, G. H. von, *Die Symbolik des Traumes*, Leipzig: Brockhaus, 4th edition, 1862, particularly pp. 148-9.

32. Stengel, E., 'Hughlings Jackson's Influence in Psychiatry', *The British Journal of Psychiatry*, Vol. 109, No. 460, 1963, pp. 348-55.

33. Sully, James, *The Human Mind: A Text-book of Psychology*, London: Longmans Green, 2 Vols., 1892.

34. Tymms, Ralph, *Doubles in Literary Psychology*, Cambridge: Bowes and Bowes, 1949.

CHAPTER FIVE

SOME ASPECTS OF FREUD'S APPROACH TO THINKING

> External perception is an internal dream which proves to be in harmony with external things: and instead of calling hallucination a false external perception, we must call external perception a *true* hallucination.
>
> HIPPOLYTE TAINE

AGAINST THE historical background sketched in Chapter Four, let us now try to say something of Freud's treatment of thinking. Broadly, what faces us is an immensely rich store of observation and insight relating to thought treated by Freud as subjectively oriented, and a much less developed and less convincing account of thinking that is objective, in the sense of being enmeshed with the world of external stimulation and shared experience and not immediately subservient to pleasure and pain. It has been a major preoccupation of later analytic writers to scrutinize and develop Freud's treatment of 'reality-oriented' thought processes. This scrutiny has led some authors, e.g. the late David Rapaport, to argue cogently that some radical modification is required in Freud's account of the equipment of human nature at the start. There is little doubt in fact that Freud's conception of 'objective' thinking cannot be made to work on the basis of the premises with which he began. To this much debated question we will return at the end of this chapter. Meanwhile, let us consider—so far as it can be done briefly—Freud's delineation of 'subjective' thinking. This involves considering first the *Project*[3]* and then Freud's more highly developed views.

* This *Project*, published posthumously, was written in 1895 and is Freud's initial sketch for a scientific psychology. It is fundamental for understanding the influence of his earlier neurological approach on his later psychological views, even though the latter developed beyond their original neurological foundations. See also MacIntyre.[13]

THE EARLY NEURO-PHYSIOLOGICAL APPROACH

The cluster of concepts at the core of Freud's initial treatment of 'subjective' thinking was formed from the following ingredients:

(a) Concepts common to the *Project* and to later views.

(i) A limited 'Quantity' or energy, biologically interpreted.

(ii) Two neurological principles: 'neuronic inertia' whereby motor neurones keep the organism free of stimulation; 'constancy', that of maintaining equilibrium.

(iii) Action occurring to reduce the tension of imbalance.

(iv) Pain and pleasure defined in terms of such tension and its reduction.

(b) Concepts sketched in neurological terms in the *Project* and echoed in psychological terms in Freud's later views of personality structure.

(i) Two main systems of neurone: ϕ reacting to external stimulation but not retentive; ψ retentive and the vehicle of psychological processes. A third group ω (perceptual neurones) then added by Freud such that ϕ neurones transfer periodicity (the basis of qualitative distinction) to ω neurones which can excite ψ neurones.

(ii) ψ neurones divisible into 2 groups, one reacting to ϕ (& ω) neurones and another nuclear group responding to continuous endogenous stimuli of cellular origin and giving rise to primary needs, e.g. hunger, respiration, sexuality.

(iii) Response of ψ neurones to external stimulation is thus indirect, via discharge of ω neurones.

(iv) Stimulation of ψ neurones from internal sources, because direct, is more intense than that from indirect external stimulation. In such endogenous stimulation lies the driving force of the psychic mechanism.

(v) At this primary level, consciousness is merely the subjective aspect of ω (perceptual) neurones discharging. Hence a vast proportion of psychically significant processes occur outside its range.

(vi) A sub-system of ψ neurones becoming organized and energized ('cathected'), such that immediate discharge of other neurones upon stimulation may be inhibited, post-poned or otherwise affected as a result of previous painful and pleasurable experience. Such inhibiting and allied pro-cesses are secondary and the sub-system of 'ψ cathexes', of which a core is permanently energized, constitutes the 'ego' as first conceived by Freud.

Most of these ingredients we have now encountered in their historical setting. Their interrelation and their development in the light of the hypothesis that subjective thinking serves biological and personal ends was part of Freud's own achieve-ment, even if we do question the ends he thought theoretically sufficient. Let us look at the ingredients a little more closely.

Freud's conception of a limited amount of 'Quantity', later designated 'libido', is, as Kris[11] has realized, Helmholtz's, Herbart's and Fechner's[2] notions fused. There emerges a kind of no-man's-land conception of action potential or 'energy'. 'No-man's-land', in so far as it remains permanently uncertain whether 'Quantity', and later libido, is physical, psychical or both. Theoretically, there is the possibility of advantage in this permanent uncertainty; for it offers to libido the status of an intervening variable. But, as Meehl[15] pointed out long ago, libido, in the course of its theoretical use, in fact acquired properties such as being 'dammed up' and of being transformed into other things and was imperceptibly changed into a hypo-thetical construct; that is to say a supposedly 'real' entity whose existence was required to underpin its alleged explana-tory powers. More recently, Hinde[9] has criticized the whole approach to motivation in terms of an energy model.

When first introduced, 'Quantity' or libido also bore a super-ficial resemblance to Spinoza's *conatus*. Superficial because for Spinoza *conatus* was that endeavour to remain itself which defines an individual. Within Spinoza's particular metaphysical system, as Stuart Hampshire has argued, *conatus* is a logical concept. Libido, for Freud, writing 200 years later, began and ended as a biological concept. A further distinction, to my mind, is that Spinoza retained the Aristotelian conviction that man's most desirable state is one of integrated active functioning. So that, for him, the individual effort after self-maintenance, if it can be described in homeostatic terms at all (which I venture to doubt), is in the direction of calibrated *activity*.

Though on the evidence of the *Outline of Psycho-analysis*,[4] posthumously published, Freud was finally undecided on this point, in the intervening years he often wrote as though libido were primarily sexual energy, the term 'sexual' being sometimes narrowly and sometimes very widely interpreted. We can leave aside the volcanic eruption of controversy that was stimulated by this. If the term 'sexual' is used narrowly, the 'sexual theory of neurosis' looks like an over-generalization from some specific but recognizable syndromes. If 'sexual' is used widely, the theory seems tautological, so long as one of the criteria of neurosis is disturbance of a person's affectional and social relations. A discussion of the uses and abuses of tautology is out of place here, so is fuller discussion of Freud's more general theory of motivation. Freud himself explicitly repudiated the allegation that he attempted to explain even dream motivation exclusively in terms of sexuality. Such denial on Freud's part was quite consistent with his emphasis on the pervasive importance of such drives, an insistence which Jung thought exaggerated. We can recognize these facts and turn attention to Freud's description of processes of thinking. This is of value, whatever theory of motivation turns out to be most appropriate; but that value can be masked by over-emphasizing the exclusively sexual motivation popularly attributed to Freud.

For understanding Freud's treatment of thinking, it is important to realize that there are also two aspects to his assumption that 'Quantity', 'libido' or energy, whatever its biological nature, is limited. On the one hand, this means no more than the common-sense belief that for any given individual there are limits to the reserves of vitality upon which he can draw. But there is more to it than this. As used by Freud the 'limitation' assumption seems also to imply that generation of extra energy by use is precluded. From the start, this limitation tended to pile up the odds in favour of a life of conflict. For if one uses energy for one thing, automatically there is less for something else. Freud inclined, in fact, to superimpose a nineteenth-century economist's account of energy on to that of a nineteenth-century physicist. The bolder notions of spending energy (or money), in the interests of generating more, were not natural to his time nor, it would seem, to him as a person— partly for reasons with which one can only sympathize.

In Freud's *Project*, as just noted, the organism, with its limited energy so conceived, was endowed (broadly) with self-preservative instincts, often illustrated by hunger and attempts to satisfy it, and by sexual desires. Later in his theorizing Freud added aggression. Deficit in the first two respects, and the pile up of unreleased aggression, created an unbalance experienced as tension. Though direct influence is uncertain, this is in line with what Spencer and Claude Bernard said of the *milieu intérieur* (and *extérieur*) working on principles designated 'homeostatic' by W. B. Cannon at a later stage. Such unbalance might be internally induced, as above, or it might arise from external stimulation, or from discrepancies between internally and externally induced states. Pain and pleasure are constituted, respectively, by increase of tension or its release. Action occurs to reduce the state of tension that is the product of unbalance. Or in Hughlings Jackson's[10] words, action occurs to restore equilibrium by expenditure of energy. To these notions must be related Freud's inveterate tendency, theoretically, to treat any stimulus from the outside world as a threat rather than an invitation.

Up to a point this tendency was consonant with nineteenth-century neurology, but only up to a point. In Breuer's hands the same principle, though suggested, possibly, by Freud, was in fact used in relation to the removal of *surplus* excitation. Breuer assumed that some degree of excitation was characteristic of any living organism, though there were individual differences in optimum level. He has some wry remarks to make on people who are very active, as well as on those with an 'inborn gift for lounging on sofas'. Freud, for reasons that are obscure, seems to have over-generalized this principle, as he did certain others, so that removal of all stimulation was the aim of nervous discharge, and *no* excitation (the state of death) was the organism's goal. In contrast to Freud's usage, Breuer's view remains consonant with mid-twentieth-century evidence on optimum level of excitation and on the organism's need of external stimulation.

On the cognitive side, Freud has been criticized by many people for saying too little about sensory awareness and the acquisition of skills. Such criticisms have been made most effectively, because sympathetically, by Ruth Munroe and there is no need to repeat them here. It is clear that Freud's own attention was slanted elsewhere. This has unfortunate consequences if his writings are torn from their historical context and treated as a rounded portrait of human development. It was in fact integral to Freud's original position that an organism was equipped physiologically to see, hear, smell, taste, touch and move. In fact it was equipped to react and respond in very complicated ways, of which Freud, as an excellent neurologist, was amply aware; but he was not very interested in writing about them.

But Freud, as a psychologizing neurologist, also took for granted a form of representative perception. The organism is not directly aware of what goes on outside it but only of that which is the product of its own receptor organs discharging. He fused this with a largely associationist account of the contents both of the resultant experience and of that experience which arises from internal deficit and desire. That which the organism lives through primarily is, in effect, the *representative* product of externally-induced change and the *immediate* product of internal stimulation. But the elements of such experience, externally or internally originating, are sensations, images, ideas, affects, states of tension, feelings of relief or satisfaction all very loosely defined. In so far as the impact of internal processes is *direct* it is liable to be more intense.

When, in his *Project*, Freud first formulated this idea about the intensity of experience internally produced, he was reading, among other people, the French psychologizing philosopher Hippolyte Taine,[20] of whom he wrote appreciatively to Fliess.[3] The understanding of Freud's treatment of primary and secondary processes is fundamental to grasping his whole position. His treatment of subjective thinking is unintelligible unless one appreciates his handling of primary processes in terms of strivings to remove unbalance, combined with the capacity to produce and reproduce ingredients of experience internally. The idea of this capacity would seem to be connected

historically with Taine's view of perception as veridical hallucination. It seems legitimate, therefore, to side-track for a moment
to consider Taine, in the interest of bringing one aspect of
Freud's primary processes into better focus.

What Taine said was:

> . . . the image, like the sensation it repeats, is, in its nature,
> *hallucinatory*. Thus the hallucination, which seems a mon-
> strosity, is the very fabric of our mental life. Considered in
> relation to things, it sometimes corresponds with them, and
> then constitutes normal external perception; sometimes, it
> does not so correspond, and then, as for instance, in dreams,
> somnambulism, hypnotism, and disease, it constitutes false
> external perception, or hallucination strictly so called.[20]

This comment, and others like it, needs to be placed in the
context of Taine's belief in two principal processes 'employed
by nature to produce the operations we term cognitions: the
one consisting *in the creation of illusions within us*; the other
consisting *in their rectification*.'[20]

By illusions Taine meant two things. First, there are the
processes whereby sensations that arise from the stimulation of
receptors, sensory nerves and corresponding central areas (and
are but representative signs of the external facts exciting them)
are projected outwards. Secondly, there are those whereby
images, that are revived sensations but often centrally aroused,
are given the status of sensation, i.e. of external production.
He believed that 'the two departments of the nervous system,
that in which sensations take effect, and that producing images,
are antagonistic—in other words, that sensations become feeble
as images become strong, and *vice versa*'.[20] But 'every image is
possessed of an automatic force, and tends spontaneously to a
particular state; to hallucination, false recollection, and the
other illusions of madness. But it is arrested in its progress by
the contradiction of a sensation, of another image, or group of
images' (*loc. cit.*). By this last Taine had in mind, for example,
the recognition of a vivid dream sequence for what it is,
because of its inconsistency with a whole coherent system of
recollections and judgments.

The operation of the two antagonistic systems, the mutual

arrest of potentially hallucinatory image and the externally
rooted sensation or rival system of images, produces an equilibrium which is the state of reasonable wakefulness. When,
writes Taine, this

> lasts over a certain time, the fatigue is too great, and we
> sleep; our images are no longer reduced and guided by
> antagonistic sensations coming from the outer world, by
> the repressive effect of combined recollections, by the
> dominion of well-connected judgments: so they then
> acquire their full development, turn into hallucinations,
> arrange themselves spontaneously according to new ten-
> dencies, and sleep, though crowded with intense dreams,
> is a rest, since, suppressing a constraint, it brings on a state
> of relaxation.[20]

Taine drew his accounts of sensation and its physiological
basis from writers as respectable as Müller, Helmholtz and
Weber. He was obviously steeped in the writings of French
medical psychologists. His associationism is of English origin.
Bain and John Stuart Mill figure among his sources. He himself
seems to have possessed extraordinarily vivid imagery, which
he could describe with a literary skill that aroused Binet's
admiration as it does ours. He writes at far too great a length;
every point is reinforced with examples and anecdotes, but
they are often vividly memorable. The blindfold chess player's
imagined board, wherein he sees the pieces but without their
shadows, is 'rectified' by the grey sensations aroused by perception of the actual wall at the distance he formerly 'saw' the
board—though the man when playing does not usually bother
to distinguish the real and imaginary pieces. The fact that
heightened imagery can have real effects is illustrated in all
sorts of ways; by Flaubert* describing the poisoning of Emma
Bovary with so strong a taste of arsenic in his mouth that he
was upset enough to throw up his dinner; by a physiologist,
who wished to obtain a quantity of saliva, tying up 'a hungry
dog a few inches from a piece of meat and collecting the liquid

---

* Binet's writers, see Chapter Seven, were somewhat sceptical of this
famous story.

which the flavour continually wished for and continually absent discharges from the animal's jaws'.[20]

Taine thought there was increased likelihood of hallucinatory experience in states of low sensory stimulation, for example alone or in the dark.[20] In ancient Greece, the Aesculapian doctors are alleged to have known and utilized this fact. In the twentieth century we think immediately of the 'coffin' experiments at McGill and the controversial issues to which they have given rise.[21] To drive home the possibility of central production of imagery in the absence of sensory stimulation, Taine uses, among other examples, Esquirol's two deaf women in the Salpêtrière disputing night and day with the voices of imaginary persons. So far as I can find, he did not hazard the guess that the production of imagery could be motivated; with the one implied exception, quoted above, where the dog *wishes* for meat, and the passing comment elsewhere that instincts are groups of images whose association is innate. This great gap returns Taine to the class of atomistically-minded sensory associationists, with whom he really belongs. But there is plenty of reason for Freud having found him interesting. And I venture to suggest that Taine's reversal of the usual approach to the relative rôles of perception and hallucination, involving as it does antagonistic and complementary nervous functioning, is fundamental for understanding Freud's primary and secondary processes. Let us return once more to Freud himself.

From general knowledge, and what we have said so far, it is easy to see how important for Freud was the concept of different levels of response, familiar to us historically from Schubert, the French psychotherapists, Galton and Hughlings Jackson, with Taine now on the wings enhancing the status of the processes producing imagery. Freud when he first made use of the notion of hierarchy, in the *Project*, did so in terms of levels of neurological functioning with different psychological significance. Ernst Kris has pointed out that modern neurologists would no longer rest content, as Freud largely did, with only *two* main levels, those of the primary and secondary processes. MacIntyre[13] has argued, correctly I think, that Freud's early neurological scaffolding served as a basis for the psychological model he adopted when moving away from neurological explanation as immediately promising. It is in Freud's initial *Project* that we find the original primary and secondary processes which, as we have said, are basic to understanding Freud's position. The primary are those immediately concerned with avoiding stimulation and maintaining equilibrium. The secondary are rooted in the need to tolerate the maintenance of some energy in order to satisfy basic drives. The permanently energized sub-system of ψ neurones (already mentioned as the ego, p. 106) is invoked to inhibit both internally-produced imagery and the immediate motor action natural at the primary level. The responses associated with this ego are secondary, i.e. acquired. They have a 'rectifying' function remarkably like Taine's.

So much, very briefly, for basic ingredients. Now let us turn at last to subjective thinking. This for Freud was that which goes on at a primary level in the service of pleasure and avoidance of pain, as so far understood. When primary processes were no longer discussed by him in terms of neurones, thought processes that are primary arise, in principle in the same way, as processes, or products of processes, offsetting unbalance. I say processes or products of processes to underline a very important point. At a practical level there was for Freud no fundamental distinction between subjective thought and action. So some thinking, e.g. phantasy in some circumstances, is an action in so far as it effects release of tension. On the other hand, as we shall see, Freud retains in his conception of unconscious as well as conscious thought some traces of an 'inspectionist' viewpoint. Even primary thought processes, therefore, may involve an element of 'experiencing' images, desires, etc. In this respect the primary processes of Freud bear no inconsiderable resemblance to the 'wind puffs of action, experience and desire' by which Schubert's[17] *die Seele* was moved when dreaming; though Freud makes the hold of these processes on the total personality much more intense biologically.

This leads us away from the *Project* to Freud's later and highly-developed treatment of subjective thinking. This I want to discuss not primarily in relation to his later conception of personality structure in terms of id, ego and superego, which we can here take for granted as familiar, but in terms of the actual processes of thought, some of which he was original in identifying, all of which he was original in describing and illustrating. For the purposes of this book I propose to concentrate on what we can extract from *The Interpretation of Dreams*,[5] including amendments made by Freud in later editions, and *The Psychopathology of Everyday Life*.[6]

THE FUNCTION OF DREAMS

Freud's treatment of dreams is based on assigning them a function within the framework of concepts we have already outlined. This involved him, initially, in argument against views with long pedigrees and still current in his day. The three most important of these were: that dreams are functionless, degenerate forms of thought that can be disregarded; that dreams, alien as they are to waking life, provide some sort of mystical (if distorted) contact with another world; that dreams are wholly explicable in terms of somatic stimulation during sleep. For Freud, disregarding dreams was to overlook a valuable source of insight into a person's (particularly a patient's) concerns. The second line, exemplified as we have seen in Schubert, could lead only into uncheckable mystification, if taken literally. The third line Freud considered of value, but inadequate if generalized as the *only* explanation. If dreams are due to somatic stimuli, he asks pertinently, why do we not dream all the time, as we are never without some such stimulation? And why do we dream of this rather than that?

Freud's alternative was to insist on dreams having a function. Dreaming is a form of wish-fulfilment, the term 'wish' having a subtle range of meanings. These seem to have affected, and been affected by, the developing state of his personality theory at the time that he wrote *The Interpretation of Dreams*. That the senses of 'wish' are different is apt to be obscured in the rigidified psycho-analytic theory, where wishes are related to three different agents, the id, ego and superego. Five nodal senses, in fact, seem worth disentangling in this context.

In the first sense, 'wish' relates to desires or impulses arising during the day, acknowledged, but unsatisfied for external reasons, and carried over into the sleeping state. These are exemplified by Anna Freud at the age of nineteen months calling out excitedly in her sleep: 'Anna Fwewd, stwawbew-wies, wild stwawbewwies, omblet, pudden!'[5] This was after she had been sick one morning and, consequently, had been kept without food all day. Except (as in this case) when such wishes are also related to continuing deficits of a biological nature, the acknowledged and conscious desires of adults are not considered by Freud to be usually strong enough *by themselves* to play a major rôle in dreaming. But see the comments on meanings four and five.

In the second sense, 'wish' means desires or impulses arising during the day but repudiated, not dealt with, and suppressed or repressed and carried over into sleeping. This seems to be exemplified by the lady

> who was rather fond of making fun of people and one of whose friends, a woman younger than herself, had just become engaged. All day long she had been asked by her acquaintances whether she knew the young man and what she thought of him. She had replied with nothing but praises with which she had silenced her real judgment; for she would have liked to tell the truth—that he was a *Dutzendmensch* [literally a 'dozen man', i.e. commonplace]. She dreamt that night that she was asked the same question and replied with the formula: '*In the case of repeat orders it is sufficient to quote the number*'.[5]

Freud's own revengeful dream on the people whom he found rude in a railway carriage[5] illustrates the same kind of wish, and underlines the implication that there are 'wishes' whose direct satisfaction would result in *un*pleasure but whose indirect outlet is a relief. As is well known, this line of thinking contributed to Freud's splintering the total personality in such a way that what is a direct *Wunsche* for one part may be repudiated by another, which 'wishes' in still other senses. It also contributed, among other things, to Freud's later postulation of innate aggression, internally directed at first and later externalized.

'Wish' in the third sense seems to cover two classes, one of which may overlap to some extent with the first meaning. The two classes in question are:

(*a*) The 'wishing' reflected in the desire to sleep or continue sleeping. Freud treats this as a function of the reality-oriented (if sleeping) personality. This wishing does indeed seem to fall into a somewhat different class from that reflected in Anna's desire for strawberries. On the other hand, its differentiation by Freud *may* be related to his tendency to think of the obvious tissue needs, hunger, thirst, sex, etc., as fundamental, while in his day, as indeed in ours too, the physiological basis and function of sleep are still uncertain.

Be that as it may, the 'wishing' for sleep is amusingly illustrated by Freud's own reaction to the bedlam of bell-ringing with which the pious Tyrolese, to this day, greet their fellow-creatures at six in the morning. Freud, exposed to this clanging, stayed asleep but dreamt that the Pope was dead. Others, with perhaps less effective wishes for sleep (and revenge!) but placed in similar circumstances, have awakened, roundly cursed his Holiness, and gone off to sleep again when the din was done. The 'wish to sleep' is something whose power we all know.

(*b*) The 'wishing' related to the satisfaction of straight physical needs arising during sleep, e.g. thirst or micturition. Many people dream of satisfying both of these in preference to awaking and getting out of bed. Although the classification is arguable, I have for the moment differentiated these from the 'wishes' of Class 1, by the fact that the needs have arisen during sleep and have not been carried over from the previous day.

To identify the fourth sense of wish, we must consider two interrelated processes implied by much of what Freud says, but whose operation remains more obscure than one might have hoped. To accommodate these kinds of 'wishing' Freud, whose mind ran to agents and agencies on the slightest provocation, invented 'agents' as 'wishers', i.e. the ego and later the superego, rather than focusing in detail on the types of 'wishing' characteristic of these hypothetical entities.

It may seem slightly irreverent to refer to these august members of the well-entrenched Freudian trinity in terms more appropriate to the Snark and the Boojum. The fact remains that at best, together with the id, they are convenient fictions, originally introduced to co-ordinate an unwieldy mass of material, relating to the relative degree of 'drive', 'reality' and 'evaluative' orientation characterizing psychological processes. Freud gave ample grounds for the interpretation that credits (or discredits) him with 'discovering' (or 'inventing') agents within, or sections of, the personality. But he also, at times, seems to have been well aware of the fictional character of his trinity. His own use of the term 'fiction' in this context is illustrated later on.

To return to this fourth kind of 'wishing', broadly, what we seem to be dealing with in the case of so-called 'ego wishes' are impulses to action (or inaction) integrated within a complex system of 'realistic' (and/or adult) assessments of the feasible, in terms of the internal and external situation of the individual personality. In the case of the superego 'demands', we are dealing with impulses integrated into complex systems of evaluation, with which the person is identified, but which may or may not be either realistic or easily made conscious.

By way of illustration, both of these senses of 'wish' seem to be involved, among other things, in Freud's account of his own complex dream of news of his son at the front. Accepting, for the moment, the existence, on Freud's part, of an element of envy of youth which might have found satisfaction in harm to the son in question, we have also to reckon with what Freud calls 'the *strength* of the painful emotion which would have arisen if such a misfortune [i.e. harm to the son] had actually happened'.[5] This seems to imply the existence and operation of an integrated set of realistic attitudes, and evaluations, in which deeply protective and allied emotions are involved and with which the envious hostility comes into unsuccessful conflict during Freud's dream. Freud seems to have allowed such systematized trends a 'wishing' or 'demanding' force, the source of which has been a question long debated by psycho-analytic theorists, the enlightened establishment of which is one purpose of psychoanalytic practice. Discussion of these issues is irrelevant for our immediate purpose. In this context, I merely want to justify inclusion of these interrelated senses of 'wish' and to make an additional comment.

In discussing the function of the ego, and the germ from which his conception of the superego developed, Freud tended to stress the corrective 'censoring' rôle of the former and the conventional, distorting function of the latter. The analogy of the 'censor' seems first to have occurred to him in a letter to Fliess. The passage is illuminating and reads as follows:

> Have you ever seen a foreign newspaper after it has passed the censorship at the Russian frontier? Words, sentences and whole paragraphs are blacked out, with the result that the remainder is unintelligible. A 'Russian censorship' occurs in the psychoses, and results in the apparently meaningless deliria.[3]

This line of thought lies behind Freud's round assertion that 'the unconscious is the true psychical reality'. But Freud seems to have been doubly ambivalent on the meaning of 'true' in this context and on his evaluation of whatever facets of any personality turned out to be most 'its own'. When the ego is censoriously corrective and the superego a conditioned hypocrite, the wishes of the id are those of man's 'true' but stifled potentiality. But at times Freud had, and indeed wanted, to allow that some of the demands/wishes of the ego (and even the superego?) were those more nearly reflecting the long-term ends of the whole person. As indeed, Freud's own desire for his son's well-being clearly outweighed his morsel of unconscious spite. So I venture to suggest that the analyst Freud did the person Freud less than justice in discussing the dreaming Freud, and that a more balanced position is reflected in a statement of Sully's, of whom Freud approved—and which I only traced through reading Freud. He quotes the first sentence without its continuation.

> We may say that, like some palimpsest, the dream discloses beneath its worthless surface-characters traces of an old and precious communication.
>
> I am well aware that most of this unveiling of the self is unpleasant and humiliating, and I am not surprised that sober-minded men should dismiss dreams from their minds as quickly as possible. Yet our slight study of the phenomena suggests that this is by no means necessary. If now and again we catch ourselves when asleep supinely obeying some gross instinct, we light at other times on worthier

selves. We do better things as well as worse things in our dreams than we are wont to do in the waking state. The stripping off of life's artificial swathings, if it sometimes gives too lively play to appetite, will also give free bound to some nobler impulse, as the perfect candour, the unstinting generosity of youth.[18]

It is interesting that the English Victorian Sully could write with so much greater equanimity of disillusion than the Jewish and Viennese Victorian Freud, and that it fell to the Swiss analyst Jung to be more sympathetic to positive unconscious wishes than Freud on the whole managed to be. It would be side-tracking to speculate on this interesting fact. Suffice it if, in this discussion, we have suggested a case for Freud's implying, if not actually using, a conception of 'wishing' integrated with reality and/or evaluative systems and operating in dreaming. We have also drawn attention to a possible double ambivalence on his part in treating and evaluating such 'wishes', as well as those more directly arising from primitive need.

We must now turn to the fifth sense of 'wish', a sense specific to Freud and one that colours much of his treatment of primary processes. More than any of the others it shows the relevance of his discussion of 'wishing' to 'thinking'.

Here we return to the notions involved in Freud's *Project*, and which he carried over into *The Interpretation of Dreams*. In brief, he reinvokes the 'constancy principle' (i.e. maintenance of equilibrium as an aim of the nervous system); takes somatic needs as basic; supposes that some object (say milk) succeeds in removing an initial state of unbalance (hunger). He then argues that the mnemic image of that which satisfied (i.e. milk) remains associated henceforth with a memory trace of the excitation produced by the need. Hence, when the need is next aroused, there is an attempt to 're-cathect' the image and re-evoke the original perception, i.e. 're-establish the situation of the original satisfaction'. 'An impulse of this kind,' writes Freud, 'is what we call a wish.'[5] And, he adds, 'Nothing prevents us from assuming that there was a primitive state of the psychical apparatus in which wishing ended in hallucinating'. 'The bitter experience of life' [e.g. of hallucinated milk not satisfying hunger] 'must have changed the primitive thought activity into a more expedient secondary one.'

It is this fifth meaning of 'wish' that shows so very clearly the close association between Freud's treatment of wishing and thinking at the primary level. At this level the processes are inseparable and both are forms of action. Their close connexion, also, with the main concepts mentioned at the start of this chapter, is apparent from the following; where Freud, in *The Interpretation*, is pulling together his account, *in principle*, of the way in which dream-thoughts, assumed by him to be rational, become the subject of distortion in sleep:

A normal train of thought is only submitted to abnormal treatment of the sort we have been describing if an unconscious wish, derived from infancy and in a state of repression, has been transferred on to it. In accordance with this thesis we have constructed our theory of dreams on the assumption that the dream-wish which provides the motive power invariably originates from the unconscious—an assumption which, as I myself am ready to admit, cannot be proved to hold generally, though neither can it be disproved. But in order to explain what is meant by 'repression', a term with which we have already made play so many times, it is necessary to proceed a stage further with our psychological scaffolding.

We have already explored the fiction of a primitive psychical apparatus whose activities are regulated by an effort to avoid an accumulation of excitation and to maintain itself as far as possible without excitation. For that reason it is built upon the plan of a reflex apparatus. The power of movement, which is in the first instance a means of bringing about internal alterations in its body, is at its disposal as the path to discharge. We went on to discuss the psychical consequences of an 'experience of satisfaction'; and in that connexion we were already able to add a second hypothesis, to the effect that the accumulation of excitation (brought about in various ways that need not concern us) is felt as unpleasure and that it sets the apparatus in action with a view to repeating the experience of satisfaction, which involves a diminution of

excitation and was felt as pleasure. A current of this kind
in the apparatus, starting from unpleasure and aiming at
pleasure, we have termed a 'wish'; and we have asserted
that only a wish is able to set the apparatus in motion and
that the course of the excitation in it is automatically
regulated by feelings of pleasure and unpleasure. The first
wishing seems to have been a hallucinatory cathecting of
the memory of satisfaction. Such hallucinations, however,
if they were not to be maintained to the point of exhaustion, proved to be inadequate to bring about the cessation
of the need, or, accordingly, the pleasure attaching to
satisfaction.

A second activity—or, as we put it, the activity of a
second system—became necessary, which would not
allow the mnemic cathexis to proceed as far as perception*
and from there to bind the psychical forces; instead, it
diverted the excitation arising from the need along a
roundabout path which ultimately, by means of voluntary
movement, altered the external world in such a way that
it became possible to arrive at a real perception of the
object of satisfaction. We have already outlined our
schematic picture of the psychical apparatus up to this
point; the two systems are the germ of what, in the fully
developed apparatus, we have described as the Unconscious and Preconscious.[5]

As already suggested, in the two 'levels' or 'systems' familiar
to nineteenth-century neurology, and in Taine's variation of
this in his conception of hallucinatory and rectifying processes,
we, in turn, can discern the germs of this theory of Freud's.

MANIFEST CONTENT

So much for the notion of 'wish' and the connexion of its
most primitive meaning with thinking at Freud's primary level.
We must now return to his distinction between the manifest
and latent content of dreams, the dream-thoughts which

* On the basis of reading Taine, I think this means re-activation of the
sense organs in the way they were originally stimulated (by, e.g. real milk)
and from which stimulation the mnemic image was derived. Such reactivation of the sense organs *originating centrally* would be genuine hallucination.

constitute the latter, and the processes of distortion that these thoughts (believed by Freud to be rational) undergo through the dream-work.

Freud's distinction between the 'manifest' and 'latent' content of dreams is so well known at a superficial level that there is little left to be said about it—at this same level. It amounts to that which the dream incorporates obviously (for example, that the Pope is dead), and that which *in its context* such dreaming symbolizes for the dreamer. In the 1909 edition of *The Interpretation*, Freud complained in a footnote[5] of the obstinacy with which readers and critics overlooked this fundamental distinction. In 1925 there was another bitter complaint about analysts who find the essence of dreams in their latent content and overlook the distinction between latent dream-thoughts and *dream-work*, i.e. the processes by which the latent thoughts are transformed into a dream.[5] Here one has some sympathy for the befuddled analysts for, as I hope to show, Freud's concept of dream-thoughts is both rich in possibilities and obscure in the extreme—again understandably so, for he had run into the question of *what is thinking?* The continuation of his 1925 complaint is, however, illuminating:

> At bottom, dreams are nothing other than a particular *form* of thinking, made possible by the condition of the state of sleep. It is the *dream-work* which creates that form, and it alone is the essence of dreaming—the explanation of its peculiar nature. . . . The fact that dreams concern themselves with attempts at solving the problems by which our mental life is faced is no more strange than that our conscious waking life should do so.[5]

Leaving aside for the moment the problem of latent dream-thoughts, let us look at the sources of manifest content. Strictly speaking *any* experience may contribute to the manifest content; as Freud says: 'All the material making up the content of a dream is in some way derived from experience, that is to say, has been reproduced or remembered in the dream—so much at least we may regard as indisputed fact.' But he quickly adds the point that in dreams we may know and remember something 'beyond the reach of our waking memory'.

Freud himself concentrates on three main sources of manifest content: events of the previous day, reactivated childhood impressions, somatic sources. In the light of his discussion it seems legitimate to add a fourth, namely: material that has already been given the semblance of judgment. Let us try to say something briefly about each of these four.

In *The Interpretation,* and referring to his own experience, Freud states: 'I must begin with an assertion that in every dream it is possible to find a point of contact with the experiences of the previous day.'[5] He gives a whole series of examples, most of which show fairly convincingly the existence of a common pivotal element between the day's experience and the dream content. For example:

DREAM: *I was visiting a house into which I had difficulty in gaining admittance . . .; in the meantime I kept a lady WAITING.*

SOURCE: I had had a conversation with a female relative the evening before in which I had told her she would have to WAIT for a purchase she wanted to make till . . . etc.

Freud cautiously relates his emphasis on the previous day, rather than a longer period of the recent past, to recall of slightly earlier events on the day in question.

Whenever it has seemed at first that the source of a dream was an impression two or three days earlier, closer inquiry has convinced me that the impression had been recalled on the previous day . . .; moreover it has been possible to indicate the contingency on the previous day which may have led to the recalling of the older impression.

Some pages later he comments from a different angle:

We must conclude that the freshness of an impression gives it some kind of psychical value for purposes of dream construction equivalent in some way to the value of emotionally coloured memories or trains of thought.[5]

The most straightforward examples of reactivated childhood

impressions are taken by Freud from Maury,[14] the enterprising author of *Le Sommeil et les Rêves* whom he admired, with ample justification.

> Maury relates how when he was a child he used often to go from Meaux, which was his birthplace, to the neighbouring village of Trilport, where his father was superintending the building of a bridge. One night in a dream he found himself in Trilport and was once more playing in the village street. A man came up to him who was wearing a sort of uniform. Maury asked him his name and he replied that he was called C. and was a watchman on the bridge. Maury awoke feeling sceptical as to the correctness of his memory, and asked an old maid-servant, who had been with him since his childhood, whether she could remember a man of that name. 'Why, yes,' was the reply, 'he was the watchman at the bridge when your father was building it'.[5]

Apropos of such dreams, Freud comments on the need for external evidence in establishing that they involve impressions from early childhood, and that there is seldom opportunity for obtaining such evidence. It is worth appreciating that in Freud's discussion of the complex operations designated 'dreamwork', he relies to a large extent on a knowledge of 'objective fact'. To give minor examples: his knowledge of Anna's 'starvation' is crucial to suggesting how her sleeping response is functioning; Freud's own Papal dream was a puzzle until his wife inquired if he had heard the bells. Facts of this sort imply that all through Freud's discussion of 'subjective' thinking, reality-oriented thinking is presupposed. But, as we shall see in discussing the status of 'dream-thoughts', an enormous question arises of how these 'thoughts' can be so known that the precise form of their distortion can be ferreted out.

I propose to make only minor comments on Freud's third source of manifest content, somatic stimuli. His main arguments for rejecting these as the sole explanation of dreaming have already been given. He provides a nice example of the manifest content of a dream neatly tailored to the type of need aroused:

If I eat anchovies or olives or any other highly salted food in the evening, I develop thirst during the night which wakes me up. But my waking is preceded by a dream; and this always has the same content, namely, that I am drinking. I dream I am swallowing down water in great gulps, and it has the delicious taste that nothing can equal but a cool drink when one is parched with thirst. Then I wake up and have a real drink.[5]

It would be irrelevant here to follow further Freud's more detailed suggestions, for example, that unpleasant somatic sensations may be linked with some wish normally repressed because it is unpleasant, and by this means the 'wish' may obtain some release. In general, Freud treats the rôle of somatic sources of stimulation as comparable to that of recent but indifferent impressions left over from the previous day. He implies that, so far as adults are concerned, these would not usually be manifest in dreaming but for connexion with an unconscious 'wish' in the fifth sense we differentiated.

This brings us to the problem of dreams in which there appear to be stretches of rational thought or judgment. The full consideration of this belongs with the treatment of dream-thoughts; Freud, however, argues that the frequent 'appearance' of rationally-worked-out arguments in dreaming is in fact misleading.

> *Everything that appears in dreams as the ostensible activity of the function of judgment is to be regarded not as an intellectual achievement of the dream-work but as belonging to the material of the dream-thoughts and as having been lifted from them into the manifest content of the dream as a ready-made structure.*[5] (His italics.)

In relation to what Freud says about secondary revision, and, with due respect, in relation to the facts, this looks suspiciously like another over-generalization on his part. But there seems little need to cavil about the generalization, to the exclusion of allowing that in sleeping, as in waking, some people's minds may travel on well-worn lines, conforming to the pattern though not the function of 'reasoning'. And Freud was obviously doing something useful in drawing attention to this possibility. Meanwhile, it seems desirable, provisionally at least, to include the incorporation of ready-made patterns of thinking as a fourth source of manifest dream content. Though I must state clearly that I am departing in this respect from what Freud actually said.

THE DREAM-WORK

All this now leads us to consider Freud's discussion of dream-work, i.e. the processes whereby ingredients from past or current experience are formed into dreams with a function, and during which our deepest concerns may be mulled over. In *The Interpretation of Dreams* Freud delineated four major processes: condensation, displacement, 'making representable' and 'secondary revision'.* In the course of discussion he also introduced other processes, for example: regression, identification and repression. But the meanings of these terms in this context do not coincide entirely with those now given to these terms when they are used to refer to 'defence mechanisms'. Let us start by considering the 'big four'—still, I may say, deferring the problem of 'dream-thoughts' and following Freud in supposing that these can be known so that the distortions of 'dream-work' can be identified.

The root processes of condensation appear to be (*a*) linking, (*b*) fusion, (*c*) complex interrelation on the basis of temporal contiguity, similarity, spatial contiguity and opposition—or all of these at once. In fact we encounter here the same root relations that underpinned our old friends the laws of association, though with 'atomism' largely dropped, a vastly greater insistence on motivation and great insight into the complexity of their operation. Freud appears to give formal priority to contiguity in time, and it is this line of thinking that suggests fundamental similarities between the Freudian and Pavlovian accounts of thought development. 'Our perceptions', writes Freud, 'are linked with one another in memory—first and foremost according to simultaneity of occurrence. We speak of

* Later said to be not strictly part of the dream-work.[5] As it is still a process whereby dream-thoughts are modified for the dreaming purpose, I have included it here.

this fact as "association".[5] He continues this statement with remarks echoing his own *Project* and leading to a position similar to one sketched by Binet, associated in our generation with the name of Hebb, and offering a theoretical framework to Professor J. Z. Young and his octopuses.

> . . . if the *Pcpt.** system has no memory whatever, it cannot retain any associative traces; the separate *Pcpt.* elements would be intolerably obstructed in performing their function if the remnant of an earlier connexion were to exercise an influence upon a fresh perception. We must therefore assume that the bases of association lie in the mnemic systems. Association would thus consist in the fact that, as a result of a diminution in resistances and of the laying down of facilitating paths, an excitation is transmitted from a given *Mnem.* element more readily to one *Mnem.* element than to another.
>
> Closer consideration will show the necessity for supposing the existence not of one but of several such *Mnem.* elements, in which one and the same excitation, transmitted by the *Pcpt.* elements, leaves a variety of different permanent records. The first of these *Mnem.* systems will naturally contain the record of association in respect to *simultaneity in time;* while the same perceptual material will be arranged in the later systems in respect of other kinds of coincidence, so that one of these later systems, for instance, will record relations of similarity, and so on with the others.[5]

But Freud seems to provide more illustrations of condensation (and indeed displacement) through similarity than through contiguity in time; so I propose to give rather more examples of this to indicate the kind of thing he says. Freud's discussion of the operation of all the processes included with 'dream-work' is so rich that only the barest outline can be given in any case.

Condensation, related, at any rate in part, to similarity, can

* This is the later method of designating the processes originally introduced with W (Wahrnemung) or ω (omega) neurones. (Compare p. 370 of *The Origins of Psycho-analysis*).[3]

occur at a superficial level and in very complex forms, with almost every degree of subtlety in between. It can occur in a verbal and a non-verbal medium. Let us start with two verbal examples of differing degrees of complexity. Freud recounts the occasion when on a journey he awoke in a train drawn up at Marburg, having dreamt that he heard:

> '*Hollthurn, ten minutes' being called out. I at once thought of holothurians [sea slugs]—of a natural history museum—that this was the spot at which valiant men had fought in vain against the superior power of the ruler of their country—yes, the Counter-Reformation in Austria—it was as though it were a place in Styria or the Tyrol.*[5] . . .

Later on in the dream a man in it asks his sister about a book by Schiller.

Freud initially inferred that he had heard 'Marburg' when it was first called out (or perhaps later) from the reference to Schiller whom, in *The Interpretation of Dreams*, he states was born at Marburg. Later, in *The Psychopathology of Everyday Life*, Freud draws attention in horror to the existence of a mistake: Schiller was born at Mar*bach* in Swabia not Mar*burg* in Styria.[6] Freud maintains he had known this all along and proceeds to hint at a motive for the waking mistake. 'Marburg' was also the name of a business friend of his father's, whom, for various reasons which Freud deliberately avoids explaining, he had some resistance to mentioning. It is both impossible and un-necessary to discuss the complexities of this situation. Enough has been shown of the operation of linking by verbal similarity both within the dream (Hollthurn, Holothurians) and in the course of recall and interpretation (Marburg, Marbach) for the reader to see the point.

Now for an example in which similarity, operating at a much more subtle level, contributes in this case to production of a neologism. Freud recounts how:

> On one occasion a medical colleague had sent me a paper he had written, in which the importance of a recent physio-logical discovery was, in my opinion, overestimated, and in which, above all, the subject was treated in too emo-

tional a manner. The next night I dreamt a sentence which clearly referred to this paper: *'It's written in a positively Norekdal style'*. The analysis of the word caused me some difficulty at first. There could be no doubt that it was a parody of the [German] superlatives *'kolossal'* and *'pyramidal'*; but its origin was not so easy to guess. At last I saw that the monstrosity was composed of the two names 'Nora' and 'Ekdal'—characters in two well-known plays of Ibsen's [*A Doll's House* and *The Wild Duck*]. Some time before, I had read a newspaper article on Ibsen by the same author whose latest work I was criticizing in the dream.[5]

The author in this case is the *same*, which provides the initial link. The neologism results from the *fusion* of two different characters. We haven't the evidence from Freud for ascertaining the nature of other relations which may have contributed to this fusion. Those familiar with *The Doll's House* and *The Wild Duck* can enjoy themselves speculating on this point. Now let us sample condensation in non-verbal material, wherein both fusion and integration can be seen to operate.

First let us illustrate Freud's 'collective figures', i.e. those wherein the actual features of two or more people are united in a single dream image. Freud's own example is that of Dr. M. in his dream of Irma's infection.

He bore the name of Dr. M., he spoke and acted like him; but his physical characteristics and his malady belonged to someone else, namely to my eldest brother. One single feature, his pale appearance, was doubly determined, since it was common to both of them in real life.[5]

Freud claims that composite figures also come into existence by a means resembling Galton's method of composite portraiture: 'namely by projecting two images on to a small plate, so that certain features common to both are emphasized, while those which fail to fit in with one another cancel one another out and are indistinct in the picture.'[5] Dr. R. in Freud's dream about his uncle with a yellow beard exemplifies this. The 'fair beard emerged prominently from a face which belonged to two people and which was consequently blurred'. A little later he

E

comments that objects too incongruous may not coalesce and a composite structure may be created 'with a comparatively distinct nucleus, accompanied by a number of less distinct features. In that case the process of unification into a single image may be said to have failed. The two representations are superimposed and produce something in the nature of a contest between the two visual images.'[5] What seems to me a good illustration of this is given by Freud much earlier in *The Interpretation* when he is talking of the rôle of memory.

I had a dream of someone who I knew in my dream was the doctor in my native town. His face was indistinct, but was confused with a picture of one of the masters at my secondary school, whom I still meet occasionally. When I woke up I could not discover what connexion there was between these two men. I made some inquiries from my mother, however, about this doctor who dated back to the earliest years of my childhood, and learnt that he had only one eye. The schoolmaster whose figure had covered that of the doctor in the dream, was also one-eyed.[5]

The way in which a whole series of linkings and fusions (on a basis including similarity in some respects) can contribute to an image becoming a kind of nodal sign of several objects (or people) thus woven into a complex interrelated system, is illustrated again in the Irma dream. For example, Irma appears with features that are her own but, thanks in part to various similarities, e.g. being a widow, and a hysterical choker, she is fused in Freud's mind with her friend and seen in the friend's position at a window. By virtue of having a diphtheritic membrane this friend is linked with an illness of Freud's daughter Mathilde, whose name is the same as that of a patient who died. Irma's friend is also linked, via her illness, with Freud's concern about his own health and with the unfortunate consequences of the famous cocaine episode. Irma's friend, being in fact very reserved, seemed unlikely to Freud to become one of his patients, but this 'recalcitrance' on her part (as he sees it) is a quality shared by still another person, a governess who was recalcitrant about admitting she had false teeth, etc. This account does no justice at all to the complexity of the ingredients or processes Freud believes to be involved in this dream, in which Irma is the main character. But probably enough has been said to suggest how one image (of Irma) may become the nodal point of a network of associations both ideational and emotional which the image can be said to 'symbolize'. If I stress that the connexions, by contiguity, similarity and the like, include the evocation of similar *responses*, e.g. anxiety, and are by no means restricted to simple perceptual relations, the reader may grasp what I have dubbed 'complex interrelation' under Freud's heading of 'condensation'.

This brings me to a major query. Freud in discussing 'condensation' refers to the 'dream-work' being 'under some kind of necessity to combine all the sources which have acted as stimuli for the dream into a single unity in the dream itself'.[5] And, as his Editor points out, in every edition of *The Interpretation* from 1909 until 1922 (after which it was omitted) Freud referred to 'this compelling impulse towards combining as an instance of "condensation"—another kind of primary psychical process'. Elsewhere in *The Interpretation* Freud makes use of the notion of the dream content 'being recast in a form designed to make sense of the situation'.[5] Some hundred pages later, he states that a dreamer's choice of a symbol, from among others, falls on that 'connected in subject matter with the rest of the material of his thoughts'.[5] It is fairly clear that what Freud has in mind in these last two passages was 'secondary revision'. It may be too facile, however, also to count the first quotation as another reference to this process. The impulse to 'single unity', there mentioned, seems somewhat different both from 'complex interrelation', in the sense already illustrated, and from the editing, for sense and respectability, characteristic of secondary revision. Freud's 'compelling impulse towards combining' looks more like a bit of insight that later got lost when psychoanalytic theory was crystallized. Moreover, it fits in so well with what Gestalt psychologists have treated as a tendency to make 'wholes', and other psychologists as an 'effort after meaning', that it should perhaps be resuscitated.

We must now try to say something briefly about displacement, 'making representable' and 'secondary revision'.

Displacement, like condensation in its various forms, seems to take place along the routes facilitated by various familiar kinds of association. Because two people are similar in some respect, one is made the bearer of a further quality in fact belonging to the other. Irma, in Freud's dream, acquires the diphtheritic membrane of her friend. In this superficial sense, displacement is often implied by condensation. The much more interesting sense in which Freud uses this term, however, relates to the transfer of emotional attitudes originally belonging to one set of ideas to another, to which their attachment is then, in fact, superficial. In the familiar example of robbers under the bed, the robbers may be imaginary, the fear is real, its source being other than these unlikely intruders. Freud says that, in transfer or displacement, we have the process whereby elements of high value are stripped of their emotional intensity and, from elements of low value, through over-determination, new values are created which thereby gain inclusion in the manifest dream content. Historically, we seem to be dealing here with a process closely resembling what Schubert called metastasis. But it is given a Herbartian setting, wherein ideas out of line with dominant interests have to be energized somehow before gaining access to dream consciousness—like the ghosts in Homer who have to be given blood before they can speak. But what a person of Freud's insight can do with these notions becomes clear from the following:

In the case of a psychical complex which has come under the influence of the censorship imposed by resistance, the *affects* are the constituent which is least influenced and which alone can give us a pointer as to how we should fill in the missing thoughts. This is seen even more clearly in the psychoneuroses than in dreams. Their affects are always appropriate, at least in their *quality*, though we must allow for their intensity being increased owing to displacements of neurotic attention. If a hysteric is surprised at having been so frightened of something trivial, or if a man suffering from obsessions is surprised at such distressing self-reproaches arising out of a mere nothing, they have both gone astray, because they regard the ideational content—the triviality—or mere nothing—as what is essential; and they put up an unsuccessful fight because they take this ideational content as the starting point of their thought activity. Psycho-analysis can put them upon the right path by recognizing the affect as being, on the contrary, justified and by seeking out the idea which belongs to it but has been repressed and replaced by a substitute. A necessary premise to all this is that the release of affect and the ideational content do not constitute the indissoluble organic unity as which we are in the habit of treating them, but that these two separate entities may be merely *soldered* together. . . .[5]

Again, in discussing the fact that latent hostility may reinforce satisfaction in 'just punishment' when some enemy involves himself in well-deserved unpleasantness, (with the result that a disproportionate attitude to the wretched wrongdoer does arise), Freud writes with an insight and a caution that shows him at his best:

A striking feature in neurotic characters—the fact that a cause capable of releasing an affect is apt to produce in them a result which is qualitatively justified but quantitatively excessive—is to be explained along these same lines, in so far as it admits of any psychological explanation at all. The excess arises from sources of affect which had previously remained unconscious and suppressed. These sources have succeeded in setting up an associative link with the *real* releasing cause, and the desired path from the release of their own affect has been opened by the *other* source of affect, which is unobjectionable and legitimate. Our attention is thus drawn to the fact that in considering the suppressed and suppressing agencies, we must not regard their relation as being exclusively one of mutual inhibition. Just as much regard must be paid to cases in which the two agencies bring about a pathological effect by working side by side and by intensifying each other.[5]

This passage has the incidental merit of illustrating both Freud's tendency to think in 'agencies' and the double relation of inhibition or reinforcement they can have to each other. As

Freud also tended to discuss displacement almost exclusively in relation to the operation of 'the censor' (i.e. because an 'idea' is 'not admissible' the affect associated with it is displaced to another and so gets release), this passage is of some importance in relation to Freud's overall opinion.

'Making representable', the third main process involved in 'dream-work', is of vast interest in connexion with 'thinking'. It is convenient to indicate the line Freud takes under three main headings: the rôle of representability in 'dream-work'; the representation of logical relations; and thirdly, 'formal' properties, exemplified in the sensory intensity and distinctness of dream images. Finally, I want to stress the possibility of accepting what Freud said descriptively but of sometimes inverting the framework of his discussion. Hence, instead of there being 'rational dream thoughts' which are distorted and turned into a medium usable in dreaming, dreaming may sometimes have the function of attempted formulation of problems and their solution, attitudes and their outcome. What therefore we can derive from Freud is a prototype account not exclusively of rational thought regressing but, in part at least, of rational thought developing. A fuller statement of this suggestion belongs with the conclusion of these two lengthy chapters. I insert this suggestion here to relieve the boredom of readers too familiar with Freud to relish shortened exposition and familiar enough with Jung to realize that this resembles in part the kind of thing he said. Now let us remind ourselves of what Freud says on 'making representable'.

In the 1914 edition of *The Interpretation* Freud borrowed from Silberer the following account of the transformation of thought into pictures in the process of forming dreams. 'If, when he [Silberer] was in a fatigued and sleepy condition, he set himself some intellectual task, he found that it often happened that the thought escaped him and that in its place a picture appeared, which he was then able to recognize as a substitute for the thought.'[5] Freud cites the following examples, among others, from Silberer.

Example 1—I thought of having to revise an uneven passage in an essay.

Symbol   —I saw myself planing a piece of wood.
Example 9—I had lost the thread in a train of thought. I
           tried to find it again, but had to admit that
           the starting-point had completely escaped me.
Symbol   —Part of a compositor's forme, with the last
           lines of the type fallen away.[5]

In principle, the rôle of this third factor of 'making represent-able' appears to be that of transforming the rational 'dream-thoughts' into the medium (that of imagery, usually visual or auditory but including verbal) which is employed in dreaming. When Freud introduces this third factor he adds:

Of the various subsidiary thoughts attached to the essential dream-thoughts, those will be preferred which admit of visual representation; and the dream-work does not shrink from the effort of recasting unadaptable thoughts into a new verbal form—even into a less usual one—provided that the process facilitates representation and so relieves the psychological pressure caused by constricted thinking. This pouring of the content of a thought into another mould may at the same time serve the purposes of the activity of condensation and may create connexions, which might not otherwise have been present, with some other thought; while this second thought itself may already have had its original form of expression changed, with a view to meeting the first one half-way.[5]

Earlier in his related discussion Freud makes the point that:

a dream-thought is unusable so long as it is expressed in an abstract form; but when once it has been transformed into pictorial language, contrasts and identifications of the kind which the dream-work requires, and which it creates if they are not already present, can be established more easily than before between the new form of expression and the remainder of the material underlying the dream.[5]

In short, the process of 'making representable' is indicated by that very phrase but carries with it implications about the other dream-work processes, e.g. condensation, and about the fact that within the medium of imagery employed in dreams there are built-in possibilities both of restriction and of new connexions. This is abundantly clear when the imagery is verbal. The replacement of simple words by ambiguous ones may result in the whole domain of verbal wit being put at the service of dream-work. (Freud's writing here echoes Schubert very closely.) That Freud had in mind determination by the medium itself, is also exemplified by the fact that in the same context he briefly refers to the way in which the second line of a poem to be written in rhyme is limited by the conditions of expressing an appropriate meaning and in a form that rhymes with the first line.

So much, briefly, for the rôle of 'making representable'; now for the difficult question of how logical relations are represented in dreams. Put another way, what characteristics of a dream would lead Freud to infer logical relations in the 'hidden dream-thoughts'? As Freud clearly realized that a fundamental question about 'thinking' lurked here, and he treated the obvious logical relations systematically under headings, it is well to follow his procedure in outline, referring the interested reader to what he says in more detail. We must not forget, however, that it is Freud's general belief that dreams that include complicated intellectual operations contain these as *'part of the material of the dream-thoughts'*. Such material *'is not a representation of intellectual work done during the dream itself'* [his italics]. What is reproduced by the ostensible thinking in the dream is the *subject matter* of the dream-thoughts and not the *mutual relations between them*, the assertion of which constitutes thinking.'[5] The existence of certain logical relations in the dream-thoughts is shown, however, according to Freud, as follows.

The existence of *some* logical connexion is generally represented by simultaneity in time. Dreams, he says, act 'like the painter who, in a picture of the School of Athens or of Parnassus, represents in one group all the philosophers or all the poets. It is true that they were never, in fact, assembled in a single hall or on a single mountain-top, but they certainly form a group in the conceptual sense.'[5]

Causal relations, Freud maintains, can be inferred from two kinds of representation. First:

> Suppose the dream-thoughts run like this: 'Since this was so and so, such and such was bound to happen.' Then the commoner method of representation would be to introduce the dependent clause as an introductory dream and to add the principal clause as the main dream. If I have interpreted aright, the temporal sequence may be reversed. But the more extensive part of the dream always corresponds to the principal clause.[5]

His exemplification of this is long and complicated and to my mind unconvincing. The reader must refer to the original context and judge the issue for himself.

The second way of representing causal connexion is by means of one image changing into another, provided 'the transformation actually occurs before our eyes'.[5] Freud does not exemplify this process but it is easy to imagine.

Either-or can be represented, Freud says, 'in any way whatever'. The alternatives are usually inserted into the text of the dream as equally valid. The dream may also be divided into two sections of equal length. Again the reader must consult *The Interpretation* for examples and for Freud's discussion of 'either-or' as used in the narration of a dream. The somewhat slender clues Freud adds for inferring 'either-or' in the dream thoughts indicates the difficulty, and the need, of providing more specific criteria for interpreting dream material in one way rather than another. I would suggest that Freud's discussion provides additional evidence that some dreaming may have a rôle in gradually formulating thought. (Cf. pp. 134, 139 and 153.)

Contraries, contradictories are treated in a 'highly remarkable' fashion, says Freud: they are 'simply disregarded'. Moreover, 'there is no way of deciding at first glance whether any element in the dream that admits of a contrary is present in the dream-thoughts as a positive or as a negative'.[5] Freud gives a complicated and plausible example wherein a dreamer's vision of herself climbing with a spray of flowers (that turn out to be red and faded) is interpreted as referring to two trains of thought diametrically opposed to each other. One involves Corpus Christi processions and reference to sexual innocence, the other via red flowers and *La Dame aux Camélias*, to its opposite. Freud goes only a little way towards providing clues that would make divination of contrary elements easier, e.g. the notion of change, or of reversal of chronological relations, being connected with the dream.

Similarity, consonance, approximation and possession of common attributes, constitute the only group of relations 'highly favoured' by dream representation. Freud provides considerable comment and illustration that cannot be summarized here. Examples can be drawn from the section on condensation (pp. 127 ff.) as Freud cites this process as one from which underlying similarity in the dream-thoughts can be inferred.

This treatment of the representation of logical relations of which Freud claims evidence through dream interpretation, while extraordinarily ingenious, obviously leaves many questions unanswered. One of the most difficult issues is raised by that of negation. Endless trouble has been caused by the apparent fact that an image may, in effect, stand for itself or its opposite, and fearful accusations can be levelled at psychoanalysts who thereby gain a theoretical position of the 'heads I win, tails you lose variety'. The position may be clarified in discussion of dream-thoughts, so I propose to pass to the 'intensity' heading.

Freud states that the intensity of dream images (not to be equated with the clarity of the whole dream) varies over the whole range from a sharpness of definition we are tempted to regard as greater than that of reality to 'an irritating vagueness . . . not completely comparable to any degree of indistinctness which we ever perceived in real objects. Furthermore we usually describe an impression which we have of an indistinct object in a dream as "fleeting" '.[5] He rejects the notion that vividness can be related to the impingement of sensory stimulation during sleep. Nor, he says (stressing the transvaluation due to the censorship), is it correlated with the psychical importance of the element in the 'dream-thoughts' which is represented. Instead, he argues that the 'elements by which the wish fulfilment is expressed are represented with special intensity' and that 'the most vivid elements of a dream are the starting point of the most numerous trains of thought. . . .' Again, 'the greatest intensity is shown by those elements of a dream on whose formation the greatest amount of condensation has been expended'. Referring to the clarity of a dream as a whole, Freud maintains both that the 'content of all dreams that occur during the same night forms part of the same whole', and that 'the first of these homologous dreams to occur is often the more distorted and timid, while the succeeding one will be more confident and distinct'.[5] One is left wondering why he does not draw the conclusion that they are successive attempts at formulating the same line of thought.

In winding up his discussion of representability, Freud introduces a notion of 'willing' closely related to the fifth notion of 'wishing' that we disentangled earlier. He comments that 'the motor paralysis accompanying sleep is precisely one of the fundamental determinants of the psychical process during dreaming. Now an impulse transmitted along the motor paths is nothing other than a volition, and the fact of our being so certain that we shall feel that impulse inhibited during sleep is what makes the whole process so admirably suited for representing an act of volition and a "no" which opposes it'.[5] This throws light on Freud's general position; but it hints at something less obvious, namely, that thinking of a symbolic kind may function as an extension, or acting out in another medium, of inhibited movement. Those already familiar with current views on the development of intelligence will see signs of the Freudian conception of thought, as essentially an experimental way of acting, fitting in with that of general and comparative psychology. But the rational 'dream-thoughts', so fundamental to Freud's general position, become increasingly puzzling the more one studies the processes of distortion to which they are allegedly subject.

Let us now turn to the fourth of these major processes, i.e. secondary revision, originally included by Freud with 'dream-work' but then said not to belong with it strictly—presumably because he thought it 'highly probable' that secondary revision was a contribution to dreaming on the part of waking thought.[5]

Freud admits 'there are dreams in which the most complicated intellectual operations take place, statements are contradicted or confirmed, ridiculed or compared, just as they are in waking life'.[5] But, as we have already seen, he thinks such appearances are deceitful and much of this material is, in effect, ready-made ratiocination taken over from the 'dream-thoughts'. 'Nevertheless', he continues in the next paragraph, 'I will not deny that critical thought activity which is not a mere repetition of material in the dream-thoughts *does* have a share in the formation of dreams.' He adds: 'this thought-activity is not produced by the dream-thoughts but by the dream itself after it has already, in a certain sense, been completed.' In a later edition he rejected the notion of a provisional dream content being put together out of the material provided and then being recast. 'This', he says, 'is scarcely probable. We must assume rather that from the very first the demands of this second factor [secondary revision] constitute one of the conditions which the dream must satisfy.'[5] On the other hand its demands 'appear to have the least cogent influence on dreams'. If it derives from waking thought and we are asleep, this is not surprising, but more of this in a moment.

For Freud, the function of this revision appears to be the creation in the dream of a connectedness which he actually regards as spurious. 'A dream', he says, 'is a conglomerate which, for purposes of investigation, must be broken up once more into fragments. On the other hand, however, it will be observed that a psychical force is at work in dreams which creates this apparent connectedness, which, that is to say, submits the material produced by the dream-work to a "secondary revision".' Elsewhere he amusingly likens the purpose of secondary revision to that 'which the poet maliciously ascribes to philosophers: it fills up the gaps in the dream-structure with shreds and patches. As a result of its efforts, the dream loses its appearance of absurdity and disconnectedness and approximates to the model of intelligible experience. But its efforts are not always crowned with success.'[5]

Freud does not wholly deny the possibility of secondary revision creating new contributions to dreams; but in his view it 'exerts its influence principally by its preferences and selections from psychical material in the dream-thoughts that has already been formed.'[5] Such psychical material may include day-dreams, already formed, or earlier phantasies which 'like any other component of the dream-thoughts, are compressed, condensed, superimposed on one another, and so on'.[5] Although in this context Freud compares the process of secondary revision in dreams to that which moulds a day-dream, he tends on the whole to give secondary revision a distorting and restricting function, somewhat akin to that of a conventional editor who likes the content of dreams to be respectable and their form shipshape. Indeed, in several passages (e.g. pp. 488 and 505 of *The Interpretation of Dreams*) Freud closely allies secondary revision with the operation of the 'censor'. This carries the implication that waking thought is constitutionally corrective, à la Taine, but also 'censorious'. Such an inference does not wholly misrepresent Freud. On the other hand, we must not overlook Freud's double ambivalence on what constituted the veridical for a given person and in evaluating the products of primary and secondary processes. Quite as much as Taine, Freud was aware that in full-scale regression to hallucination the route to madness lay.

In fact, under 'secondary revision' Freud seems to have fused two different processes. First, he is dealing with one form of the process which other psychologists have described as 'an effort after meaning'. This is reflected in the search for an order which, to the person in question, seems intelligible and acceptable. This is not incompatible with the imposition of a highly conventional and (from another viewpoint) limited and falsifying pattern on recalcitrant data. Individual differences in endurance of that which seems 'unclear' are known to be as enormous as those in response to this state, e.g. speedy relapse into ready-made explanation or long-term search for an original clarification of what is puzzling.

Secondly, Freud seems to be grappling with the gradual emergence of a veridical orientation on the dreamer's part. The effect of such gradual orientation on the dream might indeed be slight; because it is, as it were, an end product of many processes to which dreaming may make its own contribution. That some dreaming inferences appear to have genuine validity would fit in well with this possibility.

REGRESSION, IDENTIFICATION AND REPRESSION

It was stated on page 126 that, in discussing dreams, Freud also made use of concepts such as regression, identification and repression in senses somewhat different from their current popular use. As it is not part of my object to consider these processes in any detail—the literature on them is already vast—I will simply comment briefly on each in this context, because to omit any comment is to falsify Freud.

Regression

In the 1914 edition of *The Interpretation* Freud summarized what he had to say on this topic as follows:

> . . . regression plays a no less important part in the theory of the formation of neurotic symptoms than it does in that of dreams. Three kinds of regression are thus to be distinguished: (a) *topographical* regression, in the sense of the ψ-systems which we have explained above; (b) *temporal* regression, in so far as what is in question is a harking back to older psychical structures; and (c) *formal* regression, where primitive methods of expression and representation take the place of the usual ones. All these three kinds of regression are, however, one at bottom and occur together as a rule; for what is older in time is more primitive in form and in psychical topography lies nearer to the perceptual end.[5]

On the same page in the 1919 edition Freud added a paragraph which includes the following:

> dreaming is on the whole an example of regression to the dreamer's earliest condition, a revival of his childhood, of the instinctual impulses which dominated it and of the methods of expression which were then available to him.

The notion of 'topographical regression' is illuminated by Freud's earlier discussion wherein he says:

Intentional recollection and other constituent processes of our normal thinking involve a retrogressive movement in the psychical apparatus from a complex ideational act back to the raw material of the memory-traces underlying it. In the waking state, however, this backward movement never extends beyond the mnemic images; it does not succeed in producing a hallucinatory revival of the perceptual image.[5]

Such a retrogressive movement in normal waking life is contrasted by Freud with 'regression' in dreaming, when an idea is turned back into the *sensory image* from which it was derived. On the lines of the *Project* he links this up with the removal, during sleep, of a continuous current from the perceptual system to motor activity. He contrasts normal and pathological regression in waking life, implying that, in the latter, thoughts are still transformed into *sensory images*. The only thoughts that undergo such transformation, however, in Freud's view, are those intimately linked with memories that have been suppressed or have remained unconscious. Topographical regression, as thus explained, started by being extremely close to what Taine called *répression*, involved for him in rectification. Freud superimposes on Taine's view the notion of unconscious elements exercising attraction on the thoughts that are then transformed regressively. In this process, these unconscious elements achieve some sort of release themselves.

Temporal regression is clarified when Freud, discussing its hallucinatory form, refers, in effect, to regression as a mode of establishing perceptual identity between what is seen *now* and that which once corrected a deficit. The primitive mode of this is by reviving the mnemic image of what removed the deficit, e.g. milk in the case of an infant's hunger. In hallucinatory psychoses and hunger phantasies, the process goes beyond the mnemic image, as it were, to reactivation of the original sensory image; but this reactivation is, of course, centrally not sensorily induced. Very much like Taine, Freud called in the 'second system' to inhibit such regression and divert the excitation involved. From this Freud derived the possibility of voluntary movement as that which involves 'purposes remembered in advance'.[5]

Formal (and topographical) regression both find an ancestor in Hughlings Jackson's studies of aphasia, to which we have already referred. But as the reader will have divined from the brief account of dream-work (particularly of 'making representable') that we have given here, Freud's treatment is immensely richer in its implications.

Later in the history of psycho-analytic theorizing, though at what stage I am not sure, the rather specialized concept of regression here discussed acquired a *behavioural* significance; that of reverting under stress to forms of response (e.g. crying or stamping or relatively unskilled movement) characteristic of an earlier stage of a person's development.

Identification

James Strachey, in editing the standard edition of *The Interpretation*, draws attention[5] to somewhat different uses of this term on Freud's part. In the main usage, Freud, in a discussion of hysterical identification, likens it to hysterical imitation, in respect of the circumstances in which the identification is apt to occur. Hysterical identification, he writes:

> enables patients to express in their symptoms not only their own experiences but those of a large number of other people; it enables them, as it were, to suffer on behalf of a whole crowd of people and to act all the parts in a play single-handed.[5]

Freud's amplification of this comment is difficult and subtle. Put very shortly, it amounts to arguing that if, for example, a patient has an hysterical attack and other patients associate this with some event, e.g. a letter from home or the revival of some unhappy love affair, their sympathy is aroused. *Unconsciously* they draw the inference: 'If a cause like this can produce an attack like this, I may have the same kind of attack since I have the same grounds for having it.' Such inference, drawn unconsciously, may in fact result in such an attack, whereas drawn consciously it would only give rise to fear.

Hence in Freud's view, at this time, identification was not simple imitation but involved an element of 'assimilation on the basis of similar aetiological pretension; it expresses a resemblance and is derived from a common element which remains unconscious'.[5]

It is quite beyond my competence to discuss this in relation to hysterical symptomatology. Our interest here is in Freud's use of 'unconscious inference'. There is no implication that such inference is logical or even realistically probable. (Nor, on the other hand, are these alternatives both excluded.) The process is important for understanding a movement of subjective thought which may lend itself to subsequent formulation as a conscious inference.

Freud's other usage in *The Interpretation* need not here concern us, as it would seem to involve confusion of identification with motivated condensation in one of the senses already outlined. Suffice the comment that what we have called the main usage seems to have become the one most generally adopted, the original context of identification on the part of hysterical patients being dropped. Hence, when Freud speaks much later of a boy identifying with his father, this would seem to involve assimilation and production of some of the father's qualities on the basis of a root similarity of which the boy is not conscious. The unconscious movement of thought could again be formulated as an inference: alike in respect of x therefore also in respect of y.

Repression

That there is no simple answer to what Freud meant by this term can be briefly indicated by the following. In *The Interpretation* Freud used 'repression' sometimes in relation to the continued existence of wishes allowed no outlet, sometimes in relation to the separation of emotion and ideational content when the latter is not acceptable. He also referred to 'repression' in connexion with his belief that whenever there is affect in a dream there is affect in dream-thoughts, but not conversely.

Towards the end of *The Interpretation*, and when discussing perception at a *primary* level, he describes repression as the

effortless and regular avoidance by . . . memory of anything
that had once been distressing.[5]

In this sense repression seems to be a primary process. But
Freud went on almost at once to say:

Among these [unconscious] wishful impulses derived from
infancy, which can neither be destroyed nor inhibited,
there are some whose fulfilment would be a contradiction
of the purposive ideas of secondary thinking. The fulfilment of these wishes would no longer generate an effect of
pleasure but of unpleasure: and *it is precisely this transformation of affect which constitutes the essence of what we term
'repression'*.[5]

This comment makes the term somewhat more complex in
meaning, if not altering its significance almost entirely. The
quotation gives additional support to the suggestion (p. 117)
that Freud, as in the phrase 'purposive ideas of secondary
thinking', implied a sense of wish different from that operating
at a primary level.

Finally, we must remember that in the full discussion of
repression in the metapsychological paper on this topic, Freud
differentiated *primal repression*, 'which consists in a denial of
entry to consciousness to the mental (ideational) presentation
of the instinct',[7] from *repression proper*. This concerned derivatives
of that which is repressed primarily. He seems, there, either
to include or to equate these derivatives with 'such trains of
thought as, originating elsewhere, have come into associative
connexion with'[7] the element primarily repressed. In this
context he treated 'repression proper' as an 'after expulsion'
and stressed not only the rejection operating from the side of
consciousness but 'the attraction exercised by what was originally repressed upon everything with which it can establish a
connexion'.[7] This kind of comment seems to reflect a shift of
emphasis on Freud's part from treating repression as a process
operating at a primary level, and obeying the equilibrium
principle, to one linked with secondary processes, though
fundamental in understanding that which is 'unconscious'.

The interested reader must be referred to Freud himself and

the numerous discussions that exist on this topic. In the *Meta-psychology* Freud's elaboration of what happens to an 'instinctual representative, withdrawn by repression from conscious influence'[7] is in line with a very old tradition; that of observing the phantastic flowering of unchecked imagination, some of whose roots have rotted in the dark. It is of considerable interest to the reader prepared to specialize further.

It would require a book in itself to consider Freud's treatment of subjective processes of this sort in any more detail. In *The Psychopathology of Everyday Life* he sought to illustrate their operation on waking memory and action. In later works, other processes, e.g. projection, were added to those already described. Again the reader must be referred to psycho-analytic publications for further consideration of these matters.

DREAM-THOUGHTS AND DIFFERENT POSSIBLE APPROACHES TO THEM

We now come at long last to 'dream-thoughts', waking thought and Freud's treatment of reality-oriented thinking.

Throughout *The Interpretation* there is the presumption on Freud's part that the 'dream-thoughts' are 'rational' and can be known, subject to the proviso that one cannot ever be sure that a dream interpretation is complete. Perhaps Freud's clearest statement both of the nature and knowability of dream-thoughts is the following:

> We have introduced a new class of psychical material between the manifest content of dreams and the conclusions of our inquiry: namely, their *latent* content, or (as we say) the 'dream-thoughts', arrived at by means of our procedure. It is from these dream-thoughts and not from a dream's manifest content that we disentangle its meaning. . . .
>
> The dream-thoughts and the dream-content are presented to us like two versions of the same subject-matter in two different languages. Or, more properly, the dream-content seems like a transcript of the dream-thoughts into another mode of expression, whose characters and syntactic laws it is our business to discover by comparing the original and

the translation. The dream-thoughts are immediately comprehensible, as soon as we have learnt them. The dream-content, on the other hand, is expressed as it were in a pictographic script, the characters of which have to be transposed individually into the language of the dream-thoughts. If we attempted to read these characters according to their pictorial value instead of according to their symbolic relation, we should clearly be led into error.[5]

Elsewhere,[5] Freud makes a distinction between essential dream-thoughts and material of less importance. The criteria by which these are distinguished are wholly obscure to me. They may not be to a practising analyst. But, so far as I know, such criteria have not yet been formulated, and to the logically-minded outsider this is a key problem in validation. But asking for such formulation may be inquiring for the subliminal cues which lead a good clinician *correctly* to diagnose the significance of incipient gestures and hesitations, etc. To describe these cues is a task to daunt the toughest. It would be foolish to doubt that such diagnostic insight is possible. Psycho-analysts would make a vast contribution to general psychology were they able to describe such cues more adequately than seems to be the case at present.

To return to Freud's essential dream-thoughts. By juxtaposing two passages, one from the *Metapsychology* and the other still from *The Interpretation*, one can gain a little further understanding of the complexities of Freud's treatment of this subject. The first makes clear the rôle of residual thought activity and how Freud thinks it is transformed. It would allow him to include, as he does elsewhere, preoccupations and anxieties of waking life, conscious and unconscious, spilling over into sleeping activity. He says:

> One of the most common types of dream-formation may be described as follows: a train of thoughts has been aroused by the working of the mind in the day time, and retained some of its activity, escaping from the general inhibition of interests which introduces sleep and constitutes the mental preparation for sleeping. During the night this train of thoughts succeeds in finding connexions with one of the

unconscious tendencies present ever since his childhood in the mind of the dreamer, but ordinarily *repressed* and excluded from his conscious life. By the borrowed force of this unconscious help, the thoughts, the residue of the day's mental work, now become active again, and emerge into consciousness in the shape of the dream. Now three things have happened:

(1) The thoughts have undergone a change, a disguise and a distortion, which represents the part of the unconscious helpmate.

(2) The thoughts have occupied consciousness at a time when they ought not.

(3) Some part of the unconscious, which could not otherwise have done so, has emerged into consciousness.

We have learnt the art of finding out the 'residual thoughts', the *latent thoughts of the dream*, and, by comparing them with the *manifest dream*, we are able to form a judgment on the changes they underwent and the manner in which these were brought about.

The latent thoughts of the dream differ in no respect from the products of our regular conscious activity; they deserve the name of preconscious thoughts, and may indeed have been conscious at some moment of waking life. But by entering into connexion with the unconscious tendencies during the night they have become assimilated to the latter, degraded as it were to the condition of unconscious thoughts, and subjected to the laws by which unconscious activity is governed.[7]

It would seem that at different stages in Freud's formulation of his views, 'latent dream-thoughts' sometimes meant preconscious residues and sometimes tendencies or thoughts unconscious at a deeper level. This suggestion fits in with Freud's comment in *The Interpretation* that:

A dream is in general poorer in affect than the psychical material from the manipulation of which it has proceeded. When I have re-constructed the dream-thoughts, I habitually find the most intense psychical impulses in them striving to make themselves felt and struggling as a rule against others sharply opposed to them.[5]

It fits in, too, with his comment (on the same page) that 'large numbers of dreams appear to be indifferent, whereas it is never possible to enter into the dream-thoughts without being deeply moved'. If the phrase 'dream-thoughts' referred exclusively to pre-conscious residues this presumably would not be so true.

Now let us bring in the second main description of essential dream-thoughts mentioned above. Freud writes:

> These usually emerge as a complex of thoughts and memories of the most intricate possible structure, with all the attributes of the trains of thought familiar to us in waking life. They are not infrequently trains of thought starting out from more than one centre, though having points of contact. Each train of thought is almost invariably accompanied by its contradictory counterpart, linked with it by antithetical association.
>
> The different portions of this complicated structure stand, of course, in the most manifold logical relations to one another. They can represent foreground and background, digressions, illustrations, conditions, chains of evidence and counter arguments. When the whole mass of these dream-thoughts is brought under the pressure of the dream-work, and its elements are turned about, broken into fragments and jammed together—almost like pack-ice—the question arises of what happens to the logical connexions which have hitherto formed its framework.[5]

The answer Freud gave to his last question is already sketched and I do not propose to say more on it. So far as dream-thoughts are concerned, there still seems little doubt that Freud treated these as, in part at least, active or reactivated residues of pre-conscious thinking, or unconscious impulses and thought at a deeper level or, it would sometimes seem, a fusion of the lot.

This, however, still does not seem to be the whole story. I venture, therefore, to suggest that two very different approaches to the nature of dream-thoughts are compatible with what Freud said and that he, and many who followed him, veered between one and the other but with a bias to the first. To psycho-analytically-sophisticated readers each of the resulting interpretations may appear a falsification of what was intended. But the suggestion that two different approaches are remotely possible may serve to bring into focus two central questions. First, how far was Freud's treatment of conscious and unconscious thinking coloured by the tendency, current in his day, to treat all thinking on analogy with vision and as exclusively a scanning or inspectional process, in which ultimately an intelligible integration of the items scanned comes about? Secondly, was his greatest achievement an implied rejection of the adequacy of this view and its incorporation into something more complex? With these questions in mind, let us consider the two different approaches, and correlative interpretations, suggested.

On the first interpretation, Freud seems to have been guided by an unstated inclination to treat dream-thoughts as in some sense formed or formulated (hence, as it were, relatively fixed) and such that when they are 'uncovered' in the process of analysis it is possible to know 'by direct judgment' which elements 'have the highest psychical value'. (Freud's phrases.[5]) By implication, one must be able to 'know' in some such sense the latent content of which the manifest dream is a scrambled version. Freud referred in his early writings to 'unmodified mnemic residues', and this notion still survives in later works, e.g. in revised editions of *The Psychopathology of Everyday Life.* The palimpsest analogy, already quoted, fits in with this fundamentally 'inspectionist' interpretation, for its use by Freud implies that the original writing (there all along on the parchment, but overlaid by another script) can be revived and deciphered. On this view both patient and analyst will readily accept much of what is 'uncovered' in the process of analysis as remembered, and as that with which the dream, and the patient, were really concerned. But there will be gaps which the patient cannot fill. The analyst's job, on this hypothesis, is to assist the patient in coming 'face to face' with the missing unconscious train of thought, which, by virtue of greater experience and less personal involvement, the analyst may more readily divine. On this view the patient eventually comes to 'recognize' (in a sense implying remember) that which was unconscious as indeed his own.

Of the many points in this one could isolate for comment, I want to stress only one—the implied treatment of thinking on scanning or inspectional lines, which, as already suggested, has behind it the long western tradition of assimilating thought to vision. It involves treating latent thoughts as though they were formed, like engravings or inscriptions on the hidden ('unconscious') altar of a Greek Orthodox Church, to which the layman (consciousness) cannot usually penetrate. Treatment, using this analogy, would be the means whereby the analyst—a very unorthodox priest—assists the layman in overcoming a prohibition partly self- and partly culturally-induced.

This analogy, like all analogies, breaks down. But its points of collapse are interesting. Neither the Greek Orthodox priest nor the layman, when allowed to penetrate, may in fact see what is on the hidden altar, for nothing may be carved or written there. The analyst is outside the church altogether, where this for the moment symbolizes the patient and his thoughts. The analyst can at best only probe, hypothesize, divine, cross-check and work within that which the patient is ultimately able to assimilate as his own. On the patient's part, though much of what he does may be 'unconsciously performed', there is nothing corresponding to the hidden altar. Though Freud's 'agents', the id, censor, ego, superego and even 'the unconscious' (who is occasionally referred to as perceiving), sometimes appear to engage in rituals holy and unholy, Freud at his most scientifically-sophisticated referred to them as *fictions*. So we cannot seriously cast them in the rôles of priests. But the obvious breakdown of the analogy serves its purpose if it suggests that, at least on occasion, there may be no unconscious relatively formed or formulated thoughts with which patient or analyst could in any sense come *face to face*. For much of what goes on at an unconscious level, of which dreams and symptoms may be the outcome, is neither formulated nor such as could be 'scanned' or 'inspected'. Though some unconscious responses may well have a habitual quality and indeed be 'residues' in some sense, it is misleading to think of them inevitably as residues that can be reactivated and ultimately 'recognized', as distinct from assimilated, as one's own. It is worth noting that the word 'recognize' is ambiguous. Its use may presuppose retention. It may, on the other hand, signify only acceptance now and possibly in the future.

This brings us to the alternative interpretation of Freud which stresses once more the process of formulation.

This interpretation accords less strictly with what Freud wrote, though it is likely to be the one connected with his name most readily by non-psychological readers. It is an interpretation which fits in closely with the line followed by Jung, except for a fundamental fact. Jung, also 'inspectionist' in some of his treatment of thinking, can be seen locating the latent thoughts to be recognized one stage further back—in the collective unconscious. From there they must be dredged, the fallen *eidos*, counterparts of those that reigned in a Platonic heaven. There are traces of a formulation theory of a different kind, and without any such neo-platonic overtones, in Freud's approach; it often seems implied in that of Neo-Freudians.

In *The Interpretation*, Freud's discussion of dream-thoughts constantly implies a gradualness of shift from waking to sleeping, rumination on some theme, and conversely. Moreover, he frequently seems to need the concept of an uncompleted task, familiar in other fields of psychology, in order to make sense of his observations. (Non-psychological readers may need reminding of the evidence suggesting that uncompleted tasks are more readily recalled than those that are finished and done with.) And, most important, Freud often stressed the unknowable nature of unconscious thought processes and their difference from conscious ones. He contrived, the while, to stress both the 'rationality' of latent dream-thoughts and the irrationality of unconscious processes of which, as we have suggested, dream-thoughts are sometimes treated as one class.

One can unravel this apparent contradiction in several ways. For instance, one may substitute functional intelligibility for 'rationality' in the first clause and illogicality for irrationality in the second. Or we may confine rational dream-thoughts to the activities of the pre-conscious. But, as already suggested, Freud in practice does not seem to have restricted latent dream-thoughts to those that were pre-conscious. There is always the hint of something much more difficult to bring to light. A third alternative is to surmise that Freud tacitly assumed all un-conscious thoughts, however bizarre, to be theoretically *capable* of logical formulation. Though such formulation may be, in fact, a late stage in a long process, Freud tended (we are suggesting) to treat it as complete, and never fully worked out the possible alternative of gradual formulation. Freud *could* hold such a gradual formulation view; even though, in practice, none of us attains self-knowledge at a fully rational level, any more than a follower of Spinoza ever achieves complete under-standing at the third degree. Freud's description, in *Studies on Hysteria*,[1] of the analyst following a logical thread through the maze of distortion supposedly due to 'resistance' on the patient's part, has an extraordinary ring of the Spinozistic assumption that man at his core is a *rational* thinker, where this includes willingness to face any fact and unequivocal *logicality*.

But a belief in ultimately possible rationality is very different from the conviction of an original virtue in this respect, which virtue has been lost by distortion. In other words, the rational formulation of what one feels and thinks may be an end process which one indeed accepts. It may not be, unless one is a Platonist, the revealing of an earlier state of clarity which one recognizes on return to it, still less an inborn mandala. To interpret Freud on these 'gradual rational formulation' lines is to question the adequacy of the palimpsest analogy and the *exclusively* 'inspectionist' approach to thinking that goes with it.

Interpreting Freud without recourse to inspectionist terms only would imply two things. First, analysis would not be exclusively a process of 'uncovering' latent and unconscious thoughts retained from recent and more remote times. It could also be one of aided formulation. No doubt the procedure has many other functions as well. Secondly, thinking, whether conscious or unconscious, would emerge as an immensely complex process of responding, selecting, integration and formulation, whose elementary forms are actions and reactions some of which we can never know and all of which are subject to the distorting processes Freud identified. Semi-conscious and conscious scanning and interrelation of ingredients (sensory, motor and emotional, internally or externally derived) would emerge as a late product, which arises, most characteristically, when immediate action is blocked for internal or external reasons. Conscious scanning could, moreover, be a process whose operation William James[12] may have been right in suggesting we can only recognize in retrospect. At the time of fully active thinking we are usually too aware to be at the same time self-aware. So one must not equate conscious thinking with self-conscious thinking, touched as it is with the narcissistic overtones that Freud was quick to note.

Would it be wholly false to interpret Freud in this way? The answer is as usual 'Yes' and 'No'. To my mind it involves crediting Freud with probably his greatest achievement: that of contributing so much to the breakdown of the narrowly inspectionist and visual treatment of thinking, and of exploring and describing in detail possible dynamic relations between responses we undoubtedly make unawares to those which we then, or later, consciously accept as our own. Respect for such an achievement is independent of whether one happens to accept or reject Freud's general, or detailed, treatment of motivation. The interpretation suggested would be seriously false to Freud if one blandly attributed to him an exclusively formulational view either of thinking or of the analytic procedure. But is it false to the following piece of speculation which Freud entertained but, so far as I know, never returned to developing? It comes from the *Studies on Hysteria*. To return to my cairn analogy, does it point to a different route which Freud himself might have followed?

The ideas which are derived from the greatest depth and which form the nucleus of the pathogenic organization are also those which are acknowledged as memories by the patient with the greatest difficulty. Even when everything is finished and the patients have been overborne by the force of logic and have been convinced by the therapeutic effect accompanying the emergence of precisely these ideas —when, I say, the patients themselves accept the fact that they thought this or that, they often add: 'But I can't *remember* having thought it.' It is easy to come to terms with them by telling them that the thoughts were *unconscious*. But how is this state of affairs to be fitted into our own psychological views? Are we to disregard this withholding of recognition on the part of the patients, when, now that the work is finished, there is no longer any motive for their doing so? Or are we to suppose that we are really dealing with thoughts which never came about, which merely had a *possibility* of existing, so that the treatment would lie in the accomplishment of a psychical act which did not take place at the time? It is clearly impossible to say anything about this—that is, about the state which the pathogenic material was in before analysis—until we have arrived at a thorough clarification of our basic psychological view, especially on the nature of consciousness.[1]

I have sketched the implications for 'thinking', if such interpretation is not wholly false. There also follows recognition of the many-sided function of analytic procedure. Thereby hangs a very long tale, for in discussing the 'validation' of such procedure, the question, *at one stage*, of whether a patient accepts or rejects an interpretation by the analyst, and indeed the fact that much of what the analyst says is interpretative, evocative, suggestive or what not, is supremely irrelevant. For, *at that stage*, there may be no inevitable presumption of an originally, or unconsciously, formed or formulated experience which the patient can 'remember', and which the analyst's interpretation must 'match'. On a given occasion neither baby nor adult may ever have formed, to any degree, an image in any sense modality of that which satisfied or frustrated them, let alone a verbalized response;* though both may have made incipient responses below the level of activity capable of retention and later 'recognition'. There may, of course, also be recognizable ingredients from past experience; for in the process of 'thinking', roughly identified above, all degrees of formulation are possible, from a humble incipient movement

* Though Freud described unconscious tendencies in terms of active or potentially active residues of earlier experience he did not seem consistently to hold the view, popularly ascribed to him, that *nothing* is ever lost. Transitory trivia merely pass over, lose their resonance, as it were, and do not form part of that which is 'unconscious'.

to the supremely complex. 'Validation' *in another sense*, of a procedure, or part of it, wherein the existence now, or earlier, of such an incipient response (along with others more complex) is divined by an analyst, and discouraged or encouraged to develop to a recognizable form, is involved with the vast question of what criteria the analyst, the patient, or anyone else could use in hazarding that this does and that does not fit in with a given personality as it could, 'desirably', be. That problem is outside the scope of this book.

TREATMENT OF REALITY-ORIENTED THINKING

We must now pass from Freud's brilliant and suggestive treatment of 'subjective' thinking to that which is 'reality-oriented' in the sense indicated on p. 104 of being enmeshed in the world of common experience and not subservient immediately to the pleasure-pain principle. Though the 'censor' and 'super-ego' may make conventional judgments, Freud, I have suggested, also relied on another conception of reality-oriented thinking which assumed its veridical and rational status. For him, as in part for Spinoza, in the attainment of this there lay the hope of man's salvation. Hence to deduce from Freud a recommendation to indulge in abandoned 'idding' is to misunderstand everything for which he stood. However, thinking might be 'objective' in the first sense, of being enmeshed with common experience, without being reality-oriented in the second sense, in so far as it disregarded an individual's primary needs. Hence its operation in the second sense is not necessarily equivalent to integrating with the social assumptions of any known society.

Freud did not properly scrutinize the slippery concept of 'reality' and I do not think that the existence of these two possible senses was in the least clear in his mind. So in different situations he and other analysts shifted almost imperceptibly from one conception to another. As a result, they have been accused alternately of an ideal of craven adjustment to the evaluations of some given group, and of complete abandon of all the values of any known society. In this we can see, from a different angle, Freud's fundamental ambivalence about the 'unconscious' as both the 'true psychic reality' and that which is to be surpassed. Given Freud's account of primary processes, however, the derivation of 'reality testing', or reality-oriented thinking in either of the senses distinguished, is a problem. In what follows I propose, therefore, to treat both senses together, taking for granted that for Freud veridical perception lies at the root of reality-oriented thought.

Whereas in Spinoza's system the difficult question is to account for error in terms other than limitations of knowledge (and this has its own difficulties), in Freud's position one major problem is how there is anything else. For Freud attempted to derive reality-oriented thinking as a secondary process from primary processes in which ostensibly it plays no part. His attempt, ingenious as it was, serves, I believe, to throw into relief some of the weaknesses of the root assumptions we listed on pp. 105-6.

Though a sketch, the most comprehensive account Freud gave of the development of such thinking was in the *Project*. There he appeared to be trying to allow simultaneously for thought rooted in veridical perception (in contrast to hallucination), and which guides rewarding action, and thought which is 'pure' and strives to establish 'identity'. This does not lead directly to action though it may be used to serve practical ends in the long run.

Freud's main consideration of veridical thinking is embedded in discussing how the ego (in this context the sub-system of ψ neurones permanently 'cathected') can overcome two dangers. The first of these arises from failure to distinguish hallucination from externally-rooted perception, so that there is failure to reduce tension by appropriate action. A hypothetical example (not worked out by Freud) would be the abortive sucking movements of a hungry baby in the presence of imaginary milk. Secondly, there is failure to note the revival of a hostile memory image originating internally, not from the external world. Hence it is allowed to flourish and requires eventually an unnecessary outlay of defensive energy to quell it. In both cases there is needed 'an indication which will distinguish a perception from a memory (or idea)'.[3]

At an early stage of development, Freud implies, there is no way, psychologically, of distinguishing veridical, externally-induced experiences from those that are internally-produced, i.e. hallucinatory images. Thus a criterion is required. He attempts to derive such a criterion initially from the report of perceptual neurones discharging. He admits that this criterion can fail; for example, when a wished-for object is cathected to hallucinatory level. Hence this criterion needs strengthening. Freud tries to do this by invoking a capacity, on the part of the ego, to inhibit the intensity of internally-produced imagery. Thereafter the ego learns 'by biological experience' (i.e. the success of veridically and failure of non-veridically directed response) to permit action only when there are 'indications of reality'. These 'indications' seem to boil down to a greater intensity of impact from perceptual neurones discharging than from revived memories, thanks to inhibition of the full development of the latter. How, one asks, did the ego know which kind of image to inhibit initially?

To seek for the genesis of this inhibition is to inquire how the 'ego' came to be formed; this is referred to by Freud as 'the most obscure of problems'.[3] On this issue, highly controversial among psycho-analysts, I venture only one additional comment. Freud's position seems to involve, and to require, a primary capacity on the part of the organism to distinguish pleasure and pain and to distinguish and recognize (however obscurely) the stimuli associated in the past with one or the other. It is required also to discriminate between degrees of intensity of stimulation. Empirically these are not alarming presuppositions. Indeed, here again we have in Freud the germs of a genetic account of thinking and its development. But about the logic of Freud's argument one has some doubts, for it seems to be circular. That is to say, Freud's criteria by which perception and hallucination are generally distinguished (he never claimed infallibility for this distinction) rests on assuming the more subtle form of veridical response which underpins Freud's hints on the development of the ego. That he presupposes veridical discrimination and recognition becomes clearer if we look at his treatment of judgment and reflective thinking, which arise when action is blocked.

Freud says that 'judgment is a ψ process which is only made possible by the inhibition exercised by the ego and which is brought about by the difference between the wishful cathexis of a memory and a similar perceptual cathexis'.[3] Where these two coincide there is no occasion for thought, only smooth action. 'When they do *not* coincide, an impetus is given to the activity of thinking which will be brought to a close when they do coincide.'[3] Such lack of coincidence may be partial or complete.

In discussing the discrepancy between memory and perceptual image, Freud stresses the complexity of the neurones involved and uses as an explanatory model a 'wishful cathexis' attached to neurones *a* and *b* and a 'perceptual cathexis' attached to neurones *a* and *c*. In effect, action is halted by the ego because of the discrepancy between *b* and *c* and a process of search is initiated until a perceptual discharge that tallies with *b* is achieved.

Freud exemplifies his neurone model in terms of a baby faced with a different view of a nipple from that originally satisfying it and making exploratory movements to get perceptual and memory image to coincide. This and the relevant discussion show that Freud was prepared to root judgment in extremely primitive response. This is all to the good. But the reader of this section of the *Project* will note that Freud has to assume some discrimination of sensible difference* between memory and perceptual images. He also invokes 'a sensation of identity' when the images finally coincide. His example shows incidentally that he tends to credit the baby with a remarkably accurate memory image of that which satisfied. This in itself is a problem, even if Freud's early statement were modified.

Freud uses the case where discrepancy of memory and perceptual image is initially complete, to take his account of thinking further. He writes:

> . . . a perception may emerge which does not coincide in *any* way with the memory image that is wished for (which

---

* This is not accusing Freud of invoking discrimination of their status as 'imaginary' or 'real'. It would be idle to stress other weaknesses in this passage in the *Project*, as I cannot imagine that Freud would later have agreed with what he said about the infant's method of problem solving. Piaget's studies of his own small infants are singularly relevant and interesting in this connexion.

we will call $M+$). It will then become a matter of interest to cognize—to get to know—this perceptual image, so that in spite of everything it may perhaps be possible to find a way from it to $M+$.[3]

In explaining what takes place, Freud makes use of 'hyper-cathecting by the ego' of the discrepant perception. Later in the *Project* he virtually equates this with 'attention' as a process behind which he cannot go. In the immediate context we are considering, Freud remarks that the different (discrepant) portion of the cathexes 'arouse interest' which gives rise to thinking of two kinds. Either 'current' is 'directed on to revived memories, in which case an aimless activity of memory is set in operation (which will find a motive in differences, not in resemblances), or it will remain concentrated on the newly-presented portions of the perception and so set to work an equally aimless activity of judgment.' This is the kind of thinking that 'strives after identity'. It is not really clear how Freud motivates this *aimless* thinking in terms of his initial presuppositions. Again one suspects that he needs something in the nature of 'effort after meaning', exploratory drives or curiosity, in addition to the self-preservative and sexual drives allowed at this stage of his theorizing. For, although this reflective thinking is practical in the sense that it may eventually be used in relation to action, it is not evident immediately what type of tension it is reducing in terms of Freud's initial list of basic drives.

There are other aspects of this early treatment of veridical thinking by Freud that are interesting; for example, what he has to say about the connexion of thought and language and his belief that it is on a fellow human being that 'an infant learns to cognize'. This is because of being an 'object of a *similar kind* to that which was the infant's first satisfying object (and also his first hostile object) as well as his sole assisting force'.[3] To discuss this in terms of Freud's later derivation of social responses from other, mainly sexual, responses would take us too far afield. Suffice it for the moment that 'theoretical interest' in other people goes back once more to their 'similarity' to an object relevant to primary reduction (and arousal) of tension.

F

Trenchant criticisms have in fact come to be levelled against Freud's treatment of reality-oriented perception and thought. Psycho-analysts have queried the conception of primary narcissism that goes with it. Suttie,[19] nearly thirty years ago, questioned the rooting of human social response in the economic relationship just mentioned and the sexual affiliations on which Freud laid so much stress. More recently a whole group of writers, for example, Rapaport,[16] Hartmann, Kris and Loewenstein, have come to argue that the rudiments of secondary process exist from the beginning. As we have seen, Freud's secondary processes were intended to subserve the reality not, immediately, the pleasure principle. So such suggestions from among writers deeply sympathetic to a psycho-analytic viewpoint imply profound changes in psycho-analytic theory. In fact, modern focus on the psychology of the ego may lead either to rejection of the whole homeostatic model or to modification of the list of drives on which the original theory of motivation was based. Many analysts cannot accept Freud's concept of innate aggression. It remains to be seen whether they will come to accept the possibility of direct social and other interests.

No account of the development of reality-oriented perception and thinking will work without elementary and veridical processes of discrimination and recognition being assumed from the start. It is no criticism of Freud to say he assumed these. Indeed, there are hints of a theory in Freud which, as Rapaport has suggested, fit in well with Piaget's approach and are most illuminating, developmentally. The critical problem is whether their assumption can be integrated with Freud's other views. I would venture to suggest a further point: empirically, the development of these processes seems to require that they be reinforced and *shared*. It has often been suggested that man's achievements in abstract thought are related in part to his long period of dependency. It has not always been stressed that, in the course of this period of dependency, adults (as well as other children) devote a vast amount of time to reinforcing these primary cognitive activities and that in this situation *shared recognition* of discrimination and recognition may play a fundamental rôle. I will return to discussion of this in later chapters.

We must now bring this long discussion of Freud to an end, aware inevitably of gaps and of deficiencies of many other kinds. Freud was born over a century ago and died more than twenty-five years ago. It would be very surprising if some of his basic concepts did not strike a much later generation as mainly historically-rooted. The notion of the organism absorbed in divesting itself of all excitation; the notion of two or even three main levels of neurological and hence, by adaptation, of psychological functioning; the unsatisfactory, if suggestive, treatment of reality-oriented thinking, all seem to me to fall into this category. Indeed, Freud's general model of motivation, and that popular triumvirate the Id, Ego and Superego, may strike a still later generation as historical oddities. All these concepts, valuable as some of them were in their day, may now be retarding rather than advancing personality theory; for people treat them as final answers where in fact there are unsolved problems. But Freud's description and use of the processes involved in subjective thinking was so far ahead of anything up to his time, and the reorientation in our general concept of thinking, largely due to Freud, was so great, that later generations may well also find that their psychology is built in part on the original work of this man.

REFERENCES

Numbers in brackets indicate the pages in this book where
given references occur

1. Breuer, Joseph, and Freud, Sigmund, *Studies on Hysteria*, Standard Edition, edited by James Strachey, Vol. II, London: Hogarth Press, 1955, pp. 293-4 (154), 300 (155-6).

2. Flügel, J. C. 'The Death Instinct, Homeostasis and Allied Concepts' in *Studies in Feeling and Desire*, London: Duckworth, 1955.

3. Freud, Sigmund, 'Project for a Scientific Psychology' in *The Origins of Psycho-analysis*, Letters to Wilhelm Fliess, Drafts and Notes. Edited by Marie Bonaparte, Anna Freud and Ernst Kris, London: Imago, 1954, pp. 157 (109), 240 (118), 370 (127), 387 (158), 390-3 (160-1), 426 (159).

4. Freud, Sigmund, *An Outline of Psycho-analysis*, translated by James Strachey, International Psycho-Analytical Library, London: Hogarth Press, 1949.

5. —— *The Interpretation of Dreams*, translated and edited by James Strachey, London: Allen & Unwin, 1961, pp. 16 (124), 17 (130), 123 (125), 130 (115), 135 (122), 149-50 (144-5), 165-6 (123), 179 (131), 181 (123), 243 (131), 277 (147-8), 293 (129), 296 (128-9), 306 (151), 311 (148), 311-12 (150), 313 (140), 313-16 (136-7), 318 (137), 321 (144), 324 (130), 329-30 (138), 333-4 (139), 337 (139), 340 (135), 344-5 (134-5), 353 (131), 445 (125), 455-6 (128), 457 (115), 461 (132-3), 467 (150), 479 (133), 488 (141), 490 (126, 140), 491 (141), 493 (141), 499 (139, 140), 505 (141), 506-7 (122), 539 (127), 543 (143), 548 (142), 552 (115), 560 (117), 566 (119, 144), 598-9 (121), 600 (146), 604 (146).

6. —— *The Psychopathology of Everyday Life*, Standard Edition, edited by James Strachey, Vol. VI, London: Hogarth Press, 1960, p. 217.

7. —— *Papers on Metapsychology*, Collected Papers, Vol. IV, London: Hogarth Press, 1948, pp. 28-9.

8. —— *New Introductory Lectures on Psycho-Analysis*, translated by W. J. H. Sprott, London: Hogarth Press, 3rd edition, 1946.

9. Hinde, R. A., 'Energy Models of Motivation' in *Models and Analogues in Biology*, Symposia of the Society of Experimental Biology, Vol. XIV, London: Cambridge University Press, 1960, pp. 199-213.

10. Jackson, J. Hughlings, 'On Affections of Speech from Disease of the Brain', *Brain*, Vol. I, 1879, pp. 304 ff.; Vol. II, pp. 203 ff. and 323 ff.

11. Kris, Ernst, Introduction to *The Origins of Psycho-Analysis*. See Freud, 3 above.

12. James, William, *The Principles of Psychology*, London: Macmillan, 1890, Vol. I, pp. 162 ff.

13. MacIntyre, A. C., *The Unconscious*, London: Routledge and Kegan Paul, 1958.

14. Maury, L. F. Alfred, *Le Sommeil et les Rêves*, Paris: Didier, 3rd edition, 1865.

15. Meehl, P. E., and MacCorquodale, K. A., 'On a Distinc-

tion between Hypothetical Constructs and Intervening Variables', *Psychological Review*, Vol. 55, 1948, pp. 95-107.

16. Rapaport, D., 'Psycho-analysis as a Developmental Psychology' in *Perspectives in Psychological Theory*, edited by Bernard Kaplan and Seymour Wapner, New York: International Universities Press, 1960, pp. 209-55.

17. Schubert, G. H. von, *Die Symbolik des Traumes*, Leipzig: Brockhaus, 4th edition, 1862.

18. Sully, J., 'The Dream as Revelation' in *The Fortnightly Review*, Vol. 53, 1893, pp. 354-65, particularly p. 364.

19. Suttie, Ian D., *The Origins of Love and Hate*, London: Kegan Paul, 1935; Harmondsworth: Pelican edn., 1960.

20. Taine, H., *De l'Intelligence*, Paris: Hachette, 3rd edn. 1878; cf. *On Intelligence*, authorised translation by T. D. Haye, London: Reeve, 1871, pp. 42 (112), 55 (112), 71 (111), 218-19 (110), 238 (110), 239 ff. (110).

21. Zubek, J. P., 'Effects of Prolonged Sensory and Perceptual Deprivation' in *Experimental Psychology*, British Medical Bulletin, Vol. 20, No. 1, Jan. 1964, pp. 38-42.

CHAPTER SIX

INTELLIGENCE AND THINKING:
I. GALTON'S CONTRIBUTION

I have no patience with the hypothesis expressed, and often implied, especially in tales written to teach children to be good, that babies are born pretty much alike, and that the sole agencies in creating differences between boy and boy, and man and man, are steady application and moral effort.

FRANCIS GALTON

THAT INTELLIGENCE has something to do with thinking has long been taken for granted. On the other hand, within psychological circles, there is virtually a hundred years of work on assessing intelligence while studies of thinking have lagged behind. The two concepts, though related, are by no means identical. While this is not the place to embark on a detailed factual account of psychologists' efforts to define and assess intelligence, there is something to be said for a quick look at the changing concepts of intelligence that have been invoked in these activities. Exploration on these lines yields unexpected rewards. For the often criticized and despised assessors of intelligence turn out to have been taking for granted that some animals and some men can sometimes 'see the point'. All they have argued is that certain people are better at this than others, due either to innate endowment, environmental stimulus or (the only tenable hypothesis in the light of current evidence) both, and that relative ability can be very roughly assessed, with assignable degrees of probability. Logically speaking, it is not open to a consistent behaviourist to allow his subject to *see* the point. His subject, whether mouse or man, can only 'discriminate', say, cheese from soap, and this is not always feasible by one sense only. To ask the investigator how he finds out that the subject 'discriminates' in this case and not that, either raises a discussion of experimental method or what the behaviourist regards as a philosophical hare. He suspects (rightly) that his opponent is saying such discrimination must be open, not blind, and supposes that denying its *blindness* lets in a 'mentalistic' or 'soulful' entity 'which has no place in science'.

Let us chase the above-mentioned hare for another moment, however. To the outsider it looks as though even the most skilled experimenter must at some stage rely on his own unblind 'discrimination' in judging whether his subject responds in one way or another to 'different' stimuli. If the investigator's 'discrimination' is on a logical par with his subject's, then, to say whether the first investigator accurately 'discriminated' his subject's discriminations, a second investigator must 'discriminate' in checking the first one's 'observations'. Scientifically it is indeed essential that such a cross-check should be applied; for the suggestion that discrimination must not be treated as inevitably 'blind' does not imply that it is always visual, conscious or veridical. But the whole elaborate procedure of scientific checking is partly to ensure that there really was true discrimination in the first instance; it presupposes the possibility of such discrimination on the part of somebody somehow and somewhere in the series of experiments. Without this presupposition there is an infinite regress. It would seem simpler to allow *in principle* that the man might really *see*, and the mouse really *smell*, the cheese in the first instance; though it requires experiment to ascertain the conditions wherein this is done most reliably.

To approach the question in a different way: if, *à la* early Freud, man and mouse only hallucinate cheese on the basis of a previous 'reduction of primary needs and tensions', and slowly learn which hallucinations pay off, then, as we have already argued, man and mouse must be able to recognize success and failure and discriminate and recognize experiences associated with one or the other. In some cases, indeed, we must allow one or more investigators the much more dangerous privilege of knowing, with a high degree of probability, whether a public piece of cheese is, or is not, present at the time, in order to say that the subject seems to be hallucinating. Such knowing is a complex process; we do not understand either psychologically or philosophically much of what it implies. But it seems fairly clear that processes of discrimination (and recognition) in an unblind, shareable and sometimes veridical sense are integral to it, and their presupposition underpins any scientific inquiry. Hence to treat the basic observational roots of science as 'blind responses', for fear of God, mind or the devil, is a species of paranoic intellectual suicide.

The vision of the whole of behaviouristically-oriented experimentation and of psycho-analytic inquiry either involving an infinite regress or being two great systems of hallucination validated, if at all, by hallucination, is thought-provoking. But the thoughts provoked are not those which either group of investigators, with their urgent claims to be scientific, really seem to want. In any case, even hallucinations are described as 'seen' or 'heard' or otherwise experienced in some form. So whatever processes these words refer to have been smuggled into the story. They might as well be there officially from the start and the American fear that they are 'mentalistic', and the Russian terror of a lurking Deity, allayed by some other means.

As some kinds of veridical discrimination and recognition have in fact played an important rôle in theories of intelligence, this returns us to those who have attempted to study intelligence and relate it to a theory of thinking.

Galton and Binet were the founding fathers of such work. I therefore propose, in this chapter and the next, to outline their contributions, relating their treatment of intelligence to thought. Discussion of the intricacies of intelligence as assessed is not to my purpose. Binet was influenced by Galton (among others) and went much further in developing a view of thinking. This forms the background to his work on testing, a background unknown to many people, because inaccessible. It is, however, of great interest in itself. For these reasons Binet has been given much more space in Chapter Seven. The short succeeding chapter is no more than a signpost to later developments. The sources on which it is based are more readily available. With this introduction, let us turn to Galton.

A statistical concept that fundamentally influenced later treatment of intelligence was that of the Gaussian curve. Its relevance to biological data was clearly shown by Quetelet, the Belgian Astronomer Royal, in the *Letters on Probability*. An English translation of these by Downes was published in 1849 and fell into Galton's hands.

In this book Quetelet had shown how the actual distribution of the stature of some 100,000 French conscripts conformed very closely to that expected from a normal distribution curve. The same was true of the chest measurements of 5,738 Scottish soldiers. From this Galton proceeded to argue on the following analogy:

> I argue from the results obtained from Frenchmen and from Scotchmen that, if we had measurements of the adult males in the British Isles, we should find those measurements to range in close accordance with the law of deviation from the average. . . .
>
> Now if this is the case with stature, then it will be true as regards every other physical feature—as circumference of head, size of brain, weight of grey matter, number of brain fibres, &c. and thence, by a step on which no physiologist will hesitate, as regards mental capacity.
>
> This is what I am driving at—that analogy clearly shows there must be a fairly constant average mental capacity in the inhabitants of the British Isles, and that the deviations from that average—upwards towards genius, and downwards towards stupidity—must follow the law that governs deviations from all true averages.[1]

Now Galton was perfectly clear that such an application of the law in question involved a fundamental assumption, namely that height or mental capacity, or whatever it may be, is so distributed that a scale of measurement based on equal intervals applies. For those unfamiliar with the issues raised by this, let us give Galton's own example.

> Suppose 100 adult Englishmen to be selected at random, and ranged in the order of their statures in a row: the statures of the 50th and 51st men would be almost identical and would represent the average of all the statures. Then the difference, according to the law of frequency, between

them and the 63rd man would be the same as that between the 63rd and the 75th, the 75th and the 84th, the 84th and the 90th. The intervening men between these divisions, whose numbers are 13, 12, 9 and 6 form a succession of classes, diminishing as we see in numbers, but each separated from its neighbours by *equal grades* of stature. The diminution of the successive classes is thus far too small, but it would be found to proceed at an enormously accelerated rate if a much longer row than that of a 100 men were taken, and if the classification were pushed much further.[1]

There is not much biological difficulty, it seems, in accepting such an assumption with regard to height, but it is well to realize that it is an assumption and that in arguing from analogy Galton transferred it, fully aware of what he was doing, to mental capacity. Today it remains antecedently probable on the evidence available that Galton was justified. Certainly, the practical utility of intelligence tests, created on this same assumption, for sorting out, broadly, such near-random samples of young adult men and women as was obtained by National Service call-up in time of war, would suggest that Galton, thinking in equally broad terms, was not so very far out. But an assumption it remains. This means that it is theoretically possible that the true intellectual gap between someone at the 84th and another at the 90th percentile, on a modern reliable well-standardized test, is *not* equal to that between two people with scores at the 50th and 63rd percentile respectively. In short, numerical rarity of achievement, at the top and bottom of the scale, is a reflection not merely of a quantitative increase (or decrease) in an ability distributed otherwise evenly, but that the addition or subtraction of another drop of ability results in a fundamental change of potential. Hence, at the ends of the scale particularly, a quantitative increase or decrease in grade is an inadequate indicator of potential. The practical problem for those defending this position is to produce an effective measure of the 'true ability' not reflected adequately by the usual test score, interpreted according to the law of averages. This is what makes it so important to be clear about our concepts of intelligence and their relation to 'thinking'.

What was Galton's conception of the 'natural ability' so distributed? In brief it was *general* and involved ability or intellect, zeal and adequate power of doing a great deal of work. In fact it was very complex. Whence did Galton derive this conception? The answer has entertainment value as well as other merits. He was armed in the one hand with Quetelet, in the other with a species of *International Who's Who* in the shape of the *Dictionary of Men of the Time*, published by Routledge in 1865. This dictionary covered 2,500 people, of which a full half consisted of American and European celebrities. The assortment of entries has a flavour that it is a pity to lose:

> 62 actors, singers, dancers, &c.; 7 agriculturalists; 71 antiquaries, archeologists, numismatists, &c.; 20 architects; 120 artists (painters and designers); 950 authors, 400 divines, 43 engineers and mechanicians; 10 engravers; 140 lawyers, judges, barristers and legists; 94 medical practitioners, physicians, surgeons and physiologists; 39 merchants, capitalists, manufacturers and traders; 168 military officers; 12 miscellaneous; 7 moral and metaphysical philosophers, logicians; 32 musicians and composers; 67 naturalists, botanists, zoologists, &c.; 36 naval officers; 40 philologists and ethnologists; 60 poets (but also included in authors); 60 political and social economists and philanthropists; 154 men of science, astronomers, chemists, geologists, mathematicians, &c.; 29 sculptors; 64 sovereigns, members of royal families, &c.; 376 statesmen, diplomatists, colonial governors, &c.; 76 travellers and geographers.[1]

Galton on scrutinizing his list noticed the high proportion of people past fifty years of age. Of the English represented in these groups, he extracted about 850 in this category and, calculating that the equivalent British Isles' population of adult males was around two million, arrived at the conclusion that repute yields 425 to a million and high repute about 250. Galton's rough criterion of repute at this stage was 'that a man should have distinguished himself pretty frequently either by purely original work, or as a leader of opinion'. He wholly excluded 'notoriety obtained by a single act'. Nor, he intimates, did he take much notice of official rank where it was likely to have tipped the balance between two otherwise similar people gaining distinction. 'By reputation', he says elsewhere, 'I mean the opinion of contemporaries revised by posterity – the favourable result of a critical analysis of each man's character, by many biographers. I do not mean high social or official position . . . I speak of the reputation of a leader of opinion, or a man to whom the world deliberately acknowledges itself largely indebted.'

Galton then proceeded to cross-check this rough estimate against *The Times* obituary for 1868 published on January 1st, 1869. He found about fifty men in his selected class, having excluded those of high ability dying too young to have earned deservedly wide reputation, and the old of erstwhile but not current prominence. These exclusions suggested lowering his age limit to forty-five. 'Now', writes Galton, '210,000 males die annually in the British Isles above the age of forty-five; therefore the ratio of the more select portion of "Men of our Time" on these data is as 50 to 210,000, or as 238 to a million.' He cross-checked again by obituary evidence for earlier years, when the population was much smaller, and again arrived at the rough estimate of 250 in a million or 1 in 4,000 as a criterion of eminence. The fundamental point to grasp is that, in this work of Galton, we are encountering the key conception of defining high, low or medium ability in terms of the frequency with which a specified level of performance occurs in a given population. Galton cross-checked his estimate by various other means, including figures for entry to Sandhurst, examination marks for the Cambridge mathematical tripos and, at the other end of the scale, by rough estimations of the proportions of idiots and imbeciles in the British Isles' population of the time. How his estimations would work is reflected in Table 3.

These figures need not concern us further here. Nor do we need to scrutinize in detail the argument in favour of natural inheritance that Galton derived from the different approach that takes up the bulk of his book. This was an analysis of 300 families containing nearly 1,000 men, of whom 415 were

TABLE 3

Classification of Men According to their Natural Gifts

| Grades of natural ability, separated by equal intervals | | Proportionate, viz., one in | In each million of the same age | Numbers of men comprised in the several grades of natural ability, whether in respect to their general powers, or to special aptitudes. In total male population of the United Kingdom, say 15 millions, of the undermentioned ages: | | | | | |
Below average	Above average			20–30	30–40	40–50	50–60	60–70	70–80
a	A	4	256,791	641,000	495,000	391,000	268,000	171,000	77,000
b	B	6	161,279	409,000	312,000	246,000	168,000	107,000	48,000
c	C	16	63,563	161,000	123,000	96,000	66,000	42,000	19,000
d	D	64	15,696	39,800	30,300	23,900	16,400	10,400	4,700
e	E	413	2,423	6,100	4,700	3,700	2,520	1,600	729
f	F	4,300	233	590	450	355	243	155	70
g	G	79,000	14	35	27	21	15	9	4
x all grades below g	X all grades above G	1,000,000	1	3	2	2	2	—	—
On either side of average			500,000	1,268,000	964,000	761,000	521,000	332,000	149,000
Total, both sides			1,000,000	2,536,000	1,928,000	1,522,000	1,042,000	664,000	298,000

The proportions of men living at different ages are calculated from the proportions that are true for England and Wales. (*Census* 1861, Appendix, p. 107.)

Example.—The class F contains 1 in every 4,300 men. In other words, there are 233 of that class in each million of men. The same is true of class f. In the whole United Kingdom there are 590 men of class F (and the same number of f) between the ages of 20 and 30; 450 between the ages of 30 and 40; and so on.[1]

illustrious. Galton, in spite of an enterprising skirmish round the direct and collateral descendants of Popes, was not in a position to parcel out the effects of genetic inheritance and environmental stimulus. So all he really showed was the high proportion of very able men produced by very able families. This in itself is interesting, but it leaves the hen and egg question about natural inheritance and environmental stimulus unsettled. A potentially stronger argument for heredity was suggested in a later book by Galton's anecdotal evidence on twins.

Two other points, however, from *Hereditary Genius* are worth bringing in. One is of theoretical importance. The other reflects the concrete quality of Galton's own thinking and may provide a respite for readers, ill at ease with probability curves, who share Galton's feeling that a million is 'a number so enormous as to be difficult to conceive'. Here is Galton's idea of 'a standard by which to realize it'.

Mine will be understood by many Londoners; it is as follows: One summer day I passed the afternoon in Bushey Park to see the magnificent spectacle of its avenue of horse-chestnut trees, a mile long, in full flower. As the hours passed by, it occurred to me to try to count the number of spikes of flowers facing the drive on one side of the long avenue—I mean all the spikes that were visible in full sunshine on one side of the road. Accordingly, I fixed upon a tree of average bulk and flower, and drew imaginary lines—first halving the tree, then quartering, and so on, until I arrived at a subdivision that was not too large to allow of my counting the spikes of flowers it included. I did this with three different trees, and arrived at pretty much the same result: as well as I recollect, the three estimates were as nine, ten, and eleven. Then I counted the trees in the avenue, and, multiplying all together, I found the spikes to be just about 100,000 in number. Ever since then, whenever a million is mentioned, I recall the long perspective of the avenue of Bushey Park, with its stately chestnuts clothed from top to bottom with spikes of flowers, bright in the sunshine, and I imagine a similar continuous floral band, of ten miles in length.[1]

The theoretical point is important for understanding the nature of the ability Galton had in mind. First, there is no doubt that he thought of a capacity that could be reflected in more than one activity. It is not true that mathematicians are necessarily one-sided in their natural gifts, argues Galton, invoking Leibniz, Ampère, Arago, Condorcet, D'Alembert and a group of lesser-known lights to support him. 'We still find', he says, 'mediocre men whose whole energies are absorbed in getting their 237 marks for mathematics; and, on the other hand, some few senior wranglers who are at the same time high classical scholars and much more besides.' By implication, elsewhere, he contrasts such general ability with other and special natural gifts for painting, music or 'statesmanship', though he thinks that these too may be distributed normally. His emphasis is on the mistake of attributing outstanding achievement to purely special powers and, in so doing, under-estimating what is due to concentrated efforts made by men who are widely gifted:

> People lay too much stress on apparent specialities, think-ing over-rashly that, because a man is devoted to some particular pursuit, he could not possibly have succeeded in anything else. They might just as well say that, because a youth had fallen desperately in love with a brunette, he could not possibly have fallen in love with a blonde. He may or may not have more natural liking for the former type of beauty than the latter, but it is as probable as not that the affair was mainly or wholly due to a general amorousness of disposition: it is just the same with special pursuits. A gifted man is often capricious and fickle before he selects his occupation, but when it has been chosen, he devotes himself to it with a truly passionate ardour.[1]

This returns us to the complexity of Galton's conception of natural, for him inherited, general ability; for both explicitly, and by implication, he is thinking of the union of the three separate qualities already mentioned: 'intellect', 'zeal' and 'power of work'.

> By natural ability, I mean those qualities of intellect and disposition, which urge and qualify a man to perform acts

that lead to reputation. [In the sense defined on pp. 171-2.] I do not mean capacity without zeal, nor zeal without capacity, nor even a combination of both of them without an adequate power of doing a great deal of very laborious work. But I mean a nature which, when left to itself, will, urged by an inherent stimulus, climb the path that leads to eminence, and has strength to reach the summit—one which, if hindered or thwarted, will fret and strive until the hindrance is overcome, and it is again free to follow its labour-loving instinct.[1]

This trio calls for scrutiny. How far did he think *all* were inherited? If all these, *a fortiori* each one; but Galton did not quite stick to this. His discussion of statesmen and commanders makes it clear that, in spite of his enormous bias to inheritance, Galton was not entirely overlooking opportunity and stimulus:

Social advantages have enormous power in bringing a man into so prominent a position as a statesman, that it is impossible to refuse him the title of 'eminent', though it may be more than probable that if he had been changed in his cradle and reared in obscurity he would have lived and died without emerging from humble life.[1]

And Galton was aware that a man of one-sided ability might be thrown up as a demagogue, or as a leader in some strategic situation, who would not qualify as the all-rounder required for sustained command in widely different circumstances. In fact Galton wavered somewhat on the inheritance of 'zeal' when he allowed that only intellect and power of work are required by a man who is pushed into public life; for 'when he is there, the interest is so absorbing, and the competition so keen, as to supply the necessary stimulus to an ordinary mind'. But, so far as I know, Galton did not waver on intellect and power of work. What can we say about this?

Not very much, I fear. We know that Galton had originally entitled his book *Hereditary Genius* on the basis of Johnson's Dictionary definition of genius as 'a man endowed with superior faculties'. Galton preferred the word genius 'as expressing an ability that was exceptionally high, and at the

same time inborn', to that of 'ability', which to him did not
exclude the effects of education. He came to regret the title
because of other specialized implications of the word 'genius'.
But he did not withdraw his emphasis on *inborn* capacity. As
Galton never discussed systematically what he meant by
'intellect', we have, I think, to rest content with the likelihood
that his term could mean 'intelligence' in one of its much
narrower meanings, together with much else. In some cases at
least, it involved considerable powers of retention. It might
be allied (and from his examples it was in many cases) with
what we now call special aptitudes. To be effective it had to be
associated with a capacity for work which was sustained. This
last is not only stated in the passage quoted on p. 176, but is
implied by Galton's exclusion of the sporadically notorious
from his most exclusively 'eminent'. It is also implied by
incidental remarks he makes about the relevance to achievement of physical stamina and his challenge to popular belief
in the weediness of the highly endowed. On closing Galton one
is left feeling that in his highest group his debatable 'zeal' and
hard work were near to an inborn capacity for sustained
arousal (which *could* in certain cases be credited to circumstances), allied with constitutional stamina and drive.

Perhaps we should add Galton's 'few supplementary remarks
on the small effects of a good education on a mind of the highest
order', to bring into focus what he meant.

A youth of abilities G, and X, is almost independent of
ordinary school education. He does not want a master continually at his elbow to explain difficulties and select
suitable lessons. On the contrary, he is receptive at every
pore. He learns from passing hints, with a quickness and
thoroughness that others cannot comprehend. He is
omnivorous of intellectual work, devouring a vast deal
more than he can utilize, but extracting a small percentage
of nutriment, that makes, in the aggregate, an enormous
supply. The best care that a master can take of such a boy
is to leave him alone, just directing a little here and there,
and checking desultory tendencies.
    . . . the most illustrious men have frequently broken

loose from the life prescribed by their parents, and followed, careless of cost, the paramount dictation of their
own natures: in short they educated themselves. D'Alembert is a striking instance of this kind of self-reliance. He
was a foundling (afterwards shown to be well-bred as
respects ability), and put out to nurse as a pauper baby
to the wife of a poor glazier. The child's indomitable
tendency to the higher studies could not be repressed by
his foster-mother's ridicule and dissuasion, nor by the
taunts of his schoolfellows, nor by the discouragements of
his schoolmaster, who was incapable of appreciating him,
nor even by the reiterated deep disappointment of finding
that his ideas, which he knew to be original, were not
novel, but long previously discovered by others. Of course,
we should expect a boy of this kind to undergo ten or
more years of apparently hopeless strife, but we should
usually expect him to succeed at last; and D'Alembert did
succeed in attaining the front rank of celebrity, by the time
he was twenty-four.[1]

Galton's assured expectation that ability of this level is
inborn, and will rise in the teeth of almost all obstacles, is apt
to make the twentieth-century reader writhe. In our present
climate of opinion, it is as unfashionable to suppose that some
people are as incurably able as others are incurably limited as
it was unfashionable for Galton to go against the mid-Victorian
belief that 'steady application and moral effort' suffice to explain the undoubted difference in performance between individuals. On the other hand, he seems not to have been wholly
and completely wrong.

Most modern psychologists talk of 'intelligence', not 'intellect',
and, though they differ in their definitions, almost all technical
uses of 'intelligence' refer to something more specifically and
more narrowly defined than Galton's concept. Further, most
reputable modern psychologists make a distinction between
the ability or group of abilities roughly measurable in testing,
and their effective use outside the test situation.

Such a distinction between potentially intelligent responsiveness, and effective use of this potential in ordinary life, is

necessary because of the wide differences that exist in the directions and circumstances in which people are aroused to act intelligently and in which they are willing to do sustained work. So that Galton's 'zeal', and capacity for work, no longer figure in what most psychologists attempt to assess by an intelligence test as such. It by no means follows that they are unimportant. It is simply that many modern psychologists lay more stress on the intricacies and complexities of personality and situational variables, and would shudder at sweeping statements about the inheritance of the former.

It is arguable, indeed, that Galton not only emphasized inheritance too much but incorporated too many basic aspects of thinking in his conception of general ability. For he included the modern psychologist's 'general intelligence', plus special abilities (e.g. verbal or mathematical), plus retention, plus willingness to mobilize innate equipment in these respects, in sustained attack on one or a variety of matters arousing the individual's interest. Considered as a comment on thinking, Galton's stress on innate basic equipment underplays the rôle of acquired interests and the effect, particularly the cumulative effect, of acquired skills in thinking; such as are reflected, for example, in mode of attack on a problem and in mastery of the medium, linguistic or otherwise, in which it is presented. But, as we shall see in a moment, Galton was far from forgetting other processes, e.g. imaging, in which individuals differ in their facility and in their mode of thinking.

What about the more narrowly defined concept of 'intelligence'? We shall be sketching in the next chapter some of the work that gives this phrase some meaning. It suffices at the moment to comment in passing on the state of the hen and egg controversy. Was Galton wrong in saying that we had to reckon with inborn capacity? At the time of writing the answer is 'no', though he overstated his case. A sifting of current controversy suggests that the narrowly-defined but general ability reflected in much test performance involves native endowment but also acquired skill, both contributions being relevant. Current conservative estimates attribute between 60 and 70 per cent of the variance to the former, 30 to 40 per cent to acquired skill, this being a function partly of environment and training. As nobody in fact knows the genetic basis of intelligence, these estimates must be referred to the complex mass of relevant test results and controversy to be fully understood. While conservative opinion slants the answer towards Galton's 'innate endowment', current conceptions of the vast difference that 30 to 40 per cent acquired skill could make to young adult performance, works in the opposite direction. Moreover, some applied psychologists have argued (with some justice) that the hen and egg controversy is a waste of time, in view of our serious lack of scientific evidence upon the conditions encouraging or hampering effective use of such level of ability as a child displays in a test situation. While this, very broadly, is the current position on the questions Galton raised, it is also true that, with a different conception of intelligence, and a whole lot of new data, the emphasis of psychologists could alter again. This returns us to such of Galton's other work as bears on intelligence and thinking.

We have already seen, in Chapter Four, something of Galton's important studies of associations and the conclusions he drew from these. Of his other studies, by far the most interesting is the well-known investigation of imaging that he carried out by circulating the questionnaire below and encouraging people freely to supplement their replies to the set questions. It will be noticed that the heading of the questionnaire biases the inquiry to that of visual imagery, though the rôle of other kinds was suggested by the findings.

QUESTIONS ON VISUALISING AND OTHER ALLIED FACULTIES

The object of these Questions is to elicit the degree in which different persons possess the power of seeing images in their mind's eye, and of reviving past sensations.

From inquiries I have already made, it appears that remarkable variations exist both in the strength and in the quality of these faculties, and it is highly probable that a statistical inquiry into them will throw light upon more than one psychological problem.

Before addressing yourself to any of the Questions on the opposite page, think of some definite object—suppose it is your breakfast-table as you sat down to it this morning—and consider carefully the picture that rises before your mind's eye.

1. *Illumination*—Is the image dim or fairly clear? Is its brightness comparable to that of the actual scene?

2. *Definition*—Are all the objects pretty well defined at the same time, or is the place of sharpest definition at any one moment more contracted than it is in a real scene?

3. *Colouring*—Are the colours of the china, of the toast, bread crust, mustard, meat, parsley, or whatever may have been on the table, quite distinct and natural?

4. *Extent of field of view*—Call up the image of some panoramic view (the walls of your room might suffice), can you force yourself to see mentally a wider range of it than could be taken in by any single glance of the eyes? Can you mentally see more than three faces of a die, or more than one hemisphere of a globe at the same instant of time?

5. *Distance of images*—Where do mental images appear to be situated? Within the head, within the eye-ball, just in front of the eyes, or at a distance corresponding to reality? Can you project an image upon a piece of paper?

6. *Command over images*—Can you retain a mental picture steadily before the eyes? When you do so, does it grow brighter or dimmer? When the act of retaining it becomes wearisome, in what part of the head or eye-ball is the fatigue felt?

7. *Persons*—Can you recall with distinctness the features of all near relations and many other persons? Can you at will cause your mental image of any or most of them to sit, stand, or turn slowly round? Can you deliberately seat the image of a well-known person in a chair and see it with enough distinctness to enable you to sketch it leisurely (supposing yourself able to draw)?

8. *Scenery*—Do you preserve the recollection of scenery with much precision of detail, and do you find pleasure in dwelling on it? Can you easily form mental pictures from the descriptions of scenery that are so frequently met with in novels and books of travel?

9. *Comparison with reality*—What difference do you

perceive between a very vivid mental picture called up in the dark, and a real scene? Have you ever mistaken a mental image for a reality when in health and wide awake?

10. *Numerals and dates*—Are these invariably associated in your mind with any peculiar mental imagery, whether of written or printed figures, diagrams, or colours? If so, explain fully, and say if you can account for the association.

11. *Specialities*—If you happen to have special aptitudes for mechanics, mathematics (either geometry of three dimensions or pure analysis), mental arithmetic, or chess-playing blindfold, please explain fully how far your processes depend on the use of visual images, and how far otherwise.

12. Call up before your imagination the objects specified in the six following paragraphs, numbered A to F, and consider carefully whether your mental representation of them generally is in each group very faint, faint, fair, good, or vivid and comparable to the actual sensation:

A. *Light and colour*—An evenly clouded sky (omitting all landscape), first bright then gloomy. A thick surrounding haze, first white, then successively blue, yellow, green and red.

B. *Sound*—The beat of rain against the window panes, the crack of a whip, a church bell, the hum of bees, the whistle of a railway, the clinking of tea-spoons and saucers, the slam of a door.

C. *Smells*—Tar, roses, an oil-lamp blown out, hay, violets, a fur coat, gas, tobacco.

D. *Tastes*—Salt, sugar, lemon juice, raisins, chocolate, currant jelly.

E. *Touch*—Velvet, silk, soap, gum, sand, dough, a crisp dead leaf, the prick of a pin.

F. *Other sensations*—Heat, hunger, cold, thirst, fatigue, fever, drowsiness, a bad cold.

13. *Music*—Have you any aptitude for mentally recalling music, or for imagining it?

14. *At different ages*—Do you recollect what your powers

of visualizing, etc., were in childhood? Have they varied much within your recollection?

General remarks—Supplementary information written here, or on a separate piece of paper, will be acceptable.[2]

Galton circulated his questionnaire widely among adults and children, males and females. He relates his main conclusions, however, to the analysis of replies from 100 men of whom 'at least half were distinguished in science and in other fields of intellectual work'. As usual, Galton's results were interesting and his comments entertaining as well as penetrating in terms of future trends in psychology. For example, finding a relative lack of visual imagery among his scientists, Galton felt 'bound to say, that the missing faculty seems to be replaced so service- ably by other modes of conception, chiefly, I believe, con- nected with the incipient motor sense, not of the eyeballs only but of the muscles generally, that men who declare themselves entirely deficient in the power of seeing mental pictures can nevertheless give life-like descriptions of what they have seen'. Only many years afterwards, in the ingenious studies of Jacobson and of Max, in the 1930's, and more recently with the advent of the electromyograph, did investigation of the rôle of muscular tension in thinking become possible. What exactly that rôle is, is still in debate.

Meanwhile, Galton drew four main conclusions from his results. First, he stressed the wide individual variations in the extent, vividness, colour, location, flexibility of control, etc. of the imagery used by different people in thinking. Secondly, he found evidence of 'number forms', the curious patterning that some people employ in thinking of numerals and, in some cases, days, months and years. An example of such an imagined visual framework of calculation is given on p. 202, taken from Binet's study of Diamondi, one of his high-grade calculators. I am aware of no satisfactory evidence for saying that possession of such a number-form is either an advantage or disadvantage in calculation. Thirdly, Galton's results also showed the existence of synaesthesia, i.e. the close association for some people of colours with, e.g. numbers, dates, letters of the alphabet and sounds. Finally, on this and related evidence, Galton inferred continuity in the distribution of all forms of visualization, from almost total absence to that of complete hallucination. The occasional experience of this last he thought to occur more often among normal people than was then commonly supposed.

The reader must turn to Galton himself for the details that make these studies so concrete and intriguing. Meanwhile Galton's emphasis on individual differences leads us directly to Binet's invaluable contributions to the study of thought.

REFERENCES

Numbers in brackets indicate the pages in this book where given references occur

1. Galton, Francis, *Hereditary Genius: An Enquiry into its Laws and Consequences*, London: Macmillan, 2nd edition, 1892, and London: Collins, Fontana Library, 1962 (the references made are to this edition), pp. 28-9 (169-70), 50-1 (171), 53-4 (174), 64 (175), 71-2 (169), 75 (173), 77 (175-6), 82-3 (177-8), 85 (176).

2. —— *Inquiries into Human Faculty*, London: Dent, 1943, pp. 255-6.

For some of Binet's questions were distinctly provocative, and his comments not entirely tailored with tact. He had a streak both of journalist and of reformer, and was quite capable of castigating the colossal conceit of those who had helped him by completing some questionnaire. One is left in some doubt on what his subjects may have felt when they read the published reports of his researches. He might well be a menace if let loose now. But fifty years later one can enjoy this abundance, as one browses in old volumes and *L'Année Psychologique*. International chess players; eminent dramatists; startled philosophers; micro-organisms; aphasics; hysterics; feeble-minded, brilliant and very normal children; muddle-headed alienists; fanatical psycho-analysts; obsessional Germans; senile dements; maniacs, Americans and large-scale testers, all appear in turn to make their contribution, together with others not of a kind, for Binet's great belief was in individual differences. His attitude to large-scale generalities was caustic and included reserves of irony for guesses of his own.

Binet was born at Nice in 1857,[1] fourteen months after Freud. He died, at the height of his powers, in 1911,[30] on the point, it seems, of trying to integrate all he had learnt into a coherent account of thinking. Instead of a rounded, if tentative, view (for Binet was far too intelligent to claim finality), what we have is a dozen books and some 250 articles never woven into a whole, and still awaiting analysis in thorough detail. By judicious sampling (and help from Varon's monograph, published nearly thirty years ago) we can gain some indication of the direction of change Binet's own thinking took, in the light of the evidence and experience he had. One late article gives a brilliant outline of the position he left to be developed.

Apart from the emphasis on individual differences, and the massive evidence he produced for their intrinsic interest, Binet's writing has immense historical worth and, one would like to think, rather more than this. For it reflects, at one extreme, an almost purely mechanical associationism, fathered by fore-runners such as Spencer, Mill and Taine. By the end, simple associationism is completely gone. Instead we find a sketch of thinking, in dynamic terms, as a process remote from a succession of conscious states. Binet treats it indeed as an *aconscious*, because personally involved, activity. Known only as a result of its products, thinking, for him, is in some degree the activity of a whole personality, in which action, feeling and *un*conscious motor attitudes play a vital (though not an exclusive) rôle. His distinction between *a*conscious and *un*conscious is crucial; for by this, Binet retains the possibility of integrated, flexible and creative thinking, without having to claim that he can observe thought in progress or that it is essentially either reflective or the reverse. And he can also allow that much thinking is habitual. About the middle of this chronological development from associationism to a view that is very different, we find Binet writing about imageless thought. There his work impinges on the Würzburg experimenters, already dealt with in detail by Professor Humphrey. With this broad indication of whence Binet came and went, let us treat him in such detail as restricted space allows.

ASSOCIATIONIST AND PSYCHO-PHYSIOLOGICAL APPROACH TO THINKING

The Binet of rigid associationism is best shown in Varon's choice of quotation from an early article on reasoning and perception:

> The operations of the intelligence are only the diverse forms of the laws of association: it is to these laws that all psychology comes back, whether it appears simple or is recognized to be complex. Explanation in psychology, in its most scientific form, consists in showing that each mental fact is only a particular case of these general laws. . . . In applying these ideas to the subject which now occupies us, we come to say: to explain reasoning is to determine by what combination of the laws of association this mental operation took place; simple in appearance, it is in reality complex, and in the last analysis reducible to two functions of resemblance and contiguity.[32]

Binet's early studies were on perception and hallucination, and after writing several articles he brought his views together in *The Psychology of Reasoning*, published as his first book in 1886. Here we find him following Herbert Spencer in stressing awareness of relations, insisting on the affinities of perception and reasoning, and on the primacy of awareness of similarity. He also stressed the unconscious fusion of memory image and sensation where these are alike, and became involved in the following argument and hypothesis, both of which have some interest for us now.

Many psychologists in Binet's time wished to find in the properties of the nervous system an explanation of psychological phenomena. Binet's line on this was classical in simplicity:

> Here we have the opportunity to demonstrate the worth of this fashionable opinion, more correct in appearance than reality. Let us grant, for a moment, that it is not merely probable, but absolutely established that two similar states of consciousness have as a basis one single nervous element in the brain, and that this identity of site explains the two effects of similarity, namely suggestion and fusion. Is it really possible to believe that the properties of the nervous system provide a genuine explanation of the properties of similarity? That would be a curious illusion. For in this there is no explanation, but simply a transposition into physiological terms of the phenomenon that is supposed to be explained. What is this single element that is offered as the basis of similarity? How is unity to be understood without the idea of number, of plurality, and is not this idea at least more complex than that of similarity? 'Here we move in a circle', as Montaigne observed.
>
> The truth is that we can know external things only by submitting them to the laws of the mind and consequently the study of one of these objects, of a brain, for instance, cannot explain the *forms of our thought*, for these are always presupposed. To hold otherwise is to beg the question.*

* Nous trouvons ici l'occasion de montrer ce que vaut cette opinion en vogue, qui est plus juste en apparence qu'en réalité. Admettons, pendant un instant, qu'il soit non seulement probable, mais absolument démontré que deux états de conscience semblables ont pour base, dans le cerveau, *un élément nerveux unique*, et que cette unité de siège explique les deux effets de la ressemblance, la suggestion et la fusion. Croit-on par hasard que c'est là

In the course of a footnote comment Binet adds: 'we repeat that similarity is a simple, final and irreducible notion'.

Having thus delivered himself of this effective, if slightly Kantian, attack on then current reductionism, thereby avoiding the epistemological trap into which it is easy to stumble, Binet launched into a commendable foreshadowing of Hebb's[25] physiological views. For Binet in no way wished to separate psychological from physiological functioning:

. . . reasoning true, false or insane always obeys the laws of resemblance and contiguity.

That agreed, reasoning can become unconscious without necessarily implying a profound change in the phenomenon. When it is admitted that reasoning results from a faculty of the mind, is it any more embarrassing a matter to explain the unconsciousness of certain reasonings? From our point of view, nothing is simpler. Reasoning is a synthesis of images. Images are the psychic part of a psycho-physiological whole. If they are lacking, the physiological process remains; it alone is necessary and sufficient. The physiological mechanism operates as if it were accompanied by the epiphenomenon consciousness. It does its work silently and attains just as surely its final result.

This physiological process cannot be described. We are still at the stage of hypothesis; here is a schema that will serve simply to fix our ideas. To restrict the question let us take the visual perception of a particular object.

---

une véritable explication des propriétés de la ressemblance par les propriétés du système nerveux? Ce serait une singulière illusion. Car il n'y a là aucune explication, mais une simple transposition en termes physiologiques du phénomène qu'on a la prétention d'expliquer. Qu'est-ce que *cet élément unique* que nous donnons pour base à la ressemblance? Comment comprendre l'unité, si on n'a pas l'idée de nombre, de pluralité, et cette idée n'est-elle pas au moins plus complexe que celle de la ressemblance? 'Nous voilà au rouet', comme dit Montaigne.

La vérité est que nous ne pouvons connaître les choses extérieures, qu'en les soumettant aux lois de notre esprit, et que par conséquent l'étude d'un de ces objets, d'un cerveau par exemple, ne peut rendre compte des *formes de notre pensée*, car elle les suppose toujours. Ceux qui soutiennent le contraire commettent une pétition de principe.[2]

Every perception presupposes anterior states that prepare for it. In order for us to perceive the object that is
before us, recognize its nature, usage, etc., we must have
associated in our mind, by virtue of prior experiences, the
visual image of this object, or another of the same kind,
with the procession of images of all sorts which sum up
our knowledge of it. How do we express in physiological
terms the product of these previous experiences? Images
have the same cerebral location as sensations; one may
suppose that each of them results from the excitation of a
particular group of cells situated in the sensory areas of the
cortex. Let us designate the visual image of the object by
aB; these two letters are to represent the two cells of the
visual area which are assumed to vibrate when we
experience the object visually; by C.D.E.F.G.H. . . . we
shall designate the cells serving as substratum to other
images of the object, tactile, kinaesthetic, etc.

So far the hypothesis raises no difficulties. But till now
we have omitted an essential element; the *relations*.
Psychological analysis shows that there is an associative
link between the various images of an object; it is this link
that gives coherence and unity to the group, enables one
attribute of an object to suggest the others, as when a
person's voice recalls his facial appearance. How can one
translate this association into physiological terms? How
do two impressions, for example of vision and hearing,
become connected to each other in the brain? This could
not happen if they were completely isolated, one in the
visual and the other in the auditory areas. It has been
assumed that when two groups of cells—substratum of
two images—are excited at the same time, a wave of nervous activity travels from one group to the other by means
of the communicating fibres so numerous in the brain.
In the same way, as M. Fouillé remarks, when two stones
are dropped into water a short distance apart the two
resultant series of undulations travel to meet each other.
The effect is that the route between the two groups of
cells in question is facilitated, and when, later on, one of
the two groups is excited alone, the impulse from it will

follow this path in preference to any other as being the *line of least resistance* (Spencer). In this way one has translated into physiological terms the elementary fact of the association of ideas. It has been said that cell groups* excited simultaneously are interrelated by *dynamic associations* (Ribot), or again form a single, unique *stereotype block*† (Taine). Thus in our example there exists a dynamic association between the cells aB corresponding to the visual image of the object and the cells C.D.E.F.G.H. . . . corresponding to the mechanical sensations which the object evokes when handled.

Add another element and the hypothesis is complete. We have not yet spoken of the excitatory sensation supposed to make this association of cells vibrate. Analysis has taught us that, in external perception, the sensation always resembles in some degree the first image it evokes, that is to say the previous vision or visual memory of the same object that we have designated aB. One may therefore designate the cells vibrating under the influence of actual vision by the letters Aa: the little a of this formula is the name of the element common to actual vision and past vision; because we know that the psychic quality of similarity has for its physiological correlate identity of site.

When vision begins, the nervous excitation, after passing through the cell group Aa, passes into the group aB, by means of the cellular junction point afforded by the cell a. In psychological terms, the vision of the object first recalls by similarity its visual memory. Then the excitation continues on its way, thanks to the pre-established dynamic associations, and it spreads through the cell groups designated C.D.E.F.G.H. . . . At the same time the memory of all the former experiences arises in the mind; this stream of images is associated with the vision of the moment and the psychic synthesis is made.

Certainly, such a conception of the rôle of nervous centres is frankly hypothetical; we have no means of

* I have resisted the temptation to translate *groupes cellulaires* as 'cell assemblies'.

† *Cliché* in the French gives this key meaning.

observing what happens in the brain of a man who is thinking; all one can state is that reasoning could be produced by the mechanism described, because our neuro-physiological hypothesis corresponds to the subjective analysis of reasoning. Reasoning could thus be defined from the physiological point of view: the continuation of a process of which the first phase (the excitation of the cells A*a*) is the only one that corresponds to the external stimulus. It is a corollary of the psychological definition: reasoning is an extension of experience.

We leave to the reader the task of deciding whether this mechanical theory deprives the mind of all activity, reducing it to a state that is purely passive. This is a reproach often levelled at the English School, which tries to explain all the phenomena of the mind by the laws of association. But what foundation is there for this criticism? Images are not dead, inert things, they have active properties; they attract each other, they link together, they fuse. It is mistaken to treat an image as a photographic plate, fixed and unchangeable: it is a living element, something which is born, changes and grows like our nails or hair. The activity of the mind results from the activity of images in the same way as the life of the hive results from that of the bees, or rather as the life of an organism derives from that of its cells.[2]

MODIFICATION OF INITIAL VIEW

Binet had produced a physiological schema while avoiding reductionism, but he was still entangled in a treatment of reasoning in terms of a synthesis of images; even if these were becoming as active as bees and most unlike the passive revivals of past sensations stamped upon the mind by impinging objects. Binet had still a long way to go, learning, as he worked at the Salpêtrière on hysterical and hypnotic phenomena, the simple inadequacies of simple associationism. A hypnotized subject rendered deaf to the words 'book' and 'umbrella' ceased not only to hear these words but also to recognize these objects as such. A hysterical patient with an anaesthetic hand might not report pain if the hand were pricked, unseen, but would report imagery of points or bars of hallucinatory vividness.[32] Where there were no conscious sensations, something was still registered. So we find Binet (and Féré) surmising that to the law of the excitation of one idea by another one must add the law of paralysis of one idea by another. By 1887 in *Animal Magnetism* Binet and Féré were already writing so:

> We are now aware that it [suggestion] may affect all the parts of the psychical mechanism, sensation, imagination, memory, reason, will, motor power, etc., it is in a word co-extensive with intelligence. Classical psychology, which does not mention psychical paralysis, omits half the history of the mind: it describes the active impulsive forms of intelligence, without taking note of its passive, negative forms, which are equally numerous; it represents that side of the mind on which the light falls, without taking note of the side in shadow.[3]

Five years later in 1892 came *Les Altérations de la Personnalité*, wherein Binet assembled, more clearly, the evidence for supposing that a person may at the same time register but not see or consciously experience external objects. This fact he discussed in terms of the alternating, somnambulistic, subliminal and co-conscious states of which we have already seen something in Chapter Four. Association, writes Binet,

> is not sufficient to explain the development of mental life. Undoubtedly something else besides these slight bonds is necessary to connect our ideas. More profound causes, whose nature it is difficult to determine, just because they are unconscious, operate to apportion our ideas, perceptions, memories, and all our conscious states into free and independent syntheses. When we are in one of these syntheses we have difficulty in arousing an idea which belongs to another synthesis. In general, association of ideas is not enough; but when some elements of this second synthesis have once been revived for one reason or another, then the entire synthesis re-appears.[32]

This firm criticism of simple associationism marks, for Varon, the end of one stage in the progress of Binet's thinking. The

G

years 1890-5 do appear in one sense a transitional period, at least in Binet's confidence that any simple theory of thinking would prove workable. But closer scrutiny of the two dozen or more publications of this time might well show more system in his new explorations than would appear on the surface. There is, however, no shadow of doubt about the significance of some of these writings. To show this I propose to concentrate on two English articles in *The Fortnightly Review* (for 1892 and 1894 and not in Varon's bibliography), on *La psychologie des grands calculateurs et joueurs d'échecs* (1894), and on Binet's and Passy's enterprising skirmish among their contemporary dramatists.* Here we find a gallery of legendary figures, each one apparently studied in his setting, each man and setting individually different. Sardou, Dumas, Daudet, de Curel, Edmond de Goncourt (to mention only some) all gave their mites to the slaughter of theory. Not always mites indeed, when one considers the pages written by de Curel, trying to explain to Binet how he set about thinking. But we bask in wonderful French. If simple associationism had to be buried, it is lucky to have been calculated, chess-played and dramatized out in such a richly elegant and entertaining funeral. No wonder Binet noted the solemnity of the later more rigidly experimenting Würzburgers with an ever so slightly lifted eyebrow.

Let us set the stage with *The Fortnightly Review*, where Binet on 'Mental Imagery' and on 'The Mechanism of Thought' rubs shoulders with articles on Huxley's controversies, Italian bank scandals, cycling and cycles, the insurrection of women, the burden of taxation, Bernard Shaw on 'The Religion of the Pianoforte', and White on 'The Truth about the Salvation Army'. Frank Harris was as catholic an editor in interest as was his French contributor. What had Binet got to say?

The first article[4] is simple, distinctly assured, and gives us four main points. The results of introspection on the part of philosophers such as Hobbes, Locke, Berkeley and Hume had been, said Binet, the assimilation of thinking to vision and failure to realize the variety of forms that thought processes may take.

* This must have been completed by 1894, for it was included in the first volume of *L'Année Psychologique*, covering that year and published in 1895, with Beaunis and Binet as co-editors.

Not that Binet despised introspection or disliked the philosophers. But one man's comments on his own mind do not give ground for generalization, and large-scale philosophical structures may rest, he thought, on psychological premises that are insecure. Secondly, Taine, though by no means himself an experimenter, had at least considered calculators, chess players and those who hallucinate. Galton, going one stage further, had collected data suggesting lack of imagery among scientists and others accustomed to abstraction. Thirdly, on the basis of hypnotic studies, Binet argued for the affinities between imagery, perception and hallucination. To support this, he invoked, among other things, the findings of several experimenters that a subject induced to hallucinate a red cross on a white ground may spontaneously report a green after-image on looking later at a plain white page. Finally, he said, Ribot's and Charcot's studies of aphasia, and current data from high-grade calculators, underlined the importance of imagery other than visual and suggested the significance of internal speech.

The second article opens in a much more cautious vein. Binet apologizes for his ambitious title, adding:

> The problem of the mechanism of thought is one of the most profound and most complex that can be stated, and will probably only be solved by the combined efforts of many investigators. For my part I shall be very happy if I am able to discover only a small portion of the truth. . . .[5]

Again four points may be extracted from the article. After renewed emphasis on the affinities of sensation, image and hallucination, and the derivation of the last two from sensation by reference to underlying 'groups of nervous cells', Binet continues:

> It might be concluded from the preceding facts, which, although partly hypothetical, seem beautifully simple and precise, that we understand the mechanism of thought. The definition of the nature of ideas and their probable birth in the brain seems in some way to exhaust the question. This opinion has been sustained by some. It seems to me absurd, childish in its simplicity. One must

be very careless or a very bad psychologist, to imagine that thought can be defined as a mental image accompanied by consciousness—a sort of photographic proof which can be lit up at pleasure with a ray of electricity. The simplicity of this comparison is its only merit. There is something of the image in thought; but there is also something more. The image is not the thought, it is simply the object, or, so to say, the food of thought. When we think or reason, when we disengage or combine ideas, we evoke all sorts of images, some precise and others vague; it is not the image that thinks, but we who think by means of the image.[5]

So far so good. The next move is to dislodge sensation from its place of placid dominance. The numerous difficulties in treating thought probably arise from comparing it with sensation, which, says Binet, 'has no objective existence'.

Sensation is a mere abstraction; to speak exactly, there is no such thing as a sensation evoked by a piece of red stuff, but there are human beings who under certain circumstances become conscious of a sensation of the colour red, and that is altogether a different affair. In psychological terms, it may be said that the contact of the outside world produces in human beings perceptions, not simple sensations. Perception is an impression of the senses and something else besides, viz., a reaction of the mind.[5]

And Binet goes on to liken thinking to the responsive activity of a man moving around socially in the external world:

The example just given, of a person walking in the street with a friend and gesticulating, supplies an excellent image of the act of thought. Our ideas, as we have said, are merely revivals of sensations, and these revivals are in many respects independent of the presence of exterior objects. A kind of outside world, quite distinct from the original, is formed in our mind. Our memory, our imagination and our reason create an ideal world, which is distinctly visible to us in our dreams, contemplation and somnambulism. . . .
    Now, it seems to me that we behave with respect to

this ideal world in the same way as with the real one. Our images give rise to the same reactions as our sensations. We act, move and gesticulate in the midst of the world of images just as we do in the world of sensation, and Lewes has well said that the man who endeavours to solve an obscure problem resembles one feeling his way among trees and bushes.[5]

This he follows up with a discussion of perception, stressing its likeness *in principle* to reasoning, for at the roots of both lie recognition of resemblance. For Binet, this involves, in the main, unconscious comparison of that which is impinging (the limited sensation lodged in the experience) with that which is unconsciously (or consciously) recalled.

If it were possible by some artifice to eliminate from outward perception everything of the nature of memory and to leave merely the sensation actually experienced at the moment, it would indeed be astonishing to see how little there is in sensation. . . .[5]

In reality, we are obliged each time to construct the outward world with our memories; and the vision of distances, which appears the most direct and simple, results from a series of complex memories, which enable us to set each object in its place, . . . perception of an object . . . is, more than anything else, an act of unconscious comparison. . . . Resemblance is the bond uniting the present to past sensations, and allowing the transmission to our actual perception of the results of our anterior experiences and cognitions. This transmission of cognition, considered in itself, possesses all the fundamental characteristics and consequences of ratiocination. To perceive, then, is to reason.[5]

The writing strikes us now as much too 'cognitive', and so indeed it is, but its value is not nil. The significant difference between Freud and Binet is that the former failed, while the latter did not fail, to appreciate how crucial are recognition and resemblance. Binet's position is therefore in fact immeasurably stronger.

His fourth step is worthy of Locke's unfussed acceptance of

uncertainty, and of any analyst's doubts about our knowledge of ourselves: for the Frenchman Binet throws Descartes overboard. Internal, like external, perception can be illusory and 'there is no infallible criterion of truth in consciousness'. He supports this view with evidence from studies of hysteria, implying that unperceived sensations may suggest conscious ideas of whose source the person remains unaware:

> . . . modifications are continually taking place within us, which transmit unconscious impressions to our brain. And these diverse obscure impressions are capable of suggesting ideas which appear all of a sudden in the light of consciousness, without our being able to guess at their origin. Perhaps our ideas most frequently originate thus, for they seem to summarize a work that goes on in the night of the unconscious.[5]

Let us now turn to the calculators, chess players and dramatists who helped so much to change Binet's initial view.

Ian Hunter[27] recently showed once more that the study of human high-speed calculating is of intrinsic interest, and that there is more to such study than its pure enjoyment: de Groot in Holland[24] has carried further Binet's studies of chess players. What we must distil from Binet's original work is the kind of evidence with which he was faced and some of its important theoretical implications.

THE CALCULATORS

Jacques Inaudi, the first of the two calculators Binet studied in detail, was born in Piedmont in 1867 of a family impoverished by a neurotic father's extravagance. Inaudi showed signs of a passion for calculating when, as a six-year-old illiterate shepherd boy, he appears to have done sums in his head with the aid of auditory verbal imagery. His calculations extending beyond his numerical vocabulary, the little boy got others to tell him the names of numbers over 100 in order to reckon beyond this figure. When about seven years old, Jacques followed a brother vagabonding in Provence, the elder playing a street organ, the younger showing a marmoset. Jacques found he could augment their small earnings by doing calculations

for peasants and others in markets and cafés. Taken up
by an impresario, he was shown in the big towns, finally
reaching Paris in 1880, where he was presented to the Société
d'Anthropologie by Broca. He still could not read or write,
and in this combination of poor circumstances, illiteracy and
precocious reckoning, he resembles many of the historical high-
speed calculators. In February 1892 he was presented, at the
age of 24, by Darboux, a mathematician, at a meeting of the
Académie des Sciences. Various mathematicians, including
Tisserand and Poincaré, were nominated to a commission
concerning him. Charcot, as Professor at the Salpêtrière, was
asked to examine him specially from the point of view of
physiological psychology. Charcot invited Binet to assist and
the two examined Inaudi during three sessions at the Salpêtrière. Subsequently, Inaudi co-operated in some 15 sessions
of inquiry, during the two years 1892 and '93, at the Sorbonne
laboratory, where Binet had become Assistant Director under
Beaunis, whom he succeeded.

We need not concern ourselves here with Inaudi's authen-
ticity, which is unquestioned, nor with Charcot's or Binet's
psycho-physiological studies of his height, head measurements,
etc. Our main focus of interest is his way of thinking.

By 1892, Inaudi had been able to read and write some four
years. He appeared intelligent in response, but, not surprisingly,
with great gaps in his education, and very limited interests.
Binet describes him as getting up late, arriving for lunch with
eyes full of sleep, spending the afternoon peacefully playing
cards or billiards, going to a café or theatre after dinner for
his show, and getting home in the early hours. He seems to have
been highly sexed and content to live a stereotyped existence,
which in Binet's view, 'flattered his pride and subserved his
needs'. Inaudi dreamt occasionally of numbers and these were
the only dreams he remembered. His memory of facts, places
and events in daily life, and of melodies, was poor and in
sharp contrast to his retention of numbers.

Some indication of Inaudi's ability in this respect can be
gleaned from the following. In his shows at cafés and theatres,
his performance included tasks such as subtracting two series
of twenty-one digits, adding five numbers of six digits, dividing

two numbers of four digits, calculating the cube root of nine-digit numbers, or the fifth root of twelve-digit numbers. Or he would tackle problems such as the following: from Paris to Marseilles the distance is 863 km. A train leaves at 8.15 a.m. for Marseilles travelling at a speed of 39 km.p.h. Another train leaves Marseilles for Paris at 10.30 a.m. and travels at 46·5 km.p.h. Find the time, and the distances from the two cities, at which the trains meet.[6]

The usual procedure was that a spectator would give the data, e.g. a series of numbers. Inaudi's assistant would repeat them aloud (rhythmically) in the process of recording them behind Inaudi's back. Inaudi would repeat each number after these two hearings until the series was complete, and start calculating. In the course of this he gestured, showed certain tics and made habitual incidental comments to keep his audience amused. The total time, including that used in recording and repeating the data, was about ten minutes. During the process Inaudi would be dealing from memory with anything up to 300 or so digits.

The French mathematicians did not rate Inaudi as outstanding, in comparison with other calculators, in his handling of complex problems. But his power and speed are well shown in problems done under Binet's scrutiny. For example,[6] that of factorizing 13,411 and 15,663. In the first case Inaudi took no more than three minutes to produce first:

$$115 \text{ which squared} = 13,225$$
$$13 \text{ which squared} = 169$$
$$4 \text{ which squared} = 16$$
$$1 \text{ which squared} = 1$$

$$13,411$$

A minute later he gave a second solution:

$$113 \text{ which squared} = 12,769$$
$$25 \text{ which squared} = 625$$
$$4 \text{ which squared} = 16$$
$$1 \text{ which squared} = 1$$

$$13,411$$

A short time after he indicated a third:

$$
\begin{array}{r}
113 \text{ which squared} = 12{,}769 \\
23 \text{ which squared} = 529 \\
8 \text{ which squared} = 64 \\
7 \text{ which squared} = 49 \\
\hline
13{,}411
\end{array}
$$

In the case of 15,663 he found the four solutions 62, 57, 83, 41 in about fifteen minutes and the further solutions 62, 41, 97, 27 in a few more. Binet states that a reputable mathematician in those days considered fifteen days a reasonable time for calculations of this kind.

Inaudi was examined in various ways, both subjective and objective, e.g. subjective description of his method of calculation and of the imagery involved, objective assessment of: (1) the effects of their mode of presentation on immediate or longer-term memory for digits; (2) recall of verbal rather than numerical data; (3) effects of interference (e.g. being asked to hum) and of amount of material on speed of calculation; (4) reaction time to auditory and visual stimuli. Comparable data in some of these respects were obtained from the second calculator Binet studied in detail. This was the Greek Diamondi, who volunteered to co-operate. Comparative data were also collected from school children, a group of competent cashiers from the Bon Marché and from Arnould, a specialist in mnemonic systems. For the considerable detail Binet gives of these and other inquiries the reader must consult his book.

Here we must concentrate on such findings as would seem to have contributed to Binet's treatment of thinking. They can be grouped under three main headings: individual differences in imagery, as it were the medium of thinking; effects of spatial, temporal or logical grouping, either in data presentation or in the tactics of calculation, on the ease of calculation; and, thirdly, evidence of some direction, imposed by the problem, affecting the amount of data the calculators could handle. These findings may well be interrelated at a more subtle level. But for ease in grasping their bearing on the breakdown of a

simple associationist, predominantly visual, account of thinking,
I propose to illustrate each one separately.

The most striking difference in medium lay in Inaudi's
almost complete lack of visual imagery and Diamondi's almost
exclusive dependence on it. Inaudi, mentally recalling his
data, did so by hearing his own voice repeating them. Diamondi
made use of the complex number form given in Fig. 1 which

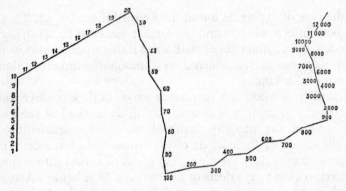

FIG. 1. Diamondi's Number Form

was superimposed on another more shadowy.[6] There is some
evidence that for Inaudi either kinaesthetic imagery or actual
laryngeal movements also contributed to his manipulation of
data. For, although he could converse while calculating, he
seems to have taken a longer time when, as in conversation with
Charcot, this was not confined to habitual comment. Hum-
ming definitely slowed him up, though, as Binet realizes, we
cannot be certain that division of attention was not the cause.
Inaudi's visual imagery seems to have been very limited, confined, for example, to noting the position of a spectator present-
ing data.

This difference in preferred medium of problem solving,
even though the numerical nature of the problem is constant,
showed up clearly when the two calculators were compared for
immediate memory for digits presented aurally. Herein Inaudi,
until recently illiterate, was assured; though his memory for
words, or for two lines of prose or poetry, was below the
average. Diamondi, with some five languages to his credit,

hesitated and failed; having, it seems, to translate the spoken French into his native Greek before the numerical visual imagery he needed would appear. Table 4 below, which bears on our second point, also seems to confirm this difference, for it shows Diamondi's greater skill in handling visually-presented data.

TABLE 4^{6*}

	Diamondi	Inaudi
	(seconds)	
Time required to repeat 25 digits from left to right	9	19
Time required to repeat the digits in the form of numbers, from left to right	9	7
Time required to repeat a square of 25 digits by descending columns	35	60
Time required to repeat a square of 25 digits by ascending columns	36	96
Time required to repeat a square of 25 digits following a spiral line from top left to centre	36	80
Time required to repeat a square of 25 digits divided diagonally by parallel lines and starting at the top right corner	53	168

In learning material aurally, the importance of rhythmic grouping is familiar to almost anyone trying it out for himself, and doubly so to those trained in Binet testing. So no one will be surprised that Inaudi, used to handling up to 300 digits presented in series (within which there was a rhythmic sub-grouping in threes), could assimilate only about an eighth, i.e. 36 digits, enunciated monotonously. This is still about five times greater than the average, but the difference according to presentation is marked. Our third factor is also involved here, namely the rôle of the directing problem or problems when

---

* By modern standards Binet's presentation of these data is inadequate; one cannot be quite sure of the precise conditions of testing, and whether, for example, Inaudi's *aural* speed (as one supposes) is compared in the first instance with Diamondi's *visual* speed and whether the learning in columns started on the left or the right. In this instance the main argument does not appear to be affected and there seems no occasion to query findings so easily confirmed on normal people.

300 digits are retained. But the importance of rhythmic grouping is too well established for question.

Its visual counterpart in mode of arrangement is less familiar.
Inaudi is said by Binet to have been four times as quick as
Diamondi in learning a series of 25 digits (45 seconds as against
3 minutes). When, however, they were both faced with visual
data, the difference between them, and within their perform-
ances according to the visual route taken in learning, becomes
apparent from Table 4.

Binet was not the first to observe our third factor,[6] that
direction to thought may be given by the problem set. He quotes
the American psychologist, Scripture, as discussing it in 1881,
when reviewing the findings on high-speed calculators prior to
these studies of Inaudi and Diamondi. The process is exemplified thus: given the digits 9 and 5, whether one thinks immediately of 14 or 45 will depend on whether one is set to add or to
multiply; under the influence of the Chancellor on income tax
one may subtract and never think of adding at all. As
Humphrey[26] has pointed out, Bradley was stating in 1887 that
'thinking is controlled by the object of thought', and from 1904
onwards the Würzburgers postulated 'determining tendencies'
and/or *Aufgabe* in addition to association. Under the heading of
'mental set' the same broad phenomenon has been the subject
of innumerable studies; though the term 'mental set' has
varied in meaning sometimes to the point where its utility was
doubtful. The excellent review of the difficulties involved,
given by J. J. Gibson,[22] will be familiar to most psychological
readers; together with Hebb's[25] conviction that psychology
cannot do without some such concept, in the face of the evidence
for central processes affecting how we perceive and think. Such
evidence fits no better with a naïve stimulus-response approach
to thinking than it did with simple associationism.

What is so interesting in Binet is the dawning realization,
in a convinced associationist, that some concept of this sort was
necessary. The kind of evidence facing him was that derived
from Inaudi enhancing the retention of digits, and their
manipulation, by grasping them relationally, thereby econo-
mizing the load on new retention and maximizing the function
of well-entrenched knowledge. The procedure is exemplified

simply when any intelligent housewife dealing with domestic bills adds on 2s. in preference to 1s. 11d. and subtracts the relevant penny at the next stage. Such a procedure may be deliberately adopted, or used without conscious awareness of it as a technique. Some such devices, adopted automatically, may not even be the most effective logically; Diamondi produces one from which neither Binet nor we can see any practical gain. Effective operation of some central control process can, however, be seen when Inaudi was asked to multiply 325 × 638 and he promptly broke the problem into 6 pieces: 300 × 600, 25 × 600, 300 × 30, 300 × 8, 25 × 30, 25 × 8, all of which multiplication it is easy to do in one's head. If asked to multiply something by 587, he did so by 600 and by 13, subtracting the product of the later calculation. To those not at home with 13 this may seem more difficult, but the example makes the interrelation of central structuring and habitual knowledge clearer.

THE CHESS PLAYERS

With our three major points in mind let us now turn to the chess players. Binet had realized that activities with relatively clear-cut criteria of effectiveness offer the best hopes of studying thought in action. Still influenced by Taine, Binet had anticipated, as well he might, that in blindfold chess-playing straight photographic visual imagery would play the fundamental rôle. But in an interview and article, Goetz, an able young exponent, claimed it was otherwise. The puzzled, and at times despairing, Binet explored. In consultation, it would seem, with Goetz and the friendly editor, Binet published a questionnaire in the chess journal *La Stratégie* (August 1892). Receiving only ten replies, he approached chess masters in France, England, Spain and Germany by letter. He attended Parisian blindfold chess sessions and persuaded some of the best-known professionals and amateurs in Paris to play in the Sorbonne laboratory. The data he obtained vary in detail. Some of the fullest comments, for example those of Tarrasch, world-renowned for his depth of play, who gave detailed answers to Binet's questionnaire, are of absorbing interest and are worth reading in full. Here we must indicate briefly what Binet has to say under the headings:

knowledge and experience, imagery, memory and recapitu-
lation.

The importance to the chess player of study and practice is
so familiar, and so obvious from Binet's data, as to seem hardly
worth mentioning. Its relevance will become clearer in connexion with current controversies over learning and insight
(Chapter Nine). Meanwhile, there is intrinsic interest in
Tarrasch declaring that the best preparation for blindfold
playing lay in study and practice with an empty board. In his
view, it was necessary to have learnt in an unconscious fashion,
and by prolonged practice, not only the position of each square
but its properties and the effects that any piece on it could
produce. Only thus would one grasp the strategies that are
necessary for understanding the potentialities of a position.

On the other hand, so Binet was assured by his subjects, the
difference between outstanding and competent players was
due more to intelligence than to practice: 'one becomes a
competent player; one is born a player of the front rank.'*
The comment is tied to the records of Blackburne and Steinitz,
who played together some twenty years, during which Steinitz
tended to have a constant nuance of advantage. Binet was given
another rider to exclusive emphasis on learning and experience
in the claim of some players that although both are crucial to
blindfold playing, capacity for this and 'power' as a player do
not entirely coincide. In blindfold playing the load on retention
is enormous; some players thought 'depth' diminished by
continuous play in such conditions.[6]†

Chess literature is riddled with comments on 'power', 'depth',
and 'style'; Binet's data are no exception. It is as difficult, if

---

* 'on devient bon joueur; on naît joueur de première force'.[6]

† Steinitz was world champion at this time, and Blackburne was the
most famous British master, known to his continental contemporaries as
'The Black Death' (Harley). In blindfold playing, an expert takes on a
group of others, seeing neither boards nor men. The moves are called by a
teller. The blindfold player has the standard advantage of playing white
and thus making the first move. His opponents have the advantage of sight
and additional time in making decisions. A good blindfold player may take
on 7 or 8 others quite regularly. 16 or 20 blindfold games played at once
was regarded in Binet's time as high. The present record, I learn from Mr.
Leonard Barden, is 52, held by the Hungarian master Janos Flesch.

not impossible, to translate their meaning as to verbalize the difference between a Richter and a Serkin. The 'objective' criterion of logical coherence or winning the game becomes inadequate at this point and one verges on personal, qualitative assessment. Binet obviously ran into this problem and it has bearing on his eventual treatment of thought. With the aid of a humble example, based on an end game of Lasker's, we may convey just a little of what is implied. The non-chess-player, provided he knows the moves and is not so 'set' by *Through the Looking Glass* as to forget that a pawn on square 8 can be either queened or knighted, may derive some fun from working out the difference in the tactics of players faced with the position in Fig. 2. Either way Black is defeated, but solution B is more elegant. (There is a third, almost brutal, solution which the reader will doubtless discover unaided.)

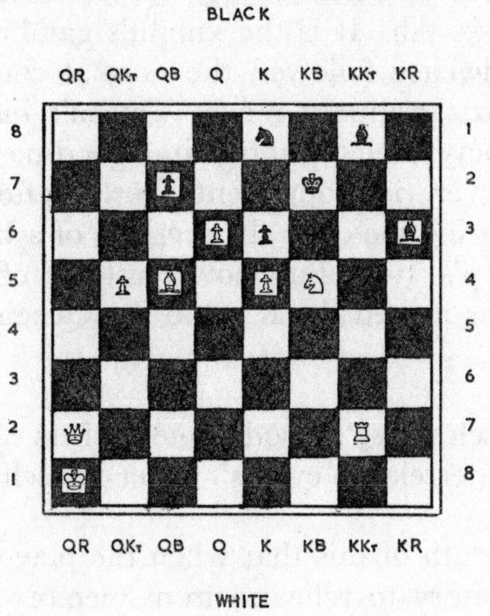

FIG. 2

Alternative solutions.

Solution A.		Solution B.	
White	*Black*	*White*	*Black*
1. P—Q7	B—Kt4	P—Q7	B—Kt4
2. R × B	B—R2	R × B	B—R2
3. Q—R8	B—Kt3	P—Q8 = Kt mate	
4. Q × Kt mate			

In blindfold playing, practice and experience showed their effects in many ways, e.g. in grasping the significance of a position as called, or giving different standard openings to different games to offset possible confusion. As Binet says, blindfold playing of eight Sicilians at once would appear almost impossible. Again, however, something 'central' seems to operate when recall of a game is aided by gradual recognition of the defence to which it conformed. From Tarrasch we get a beautiful description:

> For example, I hear the teller call, 'game four, King to Queen's square'. At this moment there is only complete chaos in my mind. I don't even know which game is meant, nor what may be the significance or implication of the move called. I merely hear the statement of my opponent's move. Then I begin to wonder which this fourth game is. Ah! It is the knight's gambit, where my opponent's defence followed the normal course until he made that extraordinary move, 'Queen's bishop's pawn one', which nevertheless put him in a good position. Fortunately, however, my opponent shortly after made the mistake of letting me offer the sacrifice of a bishop on his King's bishop's two. But now, instead of taking my bishop, he has moved the King to the Queen's square, as announced.[6]

Thus, Tarrasch adds, 'a good game of chess can be described as a series of interrelated events'. Binet himself goes on:

> Such is the truth of this that when the players consented in our laboratory to rehearse from memory some of the games played in the past—preferably those they had won, for those are better retained—we established that they more easily forgot the isolated moves which were not integrated with the rest. They retained the sequence of moves made under the influence of a controlling idea (*d'une idée directrice*) as one retains a sequence of well-connected arguments.

In short, the player succeeds in retaining a game by

fixing in his memory not only the changing visual representation of the movements of the pieces but also the ideas,
reasonings and desires that accompanied those manœuvres
and the memories of strategy that they evoke.[6]

Binet himself had moved a very long way. What did he find
out about the players' imagery? Three specially interesting
points emerge from the players' comments on this. They bear
on abstraction, on imageless thought and on the interrelation of
different processes, e.g. verbalization, visual and other imagery,
when directed to the same problem. First, let us deal with
abstraction.

Even when it was reported as clear, visual imagery was still
highly selective; resembling, as Binet suggests, a portrait with
significant omissions and emphases rather than the photograph
of popular analogy. In some degree, all the imagery described
was 'abstract', in Locke's sense of omission of individual detail.
Even Taine's[31] chess player (p. 111) had imagined his pieces
without their shadows. The significance of such comment,
however, was not lost on Binet; who, still treating images as
revived sensations, realized he must reject a simple copy theory
of both, and consider the effects of attention and attitude.

As all players could, with an effort, evoke some visual
imagery, he roughly classified reports on its *spontaneous* occurrence, according to the degree of abstraction involved. Methodologically, this is obviously a risky thing to do, but his broad
distinctions are nevertheless interesting, supported as they are
with comment and example. These reflect, fairly clearly, the
gradual omission of functionally peripheral detail, and increased focus on that which is of greatest significance to the
player for his problem-solving.

Formstreicher and Schabelsky[6] provide good examples of
those reporting the clearest visual imagery, as judged by description of the shape and colour of the chess-board and the
pieces in position. Neither had played in blindfold sessions as
such. Formstreicher, however, specialized in problem setting;
Schabelsky, a master, had gone blind six years prior to Binet's
inquiry. Formstreicher worked, it seems, not with a real chess-
board but with a visual image of the kind of diagram sent to a

newspaper. If dreaming of a problem occupying him earlier, he could often recognize its origin, e.g. French or English, by scrutinizing the dream imagery of the signs used. The piece called the bishop in English is called in French *le fou*. The signs are respectively a mitre and a jester. So with clear imagery of the signs, national identification would be quite simple. Schabelsky, retaining his chess interest though blind, found his visual memory intensified and played easily with imagery of his old board and pieces. The yellow and black colour of the squares was very distinct; that of the pieces attracted no attention, though he did not confuse the black with the white. The shape of the pieces was linked with their kind of movement. Reflecting on the state of a game, he would see the chess-board and its men as if in vision, and move the pieces in imagination as though with his hand. He remarks that, having been blind only six years, he had conserved the impression of the shape of the pieces sufficiently to dispense with actual touch in imagining them. One would like to know the cause of his blindness, for the evidence suggests central processes still in operation. Be that as it may, if 'knight to Queen's fourth' were remarked to Schabelsky this evoked the eight squares guarded by the knight. As Binet comments, the 'copy', if it is one, is not servile but intelligent.

As representing the second broad level of abstraction, we may cite Sittenfeld's use of strategically illustrative imagery.

Fig. 3. Game as played blindfold by Sittenfeld[6]

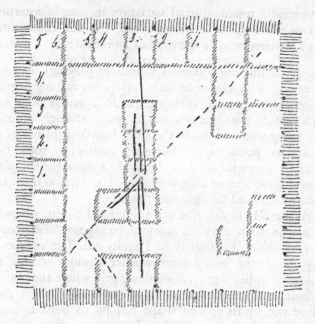

FIG. 4. Sittenfeld's sketch of his visual image of the game in Fig. 3[6]

Supposing that the game had reached the stage shown in Fig. 3 (chosen for its simplicity), Sittenfeld did his best to show, as in Fig. 4, the way he would fix the position in his memory before seeking to make a move. He explains as follows:

If now:

White	Black
1. R × P	R × R
2. R × R	R × R
3. Q × Rch	Q × Qch
4. B—Kt2	Q—Kt2
5. B × Qch	K × B
6. P—QR4	

In the first phase I see all the action concentrated round the pawn at Queen's fourth. In the second, that is to say after the disappearance of the pieces, I see that it will take me five moves to queen a pawn and that Black's King cannot prevent it because it will take him six.

Sittenfeld stressed diurnal variation in ease of interpreting notation when the board is not seen, but also commented as follows, having tried to draw what he meant:

> I explain this phenomenon (blindfold playing) by visual memory, of which my brain is capable in varying degrees. When I am intensely interested, as in a serious game such as a match, a tournament or any game strongly arousing my *amour propre*, vision of the chess-board, or rather of the successive positions, subsists very clearly for some time after the game is ended. Not only do I recall the combinations I have seen or sought during play but also those that escaped me and the mistakes made.
>
> Accurately to describe my thinking, I ought, whenever it is a question of visual memory, to say not 'chess-board' but 'position', for that is all I really see. The squares on my imaginary board have neither distinct outline nor colour: it is like a greyish shadowy grid where the position is indicated by relative intensity and I recognize a given piece not by its special shape but by its possible movement, that is to say its action. In any case the colour of a particular square is of little concern to me.[6]

We cannot complain that Binet and his subjects did not try to objectify their data.

Focus and emphasis on the piece's *mode of action* is reflected again in Goetz's comment:

> As for the pieces, I don't see their shapes, not in the least; I play my games sometimes with a Regency set and sometimes with those of the English Staunton design. Now it would be impossible for me to say if I see Staunton or Regency shapes when playing blindfold. I see only the range, the action of the pieces. Thus, for example, the rook moves in a straight line. A rook positioned somewhere has the effect on me that a gun must have on a gunner, who understands rather than sees its emplacement behind a rampart. It is the action, the range of the gun that he must envisage. Thus a bishop for my internal eye is not a piece carved in a more or less baroque fashion, it is an oblique force.[6]

Tarrasch comes in again with support. Stressing the extent to which attention is selective, even in sighted playing, how, he asks, would one see the pieces when playing blindfold? He continues:

> I can only say that I visualize for myself a fairly small chess-board, about the size of a diagram (that is to say 8 centimetres across), in order the better to grasp the whole, and enable one's mental vision to pass more quickly from one square to another. I don't see the squares as distinctly black and white but only light and dark. As for the colour of the pieces, the difference is even less marked. They look to me more as enemies or allies. The shapes of the pieces appear only indistinctly; I consider principally their capacity for action.[6]

When first encountering such remarks, Binet had been puzzled almost to the point of abandoning his inquiries. Accustomed as we are to non-visual concepts of thinking, the chess players seem intelligible almost to banality, and it is Binet's comments that appear a little strange. For at this stage in Binet's own development, Tarrasch's natural reference to enemies and allies struck him as very odd, and the hard-working players' insistence on the range and action of a piece he classes weakly (if with relief!) as 'abstract visual memory'. Abstract indeed it is, again by Locke's criterion, but the problem of how to treat all this in theory is probably still unsolved. What *is* involved in moving from imaging, in dreams or otherwise, a bishop's mitre sign, to strategic operation with lines of force connecting colourless entities in friendship or enmity?

Binet's third broad degree of abstraction landed him with the problem of imageless thought. Forsyth, a player of five games blindfold, came down flatly so: '*I do not visualize* the chess-board at all, but in spite of this, *I think* of a chess-board of the size of those with which I am accustomed to play!'[6]* (His italics.) Binet was to reach this stalemate, again, with his little daughter Marguerite, protesting that she didn't *see*, she *thought*! But this was nearly ten years later. By that time the

---

* *Je ne vois pas* du tout l'échiquier, mais, malgré cela, *je pense* à un échiquier de la grandeur de ceux sur lesquels j'ai l'habitude de jouer.

Würzburg experiments were bringing this strange concept into the centre of a controversy that lasted some dozen years, petering out eventually through exhaustion of the combatants, and temporarily eclipsing the experimental study of thought. In 1894, Binet alerted, and stalled with a cautious footnote to Forsyth: 'Note this distinction: "I do not see, I think . . ."; it probably indicates a lack of precision in mental imagery; perhaps there is something else involved. These phenomena are still very obscure.'[6] Fifty years afterwards, the whole 'frightful literature' on imageless thought seems like the dying scream of the attempt to treat *all levels of thinking* (instead of at most a few) as involving some kind of inspection, even if there were neither verbal, visual nor any other imagery there to be scanned. As we shall soon see, Binet's eventual treatment of this peculiar problem was as good as any, and probably better than most.

Here we must pick up the third point suggested by the data from chess players. Binet was convinced by their united insistence on the necessity, in blindfold playing, of being able, if need be, to recapitulate a game. He was also struck by their comparative lack of reference to verbal memory, which he believed might be more important than the players themselves realized. In the Sorbonne laboratory, Rosenthal, for example, claimed to avoid visual imagery if he could; for the realization that he 'saw' the game was a sign that he might lose. He compared his view of a chess-board during play to that of a street along which one passes without paying attention to it. But in recapitulating a game he appeared to be murmuring rapidly, and also unawares, for he denied imagery of his own voice or of any friend's.

In general, Binet's data and his discussion suggest the existence and occasional importance of internal or sub-vocal speech. It might form a constant ingredient of the process of play, but its operation could be subtle, and its importance most obvious in cases of doubt. It is clear that players, at least sometimes, cross-checked their memories by recourse to different media, and verbal memory might be the carrier of bizarre moves and oddities that did not fit in with the main development of a game. Tarrasch shows very nicely the way all this could work:

Of course internal speech goes on all the time. . . . I formulate the move announced to me as if I were writing it, for example 'King to Queen's square' as K—Q. But in order to play I must translate the hieroglyphic chess notation into actual fact. I must realize what change on the chessboard is indicated by the King's move. I hear the teller's voice or my own hardly at all. Memory of the words is on the whole subordinate to memory of the facts. Only on quite rare occasions do I have to recapitulate the whole game from the start. This, moreover, does not involve appreciating the development of the game but only the moves themselves. Because it occurs only when I am in doubt whether a move has in fact been played which had no developmental significance for the game and which, for this reason, I might perhaps have failed to make in my image of the position. Then it is that verbal memory comes into play. But this happens very rarely, since I always try to find meaning in my opponent's moves. If need be I make a mental note that at a certain point in the game an irrelevant move was made. Verbal memory is thus not wholly without importance.[6]

This is one very distinguished player* speaking, and, as we have seen, players varied in the extent of their use of different modes of thought. The point of real interest here is the power to switch from one mode to another in the interest of a centrally developing train of thinking. Without invoking the classical conception of imageless thought, we can discern here the fascinating problem of the means whereby strands of thought in different media operate to supplement, support, or indeed cancel each other out, when all are in the service of the same theme. The same phenomenon, in principle, is probably involved in conducting opera without a score. A musician maintaining that the music is 'in his head' (by which he means, in part, that one passage on completion will suggest the next) may yet evoke a visual image of the score, when in doubt, and supplement both by imagining the sound of a flute or

* Tarrasch was never world champion, but he was a player of high international repute.

clarinet, and by his grasp of the structure of the work as a whole. A young soloist playing a concerto from memory, and who has blacked out, may be brought back into action by the conductor's reassuring statement, while the orchestra goes on: 'You come in, in twenty bars, in the key of E flat.'

Some of Binet's chess players seem to have grasped very clearly the extent to which 'remember' may mean 'reconstruct', and there is no doubt that they could integrate different strands of thought. Comparing their memories with that of Inaudi, which lasted a shorter time, Binet stressed the extent to which the chess memory rested on reasoning, connexions, relationships, or

> to speak more accurately, it consists in attaching associated sensations to ideas, reasonings, emotions, desires, to psychological phenomena of all sorts; the recall of this ensemble may take place either by the direct evocation of sensation, as in memory for digits, or by recall of the intellectual and emotional conditions which accompanied this sensation initially. Such memory has greater stability, more hold, and in consequence more chance of permanence than the other.[6]

As Binet adds, this is something familiar to everyone. Indeed one may say that switching between different modes of thinking, and their successful integration (or the reverse), is familiar to us all at a much lower level in our casual discussion of some social situation, when we recall and reconstruct what we think took place.

This leads us on to Binet's dramatists reflecting on the creation of their characters.

THE DRAMATISTS

The 114 pages Binet and Passy devoted to their contemporary dramatists are admittedly no more than accounts of conversations initiated to explore 'creative imagination'. The psychologists disavow any claim to profundity or to discoveries of literary significance. They were going in a novel direction and tentatively feeling their way. Seventy years later, this lack of pretension, and the lively style, make these slight excursions attractive. But their relevance here is to Binet's treatment of thinking, and this is something we must try to show.

In the dramatists themselves, their work and their ruminations, the importance to thought of attitudes and emotions lay
there for all to see; so did that of unconscious functioning, and
Binet saw it:

> The poets say they are inspired by the muse; we say simply
> that these inspirations emanate from the unconscious.*

This was not wholly a new departure for Binet, steeped as he
was in the studies of abnormal functioning shown already in
Chapter Four. Nor does it commit him to the same views as
Freud. In spite of illuminating hints (pp. 187, 238), what Binet
meant by 'unconscious' must stay partly in doubt. He was
talking descriptively and not claiming thereby to *explain*. This
is shown very clearly by his comments on Poincaré's[29] famous
description of mathematical thought which came later.
History may show in the end the strength of Binet's position.
Meanwhile, the background from which he and Passy approached the dramatists slanted their probings to a problem
still unsolved: how really do the spontaneous and apparently
self-supporting imaginings of an artist differ from those
revealed in dissociated states? Hence the conversations sometimes revolved round the '*dédoublement*' of consciousness. This is
specially true of Alphonse Daudet and de Curel. But before
returning to this, let us sketch the general picture.

In the published article of 1894-5 Binet and Passy refer to
data from twelve writers. One occasionally senses discourage-
ment on the psychologists' part, and, indeed, an exasperation
which has its comic side:

> It was often the case that the authors did not grasp the
> interest of the questions. A very large number, moreover,
> seemed completely devoid of psychological sense and did
> not know how to look into themselves. 'I reflect, I discuss,
> I examine, I criticize; in fact I work; there is no other
> word.' One must admit that confidences of this sort do not
> take one very far.†

---

* Les poètes disent qu'elles [les idées] sont inspirées par la muse; nous
disons simplement qu'elles émanent de l'inconscient.[8]

† Il est arrivé bien souvent que les auteurs n'ont pas compris l'intérêt des
questions. Un très grand nombre, surtout, paraissent complètement

Six of the twelve authors, however, must have taken great pains to help: Sardou, Dumas fils, Alphonse Daudet, Meilhac, Pailleron and Edmond de Goncourt. The seventh, François de Curel, passionately interested in psychological processes, discussed his thinking, and also wrote to Binet at length, with a style and reflective quality that in its way is haunting. A modern psychologist must be grateful that writers of this distinction discussed their thinking at all; even if the upshot were indeed that 'creative imagination' proved a process the imaginer could not fully describe.

Emerging initially from Binet's and Passy's pages are some distinctive people, contrasting sharply in outlook and aim. Sardou, like Wagner to some and a young Napoleon to others, changed into different people as he talked. The psychologists even caught a glimpse of Holbein's Erasmus as, long-haired and velvet-capped, Sardou bent over a manuscript. He himself reported possession of vivid auditory and visual imagery, and all his comments and actions suggest that this was true. He 'saw' his characters moving on an imaginary stage, and what one person could say in the time would be tailored to his movement. Sardou supervised production to the last detail, including comment on the design and colours of the clothes. Talking of part of Paris, as it was in the past, skilfully, and without hesitation, he sketched what he 'saw'. There was a sense, it seemed, in which personality, for Sardou, lay in its means of materialization, and this gifted writer could also have been an actor or an architect.

By contrast, Dumas was solidly Dumas. The friendly note agreeing to the psychologists' *rendezvous* arrived in the neat square script of *La Dame aux Camélias*, written some fifty years before. From fifteen pictures, taken over forty years, the person seen alive in his setting also looked out. Where Sardou had kept dozens of dossiers of notes and potential plays, maturing it seems at different rates and times, Dumas worked on one thing, finished it and went off on other ploys, such as collecting

---

dénués du sens psychologique et ne savent pas regarder en eux-mêmes. . . . 'Je réfléchis, je discute, j'examine, je critique; enfin je travaille; il n'y a pas d'autre mot'. Il faut avouer que les confidences de ce genre ne nous mènent pas loin.[8]

pictures or rare literary manuscripts. Where Sardou's own manuscripts were welters of emendations, those of Dumas were as unbelievably neat. In his plays, it seemed, Dumas spoke for himself, lurking sometimes in major, sometimes in minor characters. Occasionally, 'les jeunes filles parlent à la Dumas'. Montigny, the best-known director of his day, shouldered all the business of staging and production.

Daudet, another contrast, appears an enigmatic figure, in his intense sensitivity and cool observation. Novelist and story writer, a dramatist more by chance, he presents an odd mixture of detachment and sympathy. Without any suggestion on the psychologists' part, he ruminated on the two men in himself, the one that felt and the other that watched the first and assessed him, and on the 'horrible analytic and critical faculty' accompanying him in all circumstances of life, sometimes to the point of becoming a cruel obsession. This, he thought, was not at all

> 'what is called conscience, because conscience preaches and scolds . . . and moreover one lulls that good conscience to sleep with facile excuses and subterfuges, while the witness I speak of never relaxes, does not enter into things, scrutinizes . . . like an internal watcher, impassive and unmoved, a *double*, inert and cold, which in the most violent broadsides of *Le Petit Chose* was observing all, taking notes and saying the next day: *A nous deux*!'*

And as he wrote, at fever point, and kept going by drugs, the scrutinizer in Daudet would still be questioning, for instance: would a boy of that age use that phrase with its overtones of maturity?

One final contrast, which has its entertaining side, is that between Meilhac, highly successful as a vaudeville writer, and the intensely serious and self-absorbed de Goncourt. Meilhac,

---

* 'ce qu'on appelle la conscience, car la conscience prêche, gronde . . . et puis on l'endort, cette bonne conscience, avec des faciles excuses ou des subterfuges, tandis que le témoin dont je parle ne faiblit jamais, ne se mêle de rien, surveille. . . . C'est comme un regard intérieur, impassible et fixe, un *double* inerte et froid qui, dans les plus violentes bordées du Petit Chose, observait tout, prenait des notes et disait le lendemain: A nous deux!'[8]

creator of *Froufrou*, appears in these pages engrossed in portraying gallantry, his own views on this subject thereby gaining expression. Turmoil there was, but mainly on a play's first night, when Meilhac fled from the scene until success was assured. Otherwise his time was spent mostly in the theatre, largely, it seems, for the sheer fun of it. De Goncourt the elder emerges (Jules had already died) as an attenuated embodiment of the gloom of the diaries.

The matter-of fact psychologists betray relief in remarking that, in the main, their writers had shown scant addiction to alcohol, hashish and other romantic prerequisites of creative activity. In fact, the dramatists had worked, with minor individual preferences in working conditions; then they had incubated ideas, at different rates. Then they wrote, preferably when a work felt matured, and often at high speed, with varying, but considerable, personal involvement. Sardou, indeed, wept and laughed with his characters. After which the authors set to work again, revising in various ways. More than one refers to characters altering and developing as the work progressed, Pailleron likening his key idea to a pretty woman glimpsed first in the street and changing as she is pursued. In short, the dramatists exemplified a procedure known later to many in Poincaré's familiar description of creative mathematical thought, to which we have already referred.[29]

The de Goncourts illustrate this pattern once again. But, if Edmond's comments are to be trusted, the gestation of a dramatic character could be inordinately long. There is evidence too of elaborate *Sturm und Drang* in the approach of the brothers to their varied literary tasks, notwithstanding the difference of dramatic and historical writing. As Binet and Passy remark:

> boredom, fatigue, discouragement, effort, agony, torment, torture . . . these are the expressions they use to describe what others call the joy of creation.*

They add a comment on the brothers' approach to work:

* 'ennui, fatigue, découragement, efforts, angoisses, supplice, torture . . . voilà les expressions qui leur servent à qualifier ce que d'autres appellent la joie de la production.'

It seems that, for M. de Goncourt, literary composition implies a special state of induced excitation, which in no way resembles an ordinary manner of life and which it requires some effort to maintain. . . .

To achieve this peculiar condition, the brothers de Goncourt made no use of artificial stimulants, unless one counts smoking; they employed two principal means, confinement and insomnia. They did not leave Paris in order to work—Paris, they said, is the true climate of human cerebral activity—but they cut themselves off from the world and lived a sublunary existence, following an abominably unhealthy régime, eating little, sleeping badly, talking incessantly of the work in progress, staying four days on end in their flat without emerging, disconnecting the door bell to exclude importunates because such visits were enough to upset a whole day's activity.

To this initial source of excitation—and nervous exhaustion—they added the no less efficacious one of working at night. The de Goncourts worked at night because they had observed that sleeplessness increased the power and virtuosity of the imagination. Sometimes even they utilized their dreams and nightmares.*

Binet and Passy reported, and perhaps wisely reserved their

---

* Nous croyons comprendre que la composition littéraire suppose, chez M. de Goncourt, un état particulier d'excitation factice, qui ne ressemble en rien au train ordinaire de la vie, et dans lequel on se maintient avec effort . . .

Pour atteindre cet état particulier, MM. de Goncourt ne se sont guère servis d'excitants artificiels, si ce n'est du tabac; ils ont employé deux moyens principaux, la claustration et l'insomnie. Pendant le travail, ils ne quittaient pas Paris—Paris, ont-ils dit, est le véritable climat de l'activité de la cervelle humaine—mais ils s'isolaient du monde et vivaient dans une sorte de milieu sublunaire, pratiquant une hygiène détestable, mangeant peu, dormant mal, causant sans cesse de l'oeuvre en marche, restant quatre jours de suite dans l'appartement sans sortir, enlevant la sonnette de la porte d'entrée pour supprimer la visite des importuns, car ces visites suffisent à couper l'entrain de toute une journée.

A cette première cause d'excitation—et aussi d'énervement—venait s'ajouter celle, non moins efficace, du travail de nuit. MM. de Goncourt travaillaient pendant la nuit parce qu'ils avaient remarqué que l'insomnie augmente la force et la virtuosité de l'imagination; parfois même, ils ont utilisé leurs rêves et leurs cauchemars.[8]

comments both on this and on the delicate matter of the brothers' co-operation. It is hard to be quite sure of the extent of the full picture's validity. But there seems at least something of how de Goncourt wished to be seen.

Enough has been said of the contrasting attitudes of some of the writers interviewed. Apart from this and manifestly anecdotal interest, what else can we derive from these exploratory studies?

Binet and Passy summed up under seven headings, noting particularly the straightforward, self-possessed approach of most of the authors, absorbed in work providing stimulus in itself. They noted their different attitudes, the gradual and largely unconscious maturation of key notions, the intense period of concentration, differences in degree and nature of personal involvement, differences in the nature and rôle of imagery. They remarked that the current psychology was stressing imagery too much. The rest of main value comes from de Curel, whose comments contrive to make these general ones more concrete. One can but feel too that, uninfluenced, as he must have been, by Freud or Proust, these reflections claim some intrinsic as well as historical interest.

In 1894 de Curel was about forty and had only just begun to achieve some recognition, thanks initially to Antoine, of the Théâtre-Libre. Freud's early works were largely inaccessible and Proust was as yet in his very early twenties. Only a popular dramatist once in his lifetime, with a war play of the 1920's translated as *No Man's Land*, de Curel nevertheless became respected as a stylist and dramatist of ideas. He wrote to Binet too lengthily to be quoted fully here. Three extracts, however, may show something of his reflections on relevant topics: half dissociated functioning, reverie and incubation, the revival and fusion of memories, the evolution of characters, and the complex interrelating of different modes of thinking in one main stream of creative activity. This last will return us, from a very different angle, to the related switching between different processes exemplified already in the thinking of the chess players.

De Curel had been prone to dramatic reverie ever since childhood, when his pens and pencils enacted little plays of which he himself was the hero. He eyed such egoism with ironic insight, and also the optimism of the endings of all his phantasies, contrasting this with his pessimism in the process of writing. What he wished and what he knew to be true were opposed, an opposition still apparent nearly twenty-five years later when, in the revealing Preface to his collected works,[20] he sadly implied that his dramatic characters had been his main confidants.

Let us see first something of his attempt, in response to Binet's probings, to describe his particular form of '*dédoublement*':

> For the last two or three months, I have been thinking a little about what interested us in the summer and, being engaged on a new play, I have been able to make a direct study of what happens instead of relying on memory. Hence a few further observations which I send you.
>
> Decidedly, when '*dédoublement*' occurs, there is without doubt alternation. For ten or fifteen minutes—perhaps even half an hour—my characters hold the stage and my own person fades out, then for the next two to five minutes the latter reappears while my characters retreat into the background, and so on. Those not occupying the centre of the stage never disappear completely: as I have already explained, while the characters are speaking, another person is present, making amendments, or even experiencing distractions, thinking of completely extraneous things, in which case hardly knowing what has been written down. Thus a character's speech could be riddled with my corrections and yet come as a surprise when I read it over ten minutes later. My work had been unconscious. In the same way, I have described how my characters develop while I read over what I have written, or while I am being interrupted or go and look out of the window. This development takes place entirely without my knowledge. I can stroll along the boulevards with a friend, very interested in conversation with him and absorbed in answering, and yet return home with characters much more complete than when they went out. My characters and I therefore take it in turns to be conscious and unconscious, without maybe

ever meeting at the conscious level. While my characters are in action, I am often completely unconscious, making corrections mechanically or thinking of some nonsense without being aware of it, or embarking on some reverie that I have often explored before, where my mind can travel like a blind man who walks along a road without stumbling because he knows all the turnings. My will slumbers. At the same time, my characters behave as they like, with complete spontaneity, without my will intervening in this direction either. Thus in neither of these activities is my will in any way involved, but I can nevertheless perceive a distinction between the person who amends and the characters who speak. On the one hand, I am there myself and, on the other, a group of people chattering away, seemingly outside myself. Don't you see here an indication that differentiation between 'self' and 'non-self' does not depend solely on acts of will whose resultant effects produce the sensation of 'self'?*

* Depuis deux ou trois mois j'ai un peu réfléchi à ce qui nous a intéressé cet été et, tout en écrivant une nouvelle pièce, j'ai eu occasion d'étudier les faits eux-mêmes au lieu de m'en rapporter à des souvenirs. De là, quelques observations nouvelles que je vous transmets.

Décidément, lorsqu'il y a dédoublement, les choses se passent bien par alternances. Pendant dix à quinze minutes—cela peut aller à trente—mes personnages tiennent le haut du pavé et ma propre personne s'efface, puis pendant deux à cinq minutes cette dernière reparaît, les personnages rentrant dans l'ombre, et ainsi de suite. Il n'y a jamais anéantissement complet des individus qui n'occupent pas la situation principale : comme je l'ai déjà expliqué, ou même elle a des distractions, pense à des choses complètement étrangères et dans ce cas elle ignore à peu près ce qui a été écrit. Ainsi j'ai pu saccager de mes ratures le discours d'un personnage et avoir cependant des surprises lorsque je le relis au bout de dix minutes d'écriture. Mon travail était inconscient. De même, j'ai raconté que mes personnages progressent pendant que je me relis, ou qu'on vient me déranger, ou que je vais regarder par la fenêtre. Cette progression se fait complètement à mon insu. Je puis parcourir les boulevards avec un ami, très intéressé par sa conversation, très appliqué à lui répondre, et cependant ramener au logis des personnages beaucoup plus complets qu'ils n'en étaient sortis. Mes personnages et moi nous passons donc alternativement du conscient à l'inconscient, sans nous rencontrer peut-être jamais dans le conscient. Au moment où mes personnages agissent, je suis souvent dans l'inconscience la plus complète, je rature machinalement, ou je pense à une imbécillité sans

Referring to the alternation in consciousness of himself and his characters, de Curel adds:

> This is true only during the initial composition, for if during rehearsals I have to rewrite a scene, I can very readily *get right inside the character.**

De Curel continues by suggesting that the surprise he may get from a character's ideas may depend in part on these being outside his own normal habits of thought. Also, absorbed in the characters themselves, he can give no account of how these ideas have been formed. Being prone to self-analysis, he was usually (and unusually) aware of the process of ordinary thought development. And he elaborates on a distinction between parasitical reveries, and those, *'utiles'* or *'voulus'*, which become integrated into a central theme.

Now let us look at the interrelation, for him, of different modes of thought. Considering the big question of what imagination furnishes to an author, de Curel embarks on a careful reflection on the contribution of reasoning, imagination and memory to the construction of two of his plays, *L'Envers d'une Sainte* and *L'Invitée*.[20] Both of these revolved round the feelings of a person returning after a long interval of time to the scene of earlier intense experience. De Curel credits imagination with the central theme, and ordinary reasoning with discarding its initial psychiatric setting, of

---

bien m'en rendre compte, ou je poursuis une rêverie déjà plusieurs fois parcourue et que mon esprit peut suivre comme un chemin qu'un aveugle suit sans broncher parce qu'il en connaît tous les détours. Ma volonté sommeille. A la même minute, mes personnages se conduisent comme ils l'entendent, avec une spontanéité parfaite. De leur côté non plus, ma volonté n'intervient pas. Ainsi, de part et d'autre, ma volonté se trouve n'avoir absolument rien à faire et cela ne m'empêche pourtant pas de percevoir une différence entre celui qui rature et les personnages qui parlent. Il y a moi d'un côté, et de l'autre un groupe de bavards qui me semblent hors de moi. Ne trouvez-vous pas là une indication que la différenciation du moi et du non moi ne dépend pas uniquement d'actes de ma volonté suivis d'effets, qui donnent la sensation du moi?[9]

* Cela n'est vrai que pendant la composition première, car si, pendant les répétitions, j'ai à refaire une scène, je puis très facilement me mettre *dans la peau du personnage.*

H

which he realized he knew too little of the medical and legal
aspects. Religious life, in which nuns are cut off from the
world, presented another possible context. Imagination begins
to get going again. De Curel continues.

Imagination . . . offers a new subject: a woman after
attempting a crime—reminiscence of the first idea—enters
a convent to hide her shame and do penance. The man she
loved, and could not have, dies. The nun thinks she can
now return to the world. Here is the starting point, the new
theme.

I examine it and like it. It has the advantages of the
first theme without its drawbacks. I was brought up among
Jesuits, I have seen much of monks and nuns. I am not
launching myself in unknown territory. Very quickly my
imagination furnishes me with intriguing perspectives. *I
have an over-all view of my play though as yet no knowledge of its
details nor of its characters*. I adopt the theme. All these operations, from the conception of the first idea to its final modification, have taken me altogether twenty minutes at the
most, spread over a day and a half. That gives you some
idea of the extent of the reveries, parasitical or relevant,
that intervene.

I construct my plot. Imagination plays a large part in
this, yet reasoning is not excluded. My main concern is to
visualize the setting. My imagination at once presents the
picture of a small house in a small town. Very detailed. I
see particularly clearly the garden, with its small paths
among fruit trees, ending in a thicket of hornbeam and
lilac, with a goldfish pond in the centre—the street on the
other side of the house is deserted, a cobbled street without
pavements, leading in one direction into the country and in
the other onto the high road—finally, inside the house I
know there is the drawing-room, the dining-room and a
bedroom next to the drawing-room. The house is roofed
with shallow tiles, a vine climbs over the front facing the
garden, etc. All this I perceive before I know exactly what
my characters are going to be like. Already I feel that my
nun returning here after eighteen years will find things

greatly changed in the garden. Some trees will have grown,
others will have died. The house will be the same as it used
to be. It is high summer, the season of flowers, about the
time of Corpus Christi. I am beginning to refer to the
seasons in terms of the religious festivals. Clearly the house
I am in must be one of great piety, since women leave it
only to enter a convent, a point that reasoning brings to
the notice of imagination, which nevertheless is hard at
work. Imagination conjures up scenes, not yet woven into
the play, between the ex-nun and characters as yet un-
defined but gradually taking shape precisely as a result of
these scenes. Reasoning selects from these characters appearing at random and decides how they can be worked
into the plot. All this, within the ebb and flow of reveries
both parasitical and apposite.

Here I am then, already quite attached to the peaceful
little house, watching scenes going on there but knowing
very little about the people who live in it. It is almost as if I
lived in a neighbouring house at the end of the garden,
noticing occasional voices raised, overhearing scraps of
conversation, catching a glimpse of the people through the
trees.

What is most difficult to describe is what happens now,
exactly how the characters emerge from the shadows
finally. Reasoning, pure imagination and memory are
engaged in operations so complex that one must continually speak of all these at once in order to give an idea of
what happens. You must accept then, once and for all,
that what I tell you is enormously simplified.

My characters are not determined when I begin to
write down the plot. This is just what is going to bring the
creatures into existence, for in a play of this kind to construct the plot is to establish the characters.

As I write on the paper 'Act I, Scene I', at last I get
right inside the house. I already know every corner of it,
though I have never been inside and do not know who lives
there. But now I have to know. Let us have some good,
elderly, quiet people, says reasoning, and in the midst of
this tranquillity we shall observe the outbreak of passions

in Julie (the ex-nun). But simultaneously imagination is watching scenes where these passions break out.*

* *L'imagination*, la bonne à tout faire, la compatissante personne qui tourne toutes les difficultés, apporte, pleine de zèle, un *nouveau sujet*: une femme, après avoir tenté de commettre un crime,—réminiscence du premier sujet,—entre au couvent pour cacher sa honte et faire pénitence. L'homme qu'elle aimait et ne pouvait avoir meurt. La religieuse se croit en droit de rentrer dans le monde. Voilà le point de départ, le nouveau sujet.

Je l'examine, il me plaît. Les avantages de la première donnée subsistent, et les inconvénients disparaissent. J'ai été élevé chez les jésuites, j'ai vu beaucoup de religieux et de religieuses. Je ne me lance pas en pays nouveau. Mon imagination me fait apercevoir très rapidement des perspectives séduisantes. *J'ai une vue d'ensemble de ma pièce dont je ne connais encore ni les moyens ni les personnages.* J'adopte ce sujet. Toutes ces opérations, depuis la conception de l'idée première jusqu'à la transformation définitive inclusivement m'ont pris tout au plus vingt minutes réparties sur un jour et demi. Cela vous laisse entrevoir toutes les rêveries parasites ou utiles qui sont intervenues.

Je fais mon scénario. L'imagination y a une très grande part; cependant le raisonnement n'en est pas exclu. Ma préoccupation est de voir le milieu. Mon imagination me montre immédiatement une maisonnette dans une petite ville. Très détaillée. Je vois surtout très bien le jardin avec ses petites allées bordées d'arbres fruitiers et au fond un bosquet de charmilles et de lilas, au milieu un bassin avec des poissons rouges,—la rue qui borde la maison de l'autre côté, rue déserte, pavée, sans trottoirs, aboutissant d'un côté sur la campagne, de l'autre sur la grand'rue,—enfin dans la maison je connais le salon, la salle à manger et une chambre à coucher attenant au salon. La maison est couverte en tuiles creuses, de la vigne grimpe sur la façade du jardin, etc. Je distingue tout cela avant de savoir au juste quels seront mes personnages. Je sens déjà que ma religieuse tombant là-dedans au bout de dix-huit ans, trouvera de grands changements dans le jardin. Des arbres auront poussé, d'autres seront morts. La maison sera restée telle qu'elle était. On est en plein été, la saison des fleurs, aux environs de la Fête-Dieu. Je prends l'habitude de nommer les saisons par les fêtes religieuses. Il est entendu que je suis dans un intérieur très pieux puisque les femmes n'en sortent que pour se réfugier au couvent. C'est le raisonnement qui fait observer cela à l'imagination. Celle-ci, d'ailleurs, travaille fortement. Elle aperçoit des scènes, détachées du reste de la pièce, se passant entre l'ex-religieuse et des personnages encore mal définis, mais qui précisément, grâce à ces scènes, sortent peu à peu du néant. C'est le raisonnement qui parmi ces personnages de hasard qui surgissent, fait un choix, et décide de quelle façon ils pourraient être rattachés au sujet. Tout cela, dans un méli-mélo de rêveries parasites et utiles.

Me voici donc aimant déjà cette maisonnette paisible, assistant aux scènes qui s'y passent et connaissant fort peu les personnages qui y habitent. C'est à peu près comme si je demeurais au fond du jardin, dans une autre

De Curel goes on trying to describe the rôle of different processes in producing his characters: Julie, the nun who returns, her mother, who remains momentarily vague, and Noémi, her aunt whom reasoning casts as foil to Julie, but whose personal characteristics imagination supplies. De Curel is thus led to try to clarify what he means by memory and imagination.

A word on what I mean by memory. When I create a character, it happens thus:

(1) I take over a personality from someone in real life and infuse it *in toto* into the character I need. This is a rare occurrence. . . .

(2) More often, the outline of a character is sketched by a process of reasoning, to be filled in by imagination. How does imagination set about the task? A metaphor from the microscopic world will enable me to give an idea of this. You know that the caddis larva lives in streams and that in order to move about without harmful contacts it protects itself with a sort of sheath composed of agglutinated fragments, either little bits of wood, or microscopic shells or grains of sand, according to the nature of the river bed. This produces tiny creatures that look very different from each other although they belong to the same species. Well, imagination works in exactly the same way. By the fusion

---

propriété, percevant des éclats de voix, surprenant des bouts de conversations, entrevoyant des personnages à travers les arbres.

Le plus difficile à décrire, c'est ce qui se passe à présent, la façon dont les personnages sortent définitivement de l'ombre. Le raisonnement, l'imagination pure et la mémoire se livrent à des opérations tellement complexes, qu'il faudrait sans cesse parler des trois à la fois pour donner idée de ce qui arrive. Prenez donc, une fois pour toutes, que je simplifie énormément ce que je raconte.

Mes personnages ne sont pas arrêtés que je me mets à écrire le scénario. C'est même ce qui va déterminer mes bonshommes à venir au monde, car dans une pièce de ce genre, faire le scénario, c'est établir les personnages.

En écrivant sur mon papier, acte I—scène 1, je pénètre enfin dans cette maison, dont je connais déjà tous les détours, sans y être jamais entré, ni savoir qui l'habite. Mais il faut le savoir à présent. Mettons-y de bonnes personnes, âgées, tranquilles, nous verrons éclater au milieu de cette douceur les passions de Julie (l'ex-religieuse), dit le raisonnement. Mais en même temps l'imagination voit des scènes où éclatent ces passions.[9]

of little scraps of recollection, it composes a whole which appears to be perfectly homogeneous, a person or a landscape, according to what is wanted. The small scraps of recollection from which these entities are constructed are procured by the imagination in two ways: either by searching into the past, at a definite place and time, for the required ingredient or by gathering up, as and when they are needed, reminiscences arising from sources unknown. There exists one of the infusoria, called rotifer, that lives in gutters and, although it may have been reduced to a state of inert dust by a more or less prolonged drought, returns to life when rain comes. In the same way, there exists in us a deposit of memories, specks of dust to all appearances dead, but which suddenly, under a favourable influence, begin to live again. They cannot be given temporal or spatial location without the most rigorous analysis, for the most part impracticable and not worth the effort. Imagination discovers them in plenty, turns inert dust into living matter, and lays hold of this to construct complete new entities without suspecting the nature of the material thus used.*

* Un mot sur ce que j'entends par mémoire.

Lorsque je crée un personnage il m'arrive:

1. D'emprunter à une créature vivante son caractère et de l'infuser complet au personnage dont j'ai besoin. Il est rare que j'agisse ainsi. . . .

2. Le plus souvent le raisonnement trace un patron du personnage que l'imagination se charge d'exécuter. Comment s'y prend-elle? Une comparaison tirée du monde des infiniment petits me permettra d'en donner idée. Vous savez que la larve des phryganes vit dans les ruisseaux, et que pour s'y promener à l'abri des contacts trop rudes, elle se loge dans une sorte de fourreau composé de fragments agglutinés, tantôt des parcelles de bois, tantôt des coquillages microscopiques, ou des grains de sable, suivant ce qui constitue le fond de la rivière. Cela donne en apparence des petits animaux très différents les uns des autres, bien que de même espéce. Eh bien, l'imagination emploie une méthode identique. Elle agglutine de petits bouts de souvenirs et en compose un ensemble qui paraît parfaitement homogène, personne ou paysage, suivant ce qu'on réclame d'elle. Les petits bouts de souvenirs dont l'imagination fabrique des ensembles, elle se les procure de deux façons: ou bien elle va chercher dans le passé, en un lieu et dans un temps déterminé, le fragment qu'il lui faut, ou bien elle ramasse au fur et à mesure de ses besoins des reminiscences qui surgissent on ne sait d'où. Il existe un infusoire, le rotifère, qui habite les gouttières et

De Curel contrasts a character, Noémi, who is entirely the
product of such imagination, in whose personality he can see
no trait lifted precisely from any particular living creature,
with another lifted from life. Thereby he shows again the
interplay of different processes:

> Once the character of Noémi was established, reasoning
> told me I must place beside her a very bustling sort of
> woman, in order to enliven with an almost comic touch
> this over-dismal home paved with old sorrows. Memory
> produces for me a woman I once knew who was restless,
> full of good works, knowing everything that happened
> among the poor but ignorant of what went on in her own
> house, adviser to the Lord Bishop, rival of his Assistant
> and plague of the local parson. There was just what I
> needed, ready made.*

That this is suggestive writing can hardly be questioned.
Its revelation of a high degree of semi-dissociation, in which,
however, the total personality does not disintegrate, is also
well worth pondering. Originally trained as an engineer, de
Curel saw weakness in the long stretches of reverie necessary,
in his case, for assimilating scientific material, and he classed as
'*temps perdu*' many parasitical reveries. He complained of the
occasional persistence of characters, in his life, after a play was
complete. It required some effort to get rid of these. But their

---

recommence à vivre sous la pluie après qu'une dessiccation plus ou moins
prolongée l'avait réduit à l'état de poussière inerte. De même, il existe en nous
un terreau de souvenirs, poussières mortes en apparence, mais qui tout à
coup, sous une influence favorable, se remettent à vivre. On ne peut les
situer dans le temps ou l'espace qu'au moyen d'une analyse très rigoureuse,
la plupart du temps impraticable et qui n'en vaut pas la peine. L'imagination les trouve en quantité, de poussière inerte en fait une matière vivante,
s'en empare et en compose des objets complets sans se douter même des
matériaux qu'elle agglomère.[9]

* Une fois la personne de Noémi arrêtée, le raisonnement m'a dit qu'il
fallait placer auprès d'elle une femme très remuante, pour animer d'une
note presque comique cet intérieur par trop morne et pavé de vieilles
douleurs. La mémoire m'apporte une femme que j'ai connue, agitée,
occupée de bonnes oeuvres, sachant ce qui se passe chez ses pauvres et
ignorant ce qui arrive chez elle, conseillère de monseigneur, rivale du grand
vicaire, terreur de son curé. Voilà ma besogne toute faite.[9]

imaginary status never appears in doubt. Daudet, it seemed, could genuinely hallucinate. Notwithstanding all this, Binet could not trap his authors into agreeing that in creative work, *as such*, there was the doubling of consciousness he had learnt to recognize in its abnormal form, now designated true dissociation.

These were not the only excursions by Binet and his colleagues in exotic and unexplored directions. Indeed, at one moment we glimpse Binet at a séance, together with three mediums, one of whom he persuaded to try reciting verses during possession.[9] The upshot was that her hand was found writing these instead of the spirit's supposed communications. The mediums had some trouble arguing this one away. The studies we have cited of dramatists were supplemented, in 1896, by those of actors talking of their relations to their rôles.[12] These explorations, both effective and sometimes ephemeral (that of the actors is weak), must be seen against the sober experimental background of inquiries in schools and elsewhere. So, for instance, supplementing the calculators' and chess players' rememberings are data for some 900 children which show the familiar fact that isolated words are harder to learn than phrases.[7] This question was re-studied in the Sorbonne laboratory, where better precautions could be taken against the ingenious methods of cheating that some of the school-children were observed to try.

THE CHILDREN

Prior to 1894, Binet had paid attention to psycho-physiology. Publications of the next ten years show a stream of investigations too detailed and beyond my competence to summarize critically here. Questions about emotion, respiration, heart functioning, head measurements in relation to intelligence, diet, etc. are all included. One suspects unevenness in quality, and methods now of course out of date; but these studies represent an important aspect of his interests and total output of effort to assess individual differences. In 1903 he returned to another dramatist, Paul Hervieu, de Curel's predecessor as a member of the Academy. This better-known contribution by Binet we must also omit in order to show something of his work with his own children, Marguerite and Armande, in *L'Etude*

Expérimentale de l'Intelligence.[13] Following as it did on many studies in schools, this reflects an important stage in Binet's concentrated attack on questions of individual differences and their assessment by relatively simple tests. By this time Binet, highly-sophisticated both in the pitfalls of introspection and of large-scale petty measurement, was using a combination of objectively scorable test and cautiously-elicited comment, in which the experimenter guards as well as he can against suggestion. Methodologically, this approach is the direct ancestor of Piaget's work. For Piaget was influenced by Claparède, himself one of Binet's personal friends. Binet hoped by such methods to get more insight into so-called 'higher' processes, in which he thought individual differences most clearly lay.

Binet had studied his own children earlier, at the stages of learning to walk. The one saw and made for things that would support her, the other toddled into a room and subsided in a heap. The former learnt to walk some three months earlier. At the ages of about 11½ and 10 the children came in for systematic testing by methods suggested by the following list, some norms on some of the tests being already available from schools.

List of Principal Tests used by Binet upon his Two Children
1. Writing 20 words, unobtrusively timed.
2. Verbal explanation of the associations, images, etc. involved in (1).
3. Writing 20 sentences, also timed.
4. Completing sentences, also timed.
5. Developing a theme, also timed.
6. Writing lists of 10 memories freely chosen, also timed.
7. Describing a presented object,* e.g. a cigarette or a picture.
8. Describing an event, e.g. a train journey during which Binet was in a position to note selectivity in response.

* This type of test, presumably the ancestor of projection tests as now understood, appears to have first been used with deliberate educational significance by Miss Sophie Bryant, Headmistress of the North London Collegiate School, to whom Binet gives priority. But the use of ink blots to provoke imaginative response is older and is associated with the painter Alexander Cozens and the German romantic poet Justinus Kerner.[23]

 9. Crossing out letters, timed.
10. Immediate memory for digits.
11. Copying words and lines.
12. Copying designs shown for a short interval.
13. Reaction time.
14. Memory for verses.
15. Memory for words.
16. Memory for objects (a sort of Kim's game).
17. Memory for a prose passage read.
18. Memory for designs.
19. Reproduction of lines of specified lengths with eyes closed.
20. Perception of intervals of time.

Binet submitted the data to extensive analysis and discussion. The most interesting outcomes for us can be grouped under three main headings: the further breakdown of associationism as an adequate theory, the differences in attitude and orientation the children showed, and the hints given of an 'intentional' approach to generality.

Binet was still enough of an associationist to study associations, in spite of healthy doubts about the then current amassing of unamplified associations to lists and lists of words, which was beloved by psychologists at the turn of the century. His data, now collected under more controlled conditions, showed evidence of guiding themes, very hard to explain on a mechanical model of memory, and of 'thinking' of which imaging constituted only a part. Moreover, the part that was clearly represented by some image might be important, or only accessory if judged by the central significance of a given word. Armande, responding to the word 'elephant', visualized some children waiting for a ride, but not the pachyderm itself,[13] and insisted she hadn't time to form images when limited to understanding the sense of a phrase. Binet also encountered the problem, already noted in Chapter Five on Freud [pp. 136 ff.], of how logical relationships can be represented at all if one starts only with itemized elements such as images.

The precise relation of imaging to the more complex thinking implied raises profound problems, recognized as such by Binet.

Comments from the children give some indication of what *they* believed was occurring when they 'thought'. Binet was guarding so carefully against suggestion, that we are not entitled to discard these children's interesting contributions *ab initio*; especially as Binet reports verbatim how some of these conversations went. Three extracts from the children, and a fourth from Binet's summary, may show the nature of the material and the tentative hypothesis he formed.

An immediate difference between the two children lay in the extent and nature of the imagery they seemed to possess. Marguerite could report clear-cut accurate 'pictures', whose production seemed very largely under her own control. If asked to imagine a monkey with a pipe, she 'saw' one and could add a hat or other details as requested. By contrast, Armande's imagining was much vaguer and with a tendency to develop on its own. Unlike her sister, she also claimed to think of *ensembles*, homely or even historical, like the reign of Napoleon. These were networks or junctions of several lines of reflection, seemingly different both from images or 'abstract ideas', where this phrase implies reference to a class of similar objects. She was, in fact, talking of 'concepts' in one of its modern psychological usages. In the test requiring the writing of twenty words, Armande's results revealed more unexplained transitions than did those of Marguerite. In the course of discussing these she comments so:

ARMANDE: With these words that I write almost unconsciously, the image comes only after the word is written; it comes, and, if it comes at all, is very vague and it is often effaced by the search for the next word. Sometimes, in order not to lose time, I dismiss the image myself and try to think of something else.

BINET: And if you didn't dismiss it?

ARMANDE: Then I would have a more vivid image.[13]

Some thirty pages later, in the context of exploring the relations of spontaneous and voluntary imagining, Binet quotes again:

ARMANDE: I search and I see some images which file past me as when I have nothing to do. Then I see an image

and reflect that I can use a word which relates to it. I see
an eye and I write 'look'. If I see a forest with the sky, all
together [an *ensemble*] I write 'landscape', and if there is
water, 'liquid'.

BINET: So the operation consists of two parts. . . .

ARMANDE (interrupting): Of one part which appears without my searching and I organize that with reflections in
order to call up the words.

BINET: Of these two parts, is there one more voluntary than
the other?

ARMANDE: Oh of course one is involuntary, for it is in
spite of me that the images come. The other is naturally
the more voluntary.[13]

Binet comments: 'I should have thought that the same [spon-
taneity] might be true of auditory images, and that Armande
might well be hearing words, as happens, for example, to de
Curel when he is writing, but Armande assured me that she
heard nothing and that it was "she who speaks for her images".'

Our third extract, which follows, shows us Armande
struggling directly with the relation of imagery to thought, no
mean task for someone about twelve.* Binet explains that when
he started his inquiries, the little girls understood what he
meant by images and he would inquire what imagery they
had. It was *they* who said to *him*: 'I didn't have any imagery
with this word, I only had ideas.' Sometimes they fell back on
'reflection' or 'thinking', but of the process involved they could
provide both little detail and much of worth, as we can appreciate in Armande's response to 'tomorrow'.

ARMANDE: At the start, I try, without imagery, to determine what day that will be, and what we shall do. I think
too that this is the eve of Thursday.

BINET: What images?

ARMANDE: I had a very vague image of the dining room.
These were mainly thoughts.

* We cannot unfortunately be quite certain of her age at this time. The
inquiries lasted some three years and Armande seems to have been about
ten when they began. But Binet quotes comments from different stages of the
investigation without showing clearly the children's precise ages at the
time.

BINET: Say what you mean by a thought.
ARMANDE: That which is translated by words and feelings [*sentiments*], it is vague (after reflection), it's too difficult.
BINET: Come on, courage, try to explain again.
ARMANDE: That which presents itself in several ways. Sometimes suddenly, without my expecting it. At other times following upon other thoughts.
BINET: Do you make use of words in order to think?
ARMANDE: Sometimes, but it is very much easier to make use of words, it is more precise. I hardly notice that I am thinking when I don't use words.[13]

As Binet says, Armande was well aware of the importance of internal speech. Binet, alert to the theoretical interest of this process, tried various means of elucidating its rôle, such as persuading Marguerite, like the unfortunate medium on p. 232, to divide her attention.[13] But as we can see from the close of the most relevant chapter, he remained unconvinced that verbalizing and imagining exhausted what went on. Here is Armande one more, and Binet's tentative conclusion:

BINET: Where's your hat at the moment?
ARMANDE: The one I am going to wear today is in the lamp cupboard.
BINET: How does this phrase come to you?
ARMANDE: It is prepared by several thoughts. I do not prepare the phrase. It is almost comparable to an image. The response in words appears to me like an image that interrupts the thinking. The thinking is something I know at once without having sought it by means of words; it appears to me as some sort of feeling [*sentiment*]. I don't know what to say.[13]

And talking of the feeling of negation, which for Armande preceded its verbalization, she adds firmly: 'This quite vague feeling, but which I am sure of, is a thought without words.'
Binet found himself driven to summarize as follows:

From these conversations it would seem to emerge that wordless thinking is experienced as 'feeling' [*sentiment*], and above all one has awareness of it as an experience rather than knowledge of its nature.

I surmise that the word, like the sensory image, gives precision to this 'feeling' of thinking which, without these two aids of verbalization and imagery, would remain vague indeed.

I surmise even that it is the word and the image that contribute most to bringing our thought to consciousness; thinking is an unconscious act of the mind, which needs words and images to become fully conscious. But, however difficult it is for us to be aware of a thought without the aid of words and imagery—and this is the only reason why I call it unconscious—it exists none the less. To define it by its function, it constitutes a directing and organizing force which I should like to compare—this is doubtless no more than a metaphor—to that vital force which, by the ordering of physico-chemical properties, governs the form of beings and directs their evolution, an invisible agency of whose action we see only the material results.[13]

So by 1903 Binet was well launched in the direction in which he continued.

With attitudes and generality, the two other topics of especially relevant interest emerging from this book, we must deal briefly. In earlier studies in schools Binet had been tempted to evolve a rough 'type theory' on the basis of children's approaches to description of objects.[10, 11] He distinguished four groups, represented at one extreme by restriction to accurate if selective observation and at the other by what we should now regard as a considerable infusion of projective material. It is doubtful whether the basis of this type theory stands up to scrutiny, for it appears fairly clear that Binet was imposing a typology on data that really reflect a complex continuum of response. In justice, however, we must realize that all he was doing was to imply that the descriptions given by children lend themselves to some such classification. The descriptions given by Armande and Marguerite are considered by Binet against this background. Binet made no claim to have found constitutional differences. Indeed he implies that by the close of his inquiry Armande was changing. But the kinds of differences emerging from his careful analysis of his two children's test results come very near to those of extraversion and introversion, as originally treated by Jung.

Analysis of Marguerite's responses showed predominant reference to objects visually present in the external world and whose spatial relations were veridically portrayed. Things she remembered were recent or closely related to present time. She possessed vivid imagery, under her own control, but its vividness appeared to vary with the recency of perception. On the whole she responded more slowly to stimuli than did her sister. By contrast, Armande's responses showed a higher incidence of unknown transitions, and of imaginary contents. Her memories were drawn from longer and more variable intervals of time. Her imagery seemed less clear, more spontaneous and its vividness bore no clear relation to temporal distance. She was less good than her sister in judging spatial relations and better in assessing temporal ones; less good at describing the external world, far better at identifying and describing psychological states. On the whole her responses were faster. One example, of both children's responses to the same test, must suffice to illustrate the quality of these differences in attitude, a quality confirmed by the pattern of test results as a whole. Binet quotes some of the children's responses to test 3, writing sentences, which point up Marguerite's concern with present daily affairs and the poetic (but sometimes also banal) ruminations of Armande. For us, Marguerite's also illustrate, amusingly, the perilous position of the psychologist father, with an intelligent small daughter not hesitating to prod him. The relations of father and daughters must have been very good.

MARGUERITE	ARMANDE
Yesterday Papa gave us permission to go to town this morning on our bicycles to buy a pen-holder, but I dare not ask again.	The sun is shining and the sheep are grazing in the meadow.
	A carriage stopped abruptly in front of the church.

Armande and I are very fed up.

Gyp barked quite a lot last evening, when Armande knocked at the shutters; we hope he is going to be a good watch dog.

This morning, Papa told me to come and do some experiments as soon as I had had my breakfast.

I wonder what Papa will say when he has read my first sentence.

How bored poor Armande must be waiting for me to go out on our bikes.

The other day we went with M. to get some new rolls at P.'s [probably for the pianola].

We are going with Papa to lunch at Grandma's and afterwards we hope we'll go to the Exhibition.

Papa promised this would be the last sentence, only Papa has not given me permission to go out on the bicycle (or at least he hasn't mentioned it).[13]

In a big park, in the shade of the trees, one can sit down.

On the waves, one can see in the distance little boats tossing in the wind.

Dawn breaks, the birds are singing, the flowers are opening.

It is snowing and the roofs are completely covered with its great white cloak.

Groans are heard from the poor house with the broken-down roof.

As I walked through the woods I saw a bird which had fallen out of its nest.

Umbrellas are going up, rain begins to fall and wets the roads and gardens.

It is night, a few stars are shining faintly in the sky, the quivering moon is hidden by a cloud.

The reader will be relieved to know that the children got their bicycle ride and that Binet was brought a green and yellow pen-holder! But note that it is Marguerite who tells us this the next day, while Armande continues to write down semi-poetic ruminations.

What of generality? Two suggestive points. Studies of the children's imagery, and their comments, suggested to Binet that, psychologically, the familiar epistemological distinction between particular and general does not strictly apply. Armande protested that her imaginary table was neither round nor square,[13] and, cautiously interrogated on whether the hat she thought of was particular or general, she remarked: 'It is badly expressed *in general*: I try to represent to myself one of all the objects which the word collects together, but I do not imagine any one of them.'* (For discussion of the theoretical point here, see Chapter Ten.)

This, and similar evidence of indefinite imagery, as well as other considerations, led Binet to reject as inadequate most of the varieties of nominalism, realism and conceptualism then current. His discussion has an intrinsic interest too far-reaching to explore here. His conclusion, however, is relevant once more to his steady move away from pure associationism:

> Now do such [indefinite] images in themselves constitute generality in thinking? I do not think so. For generality in thinking to be possible, something more is necessary: an intellectual act consisting in the utilization of the image. Our mind, seizing on the image, says to it, as it were: since you represent nothing in particular, I am going to make you represent everything. This attribution of function comes from the mind, and the image receives it by delegation. In other words, the idea of generality comes from a direction of thinking towards the whole group of objects; it is, to use the word in its etymological sense, an *intention* of the mind.
>
> When all has been said and done, we see that all the theorists on generality have been right; if there exists a core of truth in the most opposed systems, it is that the kind of imagery which thought uses to achieve generalization is only accessory; generality in thought is explained, properly speaking, neither by nominalism, realism or

* C'est mal dit *en général*: je cherche à me représenter un de tous ces objets que le mot rassemble, mais je ne m'en représente aucun.[13]

conceptualism, but rather, if I may be allowed a neologism, by *intentionism.**

THE STUDIES OF INTELLIGENCE

It is against this rich and varied background of interests and investigations that Binet's work, with Simon, on assessing intelligence should in part be seen. I say in part, because fully to appreciate what they tried to do one needs to know more of the practical situation within which they worked; a situation in which there were no special schools, and no objective means of assessing the nature or degree of mental defect (or of retardation) from which a child might be suffering. One infers from Binet's writings that it was also true that a child wrongly classified by an alienist as *débile* ran the risk of being despatched to a lunatic asylum, whereas those not identified remained to clutter up ordinary classes, to their own and their teachers' despair. A theoretical point is also worth remembering; namely, that Binet had taken over the term *intelligence* directly from Taine's *De l'Intelligence* in the first instance. And for Taine '*l'intelligence*' meant thinking, but explained in terms of the patterning and re-patterning of images derived from sensory experience, as outlined in Chapter Five. Hence, some of the difficulty involved in understanding what Binet thought he was measuring in his tests arises from the fact that only in the long process of devising and improving methods of comparing normal and defective children did Binet (and Simon)

---

* Maintenant, de telles images constituent-elles en elles-mêmes une pensée générale? Je ne le crois pas; pour qu'il ait pensée générale, il faut quelque chose de plus: un acte intellectuel consistant à utiliser l'image. Notre esprit, s'emparant de l'image, lui dit en quelque sorte: puisque tu ne représentes rien en particulier, je vais te faire représenter le tout. Cette attribution de fonction vient de notre esprit, et l'image la reçoit par délégation. En d'autres termes, la pensée du général vient d'une direction de la pensée vers l'ensemble des choses, c'est, pour prendre le mot dans son sens étymologique, une *intention* de l'esprit.

En fin de compte nous voyons que tous les théoriciens de la généralisation ont eu raison; s'il existe une âme de vérité dans les systèmes les plus opposés, c'est que les formes d'images dont la pensée se sert pour arriver au général ne sont qu'un accessoire; la pensée générale n'est expliquée, à proprement parler, ni par le nominalisme, ni par le réalisme, ni par le conceptualisme, mais bien, qu'on me passe ce mot nouveau, par l'intentionisme.[13]

really begin to differentiate intelligence and thought. Since, as I have been trying to illustrate, Binet's treatment of thought was developing all the time, it is no wonder that his concept of intelligence remains complex and unclear. We know the initial lines of demarcation. We do not know what else he would have done in response to detailed criticism.

The broad distinctions that do emerge arise from two main kinds of inquiry carried out by Binet and Simon between 1903 and 1911. First, there were the studies bearing directly on the construction, standardization and modification of the initial Binet-Simon Scale of 1905. Two main revisions of this were published in 1908 and 1911. Secondly, Binet and Simon did what every sensible applied psychologist has done ever since; they made special studies of the 'failures', in this case people unable to think, e.g. senile dements, paretics and severe defectives. So far as feasible, they compared the performance of these groups with each other and with those judged normal, for example, by school attainment for their age group. On the basis of these and other data,* Binet[14] and Simon can be seen gradually narrowing down intelligence, while stressing a developmental approach, in contrast to then current emphasis on integration and hierarchy as explanatory concepts.

So far as intelligence is concerned, we see four main points emerging. First, attainments arising from rote and comparable learning, and also personality traits (such as docility or rebelliousness), are explicitly excluded from the intelligence whose arrested general development constitutes mental defect. Secondly, certain aspects of attention are treated as important. Four functional levels are distinguished:

(a) Attention can be awakened and fixed on a point.
(b) Once attracted it can be held for a certain time.
(c) If diverted by distraction it can return spontaneously to the object quitted.
(d) It can resist distraction and remain fixed in spite of influences that might turn it aside.

* For example, on hysteria and other forms of psychopathology which Binet and Simon made an effort to classify more adequately during these years.[15]

Only level (*a*) is said to be characteristic of idiots, and levels (*a*) and (*b*) of imbeciles; whereas (*c*) and (*d*) represent normal functioning. Such distinctions, made more than sixty years ago, take on a new interest in relation to the reticular formation and endocrine disfunction. Thirdly, in spite of the relevance of attention, the authors insist on the arrested *general* development in defectives rather than special weakness in constituent processes, such as remembering or reasoning. However, as one key contributor to their complex notion of intelligence, they discuss judgment or the power to evoke and grasp ideas and relations which exclude illogical and unrealistic inference. They implied that native endowment could set limits to the development of intelligence, but never that it was wholly dependent on innate ability. Indeed Binet continuously referred in one context after another to social and other influences on a child's performance. Thus this kind of intelligence-testing, given Binet and Simon's insistence on the necessity of norms, became very much a process of sampling a selection of native and maturing skills in the light of empirically-obtained data on what it was reasonable to expect at different ages.

The main contributions of these studies to a theory of thinking (with asides that show the influence of Binet's earlier work) can be summarized under the three headings of *Un Schéma de la Pensée*, part of *L'Intélligence des Imbéciles*.[14] They are: direction, evolution and differentiation, and correction.

Under the first, a return was made to *l'idée directrice*, with emphasis on the complexity and persistence of a line of thinking as an indication of its power and direction. This in turn distinguished those of superior ability. But there is also the important notion of thinking being adapted to an aim or end determined largely by emotional life, the level of thought being a function of the choice of goal, intelligence being reflected in that of means to reach it. Under the second heading, we find discussion of differences in the supply of ideas and the degree of differentiation they may have. Thus thinking is likened, in part, to the trying out of keys to a locked door, some people having either a short supply of keys or ones too coarsely-cut to take effect. The suggestion is that a successful process of thinking develops from something vague to something very well defined. Under the third heading, of correction, we find, on the one hand, an echo of Taine and, on the other, a self-censoring notion that may reflect Freud's influence. At all events, thinking is taken to involve an element of criticism and judgment in which selective attention and assessment of what follows plays a part. On the other hand, the breakdown of a directive theme is not equivalent to failure of attention or memory, though one or both may be involved. Binet and Simon reject the notion of thinking as the play of distinct *faculties*. Instead, they stress a functional, not structural, approach.

CONCLUSION

This brings us to the final article in which Binet suggested his general view.[17] By this time, studies of emotion, inspired in part by Lange and James, had led him to treat this as integral to all thinking, in so far as it reflected discharge of excitation. In effect, if the discharge was powerful enough it was experienced as emotion and constituted an attitude, but some such discharge went on all the time. Between an 'intellectual' and 'emotional' attitude there was, therefore, only a matter of degree. But Binet introduces his general view of thinking with a story, important for suggesting his lack of claim to finality.

Anyone in charge of a psychological laboratory is apt to receive rather odd visits from time to time. I remember one day a stranger came to see me. As soon as he had sat down, he announced point-blank: 'Monsieur, I have brought you the secret of the world', adding casually, with a glance at a small closed box he had just laid on the table in front of me: 'The secret of the world is in that box.' I shall surprise no one by saying that despite my scepticism I regarded the box with a certain curiosity. My visitor, who seemed well versed in the art of suspense, did not open it immediately. For ten minutes I had to listen resignedly to an absolutely unintelligible harangue and, when at long last the box was opened, all I saw there was a cube of wood covered with meaningless notches. I had fallen into the trap.

I should not like to mislead the reader in a similar way by letting it be supposed I had discovered anything at all. Discoveries in psychology are rare, and I say at the outset, quite categorically, that my rôle will be the completely modest one of clarifying an idea already enunciated. I shall be happy not only if my readers privately agree that my solution is probably correct, but even more so if they add: 'Fundamentally that is what I had always thought.' The whole secret of the solution lies in a word, and that word is *attitude*.[17]

What use did Binet make of this term? As usual he was cautious. Mental attitudes, he hypothesized, were analogous to physical and involved preparation for action, a sketch of action which is not externalized but is revealed to us indirectly by accompanying sensations, images, verbalization, incipient gesture and the like. How did he weave all this together? Here again he must speak for himself, for there is no better summary possible of the position he had left and that to which he was moving in 1911.

The essential thing is to free oneself from the error of regarding the mechanism of the mind wholly in terms of states. This is the error which neither Mill nor Taine avoided, which appears again in James' theory of the emotions and which hinders any conception of the working of emotion, will and even of thought, for this involves acts, not states, and the former cannot be derived from the latter.

And it is here that the new theory breaks with the sensationalist theory. It is a dynamic view; it adds actions to apprehensions, events to states. The changed point of view can without doubt be most clearly and strikingly explained by reference to the act of understanding. According to sensationalist or intellectualist theory, to understand a word is to be able to imagine all the objects and all the meanings signified by that word. To understand the word 'house' is to be able to evoke every kind of house, in every conceivable style, period and variety, it is an imaginative capacity, a faculty of analysis, clarity, consciousness.

According to the new theory, understanding may indeed sometimes, in certain circumstances and types of individual, consist in evocations of this sort; but there exists besides a certain act of comprehension, an interior act, which no image, however clear or definite or detailed, can ever represent; for it is not enough to have a series of images before one's eyes, they must be interpreted, in short, understood; and without this necessary addition, nothing is accomplished; and, moreover, one can, as has been proved, understand without the aid of any kind of image. This understanding, according to the new theory, results from the realization of an attitude, of a particular, indefinable attitude which gives an impression of ease, of difficulty overcome, of intellectual power; there are, as it were, movements appropriate to the word we understand, movements that we feel to be right. To understand a word, then, is to feel in oneself the onset of this reaction; and, in admitting that, we have moved so far from the sensationalist theory that a supporter of that theory would be reluctant to follow; for we are admitting the paradox that one can understand without intellectual realization; one has the feeling of understanding without understanding anything at all; one understands without understanding; one has the movement, the physiognomy, the attitude of understanding, as an actor might deliver with correct intonation the words of a rôle although they were meaningless to him. In truth, this example is an excellent demonstration; it shows us very clearly the gulf separating these two conceptions of mental life: on the one hand, the older view, so rational, introducing everywhere explanation, logic, deportment, assuming that in mental life everything is explicable, co-ordinated, justifiable; and, for example, that reasoning consists of premises and conclusions, that one deduces the conclusion from the premises and only arrives at the conclusion by way of the premises. Over against this theory stands the new one, a theory of action, according to which the psychic life is by no means a rational life but a chaos of darkness streaked with flashes of light, something strange and, above all, discontinuous, which has only appeared continuous and rational because after the event it is described in a language which puts order and clarity into everything. Yet this is a factitious order, a verbal illusion, which bears no more resemblance to real life than does the declamation of classical tragedy to the unleashing of passions.

It may be that we have here the most beautiful, the most captivating and the most profound idea that has come out of those meticulous introspective studies we have been carrying out on the processes of thinking. What a subject of meditation for those who like to philosophize![17]

Would Binet have agreed with Freud? In part of course. But temperamentally the two men were poles apart, the latter at once more profoundly imaginative and more ambitious, the former with a far greater sense of evidence, and far less temptation to go beyond it. For someone of Binet's experience and generation, unconscious functioning was, of course, nothing new. He had been willing to publish an article by Jung on Freud, so was clearly far from hostile to psycho-analytic ideas. But he had reservations. And these can be detected in the last editorial summary of trends for 1910, published in the volume of *L'Année Psychologique* from which we have just quoted.

The researches in psycho-analysis of Freud and of his collaborators and pupils have aroused a great deal of curiosity in certain quarters. Some of the centenary lectures organized by the University of Hall were entrusted to Freud and Jung, who gave an interesting account of all that we owe to psycho-analysis and above all to the notion, propounded by them, that most of our thoughts and emotions derive from our sexual life and are the result of repressed sexual feelings. This idea holds a certain mystery which attracts and captivates especially minds inclined to mysticism, and Freud's theory arouses in his followers something near to fanaticism; it is so interesting to set about delving into a person's psychic life, especially into its intimate and probably shameful depths. There, one feels, is the true psychology, a thousand times more interesting than the cold graphs and tedious calculations of the dry laboratory psychology. This we will not deny; but perhaps when the charm of novelty begins to wear off it will be seen that what is lacking in psycho-analytical work are those qualities of objectivity and demonstration without which there is no science. What is to be hoped is that psycho-analysis, preserving its suggestiveness and absorbing interest, will shed the form of a psychological novel.*

Fifty years later one feels he was right.

REFERENCES

Numbers in brackets indicate the pages in this book where given references occur

1. Bancels, J. Larguier des, 'L'Oeuvre d'Alfred Binet', *L'Année Psychologique*, Vol. XVIII, 1912, pp. 15-32.
2. Binet, Alfred, *La Psychologie du Raisonnement*, Paris: Félix Alcan, 4th edition, 1907, pp. 117 (188-9), 165-8 (189-92).
3. Binet, Alfred and Féré, Charles, *Animal Magnetism*, London: Kegan Paul, 3rd edition, 1891, p. 304.
4. Binet, Alfred, 'Mental Imagery', *The Fortnightly Review*, Vol. LII, 1892, pp. 95-104.
5. —— 'The Mechanism of Thought', *The Fortnightly Review*, Vol. LV, 1894, pp. 785-99.

* Les recherches de Freud, de ses collaborateurs et de ses élèves sur la *psycho-analyse* ont éveillé, dans certains milieux, une très grande curiosité. Les conférences du centenaire qu'avait organisées l'Université de Hall ont été confiées en partie à Freud et à Jung, qui sont venus exposer d'une manière intéressante tout ce qu'on doit à la psycho-analyse et surtout à cette idée, qui est la leur, que la plupart de nos pensées et de nos émotions émergent de notre vie sexuelle, et sont un résultat de sentiments sexuels refoulés. Il y a dans cette idée un mystère qui attache, qui charme surtout les esprits mystiques, et la théorie de Freud excite chez ses adeptes presque du fanatisme; il est si intéressant de se mettre à éplucher la vie psychique d'une personne, surtout sa vie intime, profonde et comme honteuse! C'est bien là pense-t-on, de la vraie psychologie, mille fois plus intéressante que les froides courbes, les fastidieux calculs de la sèche psychologie de laboratoire; et nous n'y contredirons pas; mais peut-être que lorsque le charme de la nouveauté commencera à diminuer, on s'apercevra que ce qui manque aux travaux de psycho-analyse, c'est ce caractère de l'objectivité et de la démonstration sans lequel il n'existe aucune science. Ce qu'il faut souhaiter, c'est que la psycho-analyse, tout en gardant son caractère suggestif et attachant, perde sa forme de roman psychologique.[18]

6. Binet, Alfred, *Psychologie des Grands Calculateurs et Joueurs d'Echecs*, Paris: Hachette, 1894, pp. 77 (200), 78-9 (200-1), 115 (202), 117 (202), 147-8 (204), 241 (206), 255 (206), 268-9 (208), 269 (208-9), 274-5 (216), 288 ff. (209), 298 ff. (210-12), 303 (212), 305 (213), 306 (213-14), 358-9 (215).

7. Binet, Alfred, and Henri, Victor, 'La Mémoire des Mots' and 'La Mémoire des Phrases', *L'Année Psychologique*, Vol. I, 1895, pp. 1-23 and 24-59.

8. Binet, Alfred, and Passy, J., 'Etudes de Psychologie sur les Auteurs Dramatiques', *L'Année Psychologique*, Vol. I, 1895, pp. 60-118; particularly 91, 109, 117.

9. Binet, Alfred, and Curel, François de, 'Notes Psychologiques', *L'Année Psychologique*, Vol. I, 1895, pp. 119-73; particularly pp. 127, 138, 143, 158-61.

10. Binet, Alfred, 'Psychologie Individuelle. La Description d'un Objet', *L'Année Psychologique*, Vol. III, 1897, pp. 296-332.

11. —— 'L'Observateur et l'Imaginatif', *L'Année Psychologique*, Vol. VII, 1901, pp. 519-23.

12. —— 'Le Paradoxe de Diderot', *L'Année Psychologique*, Vol. III, 1897, pp. 279-95.

13. —— *L'Etude Expérimentale de l'Intelligence*, Paris: Schleicher Frères 1903, pp. 82 (236-7), 86 (234), 107 (237), 108 (237-8), 127 (241), 137 (235), 138 (241), 154 (241-2), 166 (235-6), 171-3 (239-40).

14. Binet, Alfred, and Simon, Th., 'L'Intelligence des Imbéciles', *L'Année Psychologique*, Vol. XV, 1909, pp. 1-147, particularly pp. 122 ff.

15. —— "Définition des Principaux Etats Mentaux de l'Aliénation', *L'Année Psychologique*, Vol. XVI, 1910, pp. 61-371.

16. Binet, Alfred, Avant-Propos. 'Le Bilan de la Psychologie en 1909', *L'Année Psychologique*, Vol. XVI, 1910, pp. i-ix.

17. —— 'Qu'est ce qu'une Emotion? Qu'est ce qu'un Acte Intellectuel?', *L'Année Psychologique*, Vol. XVII, 1911, pp. 1-47, particularly pp. 23, 46-7.

18. —— Avant-Propos. 'Le Bilan de la Psychologie en 1910', *L'Année Psychologique*, Vol. XVII, 1911, pp. i-ix.

19. Boring, E. G., *A History of Experimental Psychology*, New York: Appleton Century, 2nd edition, 1950, pp. 430, 438, 572-4.

20. Curel, François de, *Théâtre Complet*, Paris: Editions Georges Crés, 2 vols., 1920.
21. Flügel, J. C., *A Hundred Years of Psychology*, London: Duckworth, 2nd edition, 1953.
22. Gibson, J. J., 'A Critical Review of the Concept of Set in Contemporary Experimental Psychology', *Psychological Bulletin*, Vol. 38, 1941, pp. 781-817.
23. Gombrich, E. H., *Art and Illusion*, London: Phaidon Press, 1960, pp. 133 ff.
24. Groot, A. D. de, *Thought and Choice in Chess*, The Hague: Mouton, 1965 (first published in 1946 and now translated).
25. Hebb, D. O., *The Organization of Behaviour*, London: Chapman & Hall, 1949.
26. Humphrey, George, *Thinking: An Introduction to its Experimental Psychology*, London: Methuen, 1951.
27. Hunter, I. M. L., 'An Exceptional Talent for Calculative Thinking', *British Journal of Psychology*, Vol. 53, 1962, pp. 243-58.
28. Murphy, Gardner, *Historical Introduction to Modern Psychology*, London: Routledge & Kegan Paul, 5th edition revised, 1956.
29. Poincaré, Henri, 'Mathematical Creation' in *The Creative Process*, Ghiselin, Brewster (Editor), Berkeley, Los Angeles: University of California Press, 1952, pp. 22-31. Cf. *L'Année Psychologique*, Vol. XV, 1909, pp. 445-59.
30. Simon, Th., Obituary Notice. 'Alfred Binet', *L'Année Psychologique*, Vol. XVIII, 1912, pp. 1-14.
31. Taine, Hippolyte, *De l'Intelligence*, Paris: Hachette, 3rd edition, 1878. English authorized translation by T. D. Haye, *On Intelligence*, London: L. Reeve & Co., 1871.
32. Varon, Edith J., 'The Development of Alfred Binet's Psychology', Princeton: Psychological Review Co., *Psychological Monographs*, Vol. XLVI, 1934-5, No. 207, pp. 1 (187), 12 (193), 22 (193). This includes a very full bibliography.

CHAPTER EIGHT

INTELLIGENCE AND THINKING:
III. SOME OTHER VIEWS

The structuralist is interested primarily in discovering what the
momentary mental state is. The functionalist is more interested in
discovering how the momentary mental state shifts and resolves.
The behaviourist is primarily interested in behaviour itself.

L. L. THURSTONE

BINET'S VIEW of thinking, described in Chapter Seven, needs to
be flanked by four main trends in psychological inquiry for its
full significance to be grasped: (1) experimental studies of
thinking carried out by his contemporaries, the Würzburgers;
(2) contemporary and later views on intelligence and its
assessment, in particular those of Spearman, Thurstone,
Vernon, Hebb and Piaget; (3) the attack on associationism
(from a different angle) that developed into Gestalt psychology; and (4) the behaviouristic approaches to thinking that
arose from the ashes of introspective accounts. Volumes have
been, and still could be, written on these main trends. It is
quite outside the scope of this chapter and the next to do more
than suggest how different strands of this changing pattern
might be related to each other in the light of the general position Binet sketched.

Professor Humphrey[4] has sifted, summarized and commented
on the Würzburg experiments. Two immediately relevant
points emerge from his account. First, the experimenters seem
to have shown convincingly, and under controlled conditions,
that a line of thinking could not be described exclusively in
terms of a procession of ideas and images obeying the laws of
association by contiguity and likeness. There were many
reasons for this; the most interesting, here, is that dominant

themes and the nature of the problem set, both frequently operating outside conscious awareness, could be shown to affect the course of development taken by a process of thinking. Secondly, the Würzburgers reported, as had Binet's children, something they designated 'imageless thought'. As already noted, this concept became the focal point of a controversy, which may have been rendered fruitless by false assumptions on both sides. Broadly, the Würzburgers, on the one hand, and Titchener,[12] who defended a thorough-going sensory elementarism, on the other, argued in terms of an approach to thinking which tacitly involved treating it by analogy with vision, and in terms of states or structures rather than processes and functions.

Titchener's[12] short and readable lectures on the *Experimental Psychology of the Thought Processes* still betray this attitude. In spite of his defence of kinaesthetic imagery as an element overlooked by the Würzburgers, his approach is that of an 'inspectionist' and 'structuralist'; the contents of psychic life are to be analysed into elements derived from the senses. Considered from this standpoint, the notion of 'imageless thought' is senseless; for, in effect, one is being asked to inspect that which by definition is not capable of inspection. Titchener does not seem fully to have grasped the significance of Binet's move towards treating thinking on analogy with action instead of vision, though the notes to his lectures show that in 1909 he was up-to-date with Binet's writing. Instead of appreciating the change from structure to function, state to process, he remarks (correctly, however) on the similarity of Binet's stress on 'feeling' to a position advocated by Wundt.

For the Würzburg protagonists, writing in the German tradition with its Kantian heritage of 'pure reason', the supposition that thinking might have a core of muscular movement must have seemed well-nigh immoral. Moreover, Spinoza's third degree of knowledge (probably also his second), and those processes we designate as intelligent reasoning or insight, seem impossible to treat without presupposing some degree of cognitive discrimination, recognition and even 'grasping', which it is tempting to treat on 'inspectionist' lines. German defence of 'imageless thought', as found in experiments on the process of judgment, may well have involved some awareness of this theoretical point.

However, Titchener produced in passing one key idea, possibly inconsistent with his main position, and for which he is gently criticized by Humphrey. That is the notion that recognition could occur without conscious awareness. The concept of a visual (and non-visual) but non-conscious form of *recognition*, which may become conscious if adequately reinforced and shared, seems, however, exactly the notion needed for unravelling a whole network of problems.

As I have tried to show in Chapter Five, Freud needed processes of discrimination and recognition as a basis for developing an ego psychology. Binet never jettisoned his belief in the importance of recognition as the root of thinking, especially where he treats this as on a continuum with perception and implies that it is intelligent and critical. But in the wide conception of thinking he had reached by 1911, we are left a little uncertain how critical thinking, as an effective form of conscious response, would differ from that involved in the unconscious attitudes that Binet regarded as habitual and, in modern parlance, as stimulus-bound. It would seem that discrimination and recognition, of which one may be either aware or unaware at a primitive level, and which may be unlearned at a primitive level and presuppose learning at a complex one, is the concept that both Freud and Binet need. Superficially, there seems no very great difficulty in allowing for such a process either at the level of common sense, or on the basis of experimental evidence. We seem also to be constantly recognizing as well as discriminating non-visually, e.g. by touch or hearing. Experimentally, recent studies of sleep, as reported by Oswald,[7] suggest further that people are quite capable of discriminating, if not recognizing, while still asleep: in so far as they may awake, for example, to their own names and stay asleep while others from a list are read. Evidence of learning during sleep is less convincing. So 'recognition', though not necessarily consciously performed, might still require wakefulness. We shall return to other aspects of this problem in Chapters Nine and Ten.

Meanwhile, we are led back to the views of intelligence

associated with the authors listed on p. 252, for the early attempts to assess intelligence, made by psychologists other than Binet, were focused on discrimination at a sensory level. Later attempts at assessment took a different but related turn.

History shows us several things. Galton's work, carried to America in the late nineteenth century by McKeen Cattell (who was also influenced by Wundt), provoked the plague of petty measurements to which Binet took exception and of which Wissler showed the inadequacy. Class standing in Latin and Greek might intercorrelate + ·75 but class standing and strength of hand came out, not very surprisingly, at − ·08. The reader can find further relevant details in Jenkins and Paterson.[6] In 1904, Spearman[9] appeared on the scene. Inspired by passionate moral objections to associationism,* he attempted to correlate school performance and discrimination, as indicated by response to a variety of sensory tests. In effect, he presented stimuli varying in degree of physical difference and asked both how great the difference had to be for his different subjects to respond to it and whether their capacities in this respect varied with other achievements. Spearman's approach was avowedly opposed to that of Binet, the nature of this opposition being clear from the following:

> The practical advantages proffered by their [Binet's and Ebbinghaus'] more complex operations have been unreservedly rejected in favour of the theoretical gain promised by utmost simplicity and unequivocality; there has been no search after condensed psychological extracts to be on occasion conveniently substituted for regular examinations; regardless of all useful application, that form of psychical activity has been chosen which introspectively appeared to me as the simplest and yet

* The strength and emotional colouring of these objections becomes clear only in Spearman's[10] autobiography, where he refers to the intensely negative attitude to associationism inspired in him by Hume, Hartley, the two Mills and Bain. Spearman attributes the main source of this heat to an *ethical* objection. 'Sensualism and associationism tend to go with hedonism; and this latter was (and is) to me an abomination.' This curious comment fits in with the suggestion that intelligence and its testing has been a stronghold of belief in some species of rational insight.

pre-eminently intellective. This is the act of distinguishing one sensation from another.[9]

It is not completely clear to me what precise process Spearman assessed by his early tests of discrimination. Recognition may or may not have been involved. Later he re-defined what he set out to assess. Suffice it that results correlated with other criteria which, in these early studies of 1904, were teachers' and peer ratings in various subjects for twenty-four children in a village school, and examination marks for thirty-two other children in an upper-class preparatory school. Spearman's methods of handling these data are now regarded with some doubt, this being offset by respect for pioneering. The correlations, nevertheless, are historically interesting; for they give us the initial evidence that set Spearman sleuthing after a different concept of intelligence, namely, g, that general factor which accounts for positive correlations such as are shown in Table 5. The logic of the argument, for those unfamiliar with it, is that to the extent that different gradings of performance are found to agree, the assessments of performance are of the same process, provided the correlations satisfy the tetrad equation.

TABLE 5[9]

Intercorrelations of Ratings

		Classics	French	English	Maths	Discrimination	Music
Classics			·83	·78	·70	·66	·63
French	+	·83		·67	·67	·65	·57
English*	+	·78	·67		·64	·54	·51
Mathematics	+	·70	·67	·64		·45	·51
Discrimination	+	·66	·65	·54	·45		·40
Music	+	·63	·57	·51	·51	·40	

* This included subjects with a verbal content and taught in English, such as History.

It is well to realize that supplementing Spearman's insistence on g, later to be roughly described in terms of self-awareness, and perceiving and educing relations, was his predisposition to side with those who believed in 'imageless thought'. Spearman, even earlier, had tried research of his own in this field and was sympathetic to Bühler, Ach, T. V. Moore, Aveling, Thorndike, and to others who argued that excellence of imagery did not correlate with excellence of thought, whether or not they subscribed to the 'imageless thought' concept. So, in a sense, Spearman's later theory, developed in full in the late 1920's, harks back both to the insistence of Spencer, Bain and others on awareness of relations, as well as to the Würzburgers. But it also involves insistence on *active* perceiving or relating. Spearman's mathematical approach, defining what he assessed initially in terms of the unknown that accounted for the correlations found, was, of course, the forerunner of the vast amount of later work using factor analysis.

Spearman's subsequent re-translation of *g* into psychological terms was avowedly tentative. Those who see factor analysis, logically, as a complex statistical technique by which initial assumptions about the number and nature of the ingredients affecting test performance are cross-checked, can fairly easily appreciate three aspects of Spearman's position, and of those like Vernon's which derive from it, without becoming involved in intricate calculations.

First, there is Spearman's caution in translating into psychological terms the *g*, or general factor, to which he believed the statistical analysis of all his amassed data still pointed, when he published his major books in the late 1920's. Secondly, there is the type of translation he made. As is well known, he did this in terms of three noegenetic principles, stressing their relevance for understanding how *new* cognition is ever possible. Thirdly, this stress on new cognition is worth emphasis in the light of its intrinsic importance, and of the account Spearman gives in his autobiography of its very practical origin. This, it seems, was a wartime episode when the commander of a training station for submarine officers made short shrift of Spearman's efforts to discuss the production of new plans in terms of the reproduction of past experience. Forthright naval comment on the disasters that could follow *merely* reproductive planning seem to have blown the last traces of associationism and the like from Spearman's thinking. Thus he came to argue that though, even in the most original behaviour, relations, form or method might be reproduced from past experience, their application in a new setting was capable of generating genuine novelty. It is in this

I

context that one must look at the noegenetic principles, intended as they are to underpin 'new cognition', or, in Spearman's words, 'all cognition that is not merely reproductive'.

The three noegenetic principles are familiar, and have been formulated in various ways. The first with its overtones of 'self-awareness' is often forgotten. So it is worth reminding the reader briefly of one of Spearman's expositions, that in *The Abilities of Man*,[9] with such amplifying comment as is immediately relevant. The principles are:

(1) *The apprehension of one's own experience.*
. . . a person has more or less power to observe what goes on in his own mind. He not only feels, but also knows what he feels; he not only strives, but knows that he strives; he not only knows, but knows that he knows.

Spearman added a comment suggesting that *g* was only one factor in this and he allowed for variations in the clearness of awareness down to zero, at which point knowledge, but not the experience, vanishes. So his position was not incompatible with any of the obvious findings of psychopathology.

(2) *The eduction of relations.*
. . . when a person has in mind any two or more ideas (using this word to embrace any items of mental content, whether perceived or thought of), he has more or less power to bring to mind any relations that essentially hold between them.

Spearman remarks that the law seems indisputable enough, and is instanced when someone becomes aware 'that beer tastes something like weak quinine, that the number seven is larger than five, or that the proposition "All A is B" proves the proposition "Some A is B" '. Since Spearman inclined to caution on the rôle of innate endowment versus acquired experience, we need not immediately take him to task on the background experience necessary to know the taste of quinine! More of this in a moment. Meanwhile, the familiar abstract formulation of this second law is shown in the diagram below, in which f^1 and f^2 indicate the given terms and r their essential

relations (i.e. those deriving from the nature of the terms),
which people may vary in their capacity to grasp.

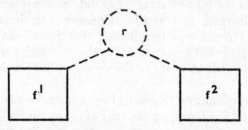

FIG 5. Illustrative schema of educing relations (adapted from Spearman[9])

Spearman had in mind such relations as resemblances, comparative size and logical implication. His classifications of
these never seemed satisfactory, but it would take us too far
afield to discuss this now. Suffice it that processes of discrimination and recognition are clearly involved.

(3) *The eduction of correlates.*

... when a person has in mind any idea together with a
relation, he has more or less power to bring up into mind
the correlative idea.

For example, says Spearman, if someone hears a musical note
and tries to imagine the one a fifth higher, if he understands the
relation 'fifth' and possesses an ear for music, he will more or
less accurately accomplish the task. Schematically the process
is illustrated thus:

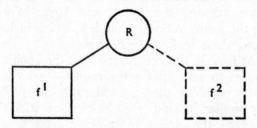

FIG. 6. Illustrative schema of educing correlates (adapted from Spearman[9])

In this immediate context, Spearman did not discuss the rôle
of learning. Instead, the given example shows nicely the interplay between his alleged general ability and the 'S's', or factors

specific to given kinds of test material, which factors he invoked to supplement g. Discrimination and recognition of the initial note, and of the musical interval, could, from our point of view, be both learned and partly dependent on innate special abilities. It could still be allowed that Spearman might be right in saying that power to evoke the correlative term, under specified conditions, is one of the processes basic to insight that is new.

Later practical and theoretical work on assessment of intelligence led to insistence, on the part of many psychologists, that Spearman's s factors were of greater generality than he had originally supposed. Hence there emerged the current form of the hierarchical conception of cognitive capacities: g the most general, group factors still general but less so, and specific factors of more limited range. Such views are associated with Vernon's [13, 14, 15] and with Burt's treatment of intelligence and special abilities. The reader must refer to these authors for the mass of evidence available on this topic and for its theoretical analysis.

Spearman's theory was opposed by various writers, including Godfrey Thompson and L. L. Thurstone, who gave different theoretical analyses of the available data. Certain features of Thurstone's position bear on treatments of thinking, and to these we must turn.

There are two very different aspects of Thurstone's approach to intelligence. The one, much better known to psychologists, derived from factor analysis and was the focus of interest in controversies, during the 1930's and '40's, between those defending the modified Spearman view, which included group factors, and those in favour of Thurstone's primary mental abilities. At issue in this controversy was the choice of a theoretical model to account for the results obtained by actual testing, with problems that, from the subject's point of view, seem very similar in kind. For detailed consideration of the issues involved the reader must again refer to the highly technical publications already mentioned. Here we need mainly to remember that Thurstonians viewed their tests as measures of the following seven capacities: verbal ability, verbal fluency, numerical ability, spatial ability, perceptual ability, inductive reasoning, and memory. These are discussed and illustrated in Eysenck's easily available *Uses and Abuses of Psychology*[2]. I propose to add only two comments.

Any test constructed by these, or other, rival schools seems largely a measure of how, and how quickly, the person doing it can cope with detecting the nature of a problem *when he has all the relevant data*. This is due partly to the effort made, in test construction, to exclude such content (the *obvious* product of learning) as would invalidate comparison even within relatively homogeneous groups. Those who have had to construct or use tests with random samples of the school or young adult population, can never escape awareness of the need to exclude, for example, ranges of vocabulary or bits of factual information which are outside the normal equipment of different socio-economic, educational or geographical groups. Few non-psychological readers seem to appreciate that part of the purpose of care in test construction is to ensure that the material within which a problem is posed draws only on such acquired content of knowledge as all of those tested may be expected to have ready to hand. To the extent that such precautions are successful, the test is so much the better as a measure of basic skill, intelligence B. This has been treated, since Hebb, as partly learnt but rooted in a native potential, intelligence A, that can never be assessed in isolation and is a function of constitutional neuro-endocrinological factors.

Assuming, however, that the content of any given test is appropriate for the group of people for whom the test is designed, a further point is worth remembering. The fact that the data relevant to solving the problems are given, means that, *ab initio*, the test is focused on the speed and subtlety of the person's immediate grasp of such relevance. This may well involve, as Vernon[12] has suggested, an indication of the facility with which a person may shift from one schema, or frame of reference, to another in problem-solving. It usually implies in practice that, however difficult the logical or other inference required to solve a problem, it is rare for a conventional intelligence test item to invoke as many as three moves at a symbolic level. Thus it is not primarily, nor is it intended to be, an indication of power of *sustained* thought. For here the thinker

himself has to evoke relevant data, keep this relevant information actively in mind, and, as it were, process it, often switching
(as did Binet's chess players) from one medium to another,
without losing the thread as a problem ramifies.

Except for what it may reveal of facility in changing frames
of reference, no claim is made that an intelligence test is a
measure of richness or variety in thinking. Other things being
equal, however, a person doing badly (and whose test limitations were supported by other evidence) might be expected to
have difficulty in mastering the wide range of reference upon
which, superficially at any rate, such richness and variety
in thinking might be expected in part to depend. Thus
the capacity, or capacities, assessed by intelligence tests,
though not sufficient, may well be necessary conditions of
thinking.

This returns us to Thurstone's[11] lesser-known approach, in
which the motivational and emotional roots of thinking (and
intelligence) were taken into account. Though it seems likely,
it is not certain that Thurstone studied Binet's untranslated
articles. Be that as it may, he wrote of intelligence and thought
as active processes coming into operation when overt action was
blocked, either by conflict between opposing drives and attitudes or, presumably, by external obstacles. Thurstone was far
from being a behaviourist. He treated the organism as initiating
action, not as a mechanically-operating victim of stimulation.
And he attached importance to its observations fitting (or not)
with conscious or unconscious expectation. But he was sympathetic to methodological behaviourism, so far as it stressed
the psychological interest of the formulated observable response.
In developing a functional account of thinking and intelligence,
he saw them, in part, as the thinker's active means of expressing
needs, attitudes and emotions, which might, initially, be vague
in the extreme, and indicated at the next level only by a
lowered threshold of response. According to circumstances they
might, thereafter, develop into complex, more or less integrated
trains of imagery and symbolization (e.g. verbal or mathematical) intervening, or mediating, between the thinker's state
and situation at one time and his overt action at another. It is
open to Thurstone to have allowed that some such thought

activities do not issue in action at all, and he carefully distinguished his view from that designated 'ideo-motor'.

Thurstone came closest to Binet in treating thought as developing from the vague to the particularized. His further comments on development are obviously sketchy, though far from incompatible with more detailed views on this, such as are exemplified in Piaget's work. At the time of writing *The Nature of Intelligence*,[11] Thurstone seems also to have stuck to a rough and ready need-reduction model of motivation, at whose limitations we have hinted in Chapter Five. But his discussion carries two implications of interest to us now. One is that high level of ability may be reflected in the relatively early stage of their formation at which a thinker can bring into focus his impulses and intentions. This suggests good possibilities for dealing with freshness of thought in any direction. The original thinker, may, as it were, mint his thoughts at a stage nearer to individual experience than the conventional coinage of the culture easily permits to lesser mortals. There is no implication here about the currency (or the medium) that he uses, which could, of course, be verbal, visual, musical or a variety of others.

Secondly, if Thurstone were right in treating the motives and emotions stimulating thought as often extremely vague and ill-defined, then efforts to be very specific about their nature automatically falsify. This is to emphasize rather than deny their possible depth. But it also means one must scrutinize the history, function and formulation of a whole thought process when trying to gauge its significance. Thus, to give a non-Thurstonian example, it would be only at the most general level that one might class Dvorak's Fourth, Mendelssohn's 'Italian' and Beethoven's Ninth Symphonies as expressing 'joy', or the Verdi Requiem and those of Mozart, Rossini, Dvorak, Fauré or Britten, as concerned with death. They are, but differently; and no psychological approach to thinking that overlooks this can possibly be useful.

Clemen's[1] interesting study of Shakespeare's imagery provides one of the best illustrations of development in skill, in attitude and in their depth of integration. In an early play, such as *Titus Andronicus*, for example, images, some even conventional, are apt to occur in rather loosely-integrated similes introduced by 'like' and 'as', and in some passages the use of an image by a given character is implausible. This gives way, in the middle period and the great tragedies, to metaphors which have a far more organic function in the structure of the drama as a whole. By this Clemen[1] means that the image involved may have a closer logical connexion with the situation giving rise to it, or it more nearly fits the character of the person employing it, or the relation of the image either to the atmosphere of the play or to its theme is closer.

For example, in *Titus* one may get lines such as:

> . . . then fresh tears
> Stood on her cheeks, as doth the honey-dew
> Upon a gather'd lily almost withered.

By the time we reach *Romeo and Juliet*, however, there are passages in which the imagery has the triple function of expressing Romeo's personality, of characterizing Juliet (by light) and, simultaneously, of creating atmosphere.

> O, speak again, bright angel, for thou art
> As glorious to this night, being o'er my head,
> As is a winged messenger of heaven
> Unto the white upturned wondering eyes
> Of mortals that fall back to gaze on him,
> When he bestrides the lazy-pacing clouds
> And sails upon the bosom of the air.

In *Hamlet*, the ghost's vivid description of his poisoning, dominated as it is by the image of an ulcer infecting and eating away the whole body, comes to symbolize a central theme in the play. Corruption of the land and people, throughout Denmark, is portrayed as an imperceptible and irresistible process of poisoning, this imagery linking with the action of the play, as in the dumb-show poisoning as well as the real poisoning of the major characters in the last act. Thus imagery and action are dynamically related. As indeed they are again in Macbeth's magnificent projection of his state of mind into nature:

> . . . Come, seeling night,
> Scarf up the tender eye of pitiful day;

And with thy bloody and invisible hand
Cancel and tear to pieces that great bond
Which keeps me pale! Light thickens; and the crow
Makes wing to the rooky wood:
Good things of day begin to droop and drowse;
Whiles night's black agents to their preys do rouse.

In short, the passionate search for specific motives underlying major works of art or science, as if the motives and
insights were already formed and then externalized, runs the
risk of being both puerile and irrelevant. It is on a par with
the older approach to language that treated 'ideas' as fully
formed, but naked and subsequently 'clothed in words'. Such
an approach leaves out all the implications and overtones of
the process of formulation, in which the thinker's attitudes,
emotions, and viewpoint may change, in which he may draw
on an array of experiences and skills, and to which, as Professor
Gombrich has argued so brilliantly, traditional skill and
schema may make their own contribution, for better or for
worse. This general comment bears on the dual interpretation
of Freud that we have suggested in Chapter Five.

We must now conclude this somewhat summary discussion
of developments after Binet with a brief indication of Piaget's[8]
position. I make no pretence of being qualified to discuss his
work in detail. But in studying Binet one begins to appreciate
the tradition to which Piaget belongs. In the light of this, and
of Flavell's[3] and Mc. V. Hunt's[5] careful expositions, one gains
some useful threads for exploring the vast Minoan palace of
Piaget's publications.

Like Binet, Piaget, though distinguishing affective from
intellectual aspects of thinking, in fact regards these as inseparable: 'all interaction with the environment involves both a
structuring and a valuation . . . we cannot reason, even in pure
mathematics, without experiencing certain feelings, and conversely, no affect can exist without a minimum of understanding or of discrimination.' Piaget's approach complements that
of Freud, in so far as it concentrates on the cognitive rather
than motivational aspects of thought.

At the roots of Piaget's account of the development of

thinking from infancy onwards lie three main conceptions. First, he treats the new-born infant as equipped cognitively with ready-made modes of sensory organization, exemplified in sucking, looking at lights, vocalizing, listening to sounds, moving its limbs and grasping what touches the palms of its hands. Secondly, Piaget invokes *assimilation*, by which he means, very generally, 'the action of the organism on surrounding objects, in so far as this action depends on previous behaviour involving the same or similar objects'. In Mc. V. Hunt's formulation, psychologically, 'assimilation operates whenever the organism sees something new in terms of something familiar, whenever it acts in a new situation as it has acted in other situations in the past, whenever it invests anything with familiarity (recognition), importance, or value'. As he points out, this would cover the phenomena called by Pavlov 'conditioning' and by Hull and others 'stimulus generalization' or 'response generalization'. But these terms have referred to 'associative or connective relations between stimulus and response'. One might add, from a historical viewpoint, itemized stimuli and responses; for it has been a characteristic of the behaviourist tradition to translate the elementarism of the associationists into physiological or behavioural terms. By contrast, Piaget is thinking in terms of active, centrally organized, structuring of experience, more on the lines advocated by Gestalt psychologists though stopping short of the treatment of insight as essentially unlearnt. By virtue of assimilation, the passively-evoked responses, arising from inborn schemata, develop into the active ones, characteristic of expectation.

Thirdly, Piaget invokes *accommodation*: the process by which ready-made structurings of experience are capable of modification by environment and experience. Hence the development of thinking is worked out, in principle, in terms of initial, relatively simple, organizing processes, which by virtue of assimilation and accommodation are progressively modified and transformed into more subtle and infinitely more complex modes of organization still designated concepts or schemata.

It is not clear to me how this complex thinking comes to be enmeshed with that of other people, unless *either* this rests on 'recurrent sames' in nature, plus species similarities in innate structurings, *or* somewhere in Piaget's voluminous writings there is more genuine allowance for social and shared recognition than would appear on the surface. It is abundantly clear, however, that Piaget treats the exercise of already formed integrated activities (schemata) as intrinsically pleasant. Thus he is not open to the criticism that 'pleasure' is defined only in terms of need or tension reduction: unless 'structuring' is itself a need, which it might be on the evidence of exploratory drives invoked by learning theorists. But Piaget's detailed descriptions of children suggest their positive enjoyment of the exercise of skills, the formation and use of schemata and the restructuring of experience. For Freud, disappointed expectation was our main teacher. For Piaget, we also learn when expectation is fulfilled.

REFERENCES

Numbers in brackets indicate the pages in this book where given references occur

1. Clemen, W. H., *The Development of Shakespeare's Imagery*, London: Methuen, 1951.
2. Eysenck, H. J., *Uses and Abuses of Psychology*, Harmondsworth: Penguin Books, 1953.
3. Flavell, J. H., *The Developmental Psychology of Jean Piaget*, New York and London: Van Nostrand, 1963.
4. Humphrey, George, *Thinking: An Introduction to its Experimental Psychology*, London: Methuen, 1951.
5. Hunt, J. Mc. V., *Intelligence and Experience*, New York: Ronald Press Co., 1961.
6. Jenkins, James, and Paterson, Donald G., Editors, *Studies in Individual Differences*, London: Methuen, 1961, pp. 68 (255-6), 70 (256).
7. Oswald, Ian, *Sleeping and Waking: Physiology and Psychology*, Amsterdam: Elsevier, 1962.
8. Piaget, Jean, *The Psychology of Intelligence*, translated by Malcolm Piercy and D. E. Berlyne, London: Routledge and Kegan Paul, 1950.
9. Spearman, C., *The Abilities of Man, their Nature and Measurement*, London: Macmillan, 1927.

CHAPTER NINE

INSIGHT AND MEDIATION

In a word, since Ideas are both *Unintelligible*, and altogether *Useless*, and (I fear) *Ill Use* is made of them, contrary to the intention of their Authors; it seems but fitting that the *Way of Ideas* should be *lay'd aside*; nay, that the very *Word* which has got such a *Vogue*, should be no longer heard of, unless a good reason may be given why we should use *Such Words* as *no Man understands*.

JOHN SERGEANT, 1700,
quoted by YOLTON[6]

Association theorists know and recognize what one calls insight in man, and contend that they can explain this by their principles just as well as the simplest association (or reproduction) by contiguity. The only thing that follows for animal behaviour is that, where it has an intelligent character, they will treat it in the same way; but not at all that the animal lacks that which is usually called insight in man.

WOLFGANG KÖHLER

IN THIS short chapter I am concerned to do two things. One is to bring in the views on thinking of a sophisticated writer in the tradition of methodological behaviourism, Professor Osgood. The second is to try to say something of the contrast between those who wish to explain thinking and problem-solving assuming only discrimination, and some kind of conditioning, and those, such as Köhler, who invoke some form of 'insight'.

The problem on which Osgood's[4] account of thinking is focused is that of how something becomes a sign. His approach and that of the philosopher Price, outlined in Chapter Ten, are thus complementary. Let us follow Osgood closely in identifying the problem as he sees it.

He starts with a child who says 'Kitty' to a furry four-legged object, but comments that the child's response is no guarantee that the noise 'represents' anything to her. 'Now suppose the child's mother asks, "Where is Kitty?" and she immediately starts searching—in the sunny corner of the porch by the cat's dinner plate. Does "Kitty" now have meaning? Is it functioning as a sign?' It would seem so. The child, says Osgood, 'is responding to a stimulus that is not the object (to the word "Kitty") in a manner that is relevant to the object signified: the child's behaviour is apparently organized and directed by some implicit process initiated by the word'. Osgood's problem is thus to differentiate the conditions under which a pattern of stimulation (which can be anything experiencible, from a gust of cold wind to a Prokofiev piano concerto) is a sign of something else, from those conditions in which it is not.

Still following Osgood, one can state this question more formally so:

$\dot{S}$ = object = any pattern of stimulation which evokes reactions on the part of an organism.

[S] = sign = any pattern of stimulation which is not $\dot{S}$ and yet evokes reaction relevant to S.

How does [S] come to operate in this way?

In the past and recent past, three accounts have been given of the process whereby something observable becomes a sign: that in terms of ideas, that of early behaviourists in terms of Pavlovian conditioning, that in terms of set or disposition. Let us say something briefly of each.

In spite of the trenchant criticism of ideas written in 1700, and quoted at the head of this chapter, explanations of signs in terms of ideas were current until the beginning of this century, and in ordinary life and language still are so. Hence on this theory [S] would become a sign by evoking ideas in the mind of the observer x. Perception of a hammer gives rise to the idea of that object, the word 'hammer' is associated with the perception and, in due season, the word evokes the idea of a hammer in the minds of user and recipient alike. Such a view of signs goes with an approach to language in terms of the exchange and barter of ideas. Experimental psychologists regard this view with misgiving, feeling that a mind-body problem lurks below its surface and that the theory is untestable. It substitutes the word 'idea' for an explanation, presupposing that 'idea' is understood. One might add that, like 'image', the term savours to some of an approach to thinking in terms of elements and states, and this may mask the nature of the processes for which in common speech the word is still needed, e.g. the more complex activities reflected in Binet's examples.

The immediate alternative offered when ideas began to go out of fashion, between 1910 and 1920, was the naïve application of Pavlovian conditioning principles by early behaviourists. On this view, signs achieved their meaning by being conditioned to the same reactions originally made to the objects signified. An object evokes certain behaviour from an animal or human being, e.g. food evokes salivation in a hungry dog and bright light may evoke blinking in a human being. If any other stimulus pattern, e.g. Pavlov's famous bell, is consistently paired with the original object, it becomes conditioned to the same response and thus gets its meaning. To return to the earlier example, the actual cat evokes certain responses in the child and if 'Kitty' is repeatedly said at the same time, 'Kitty' comes to elicit those responses. As Osgood says, the very simplicity of this theory highlights its inadequacy. Signs almost never evoke the same responses as do the objects they represent. The word 'fire' has meaning for the hearer without sending him into wild flight; the word 'apple' has meaning without eliciting chewing or peeling responses.

The third approach in terms of set and disposition is characteristic of Charles Morris, influenced in his turn by Pierce, the logician, and by behaviour theorists such as Tolman and Hull. Osgood summarizes this view as follows: 'Any pattern of stimulation which is not the object becomes a sign if it produces in an organism a "disposition" to make any of the responses previously elicited by the object'. 'Disposition' is a vague term. One can start to unravel its usage in this context by saying, as Morris does, that 'a disposition to respond to something in a certain way is a state of an organism at a given time such that under certain additional conditions the response in question takes place'. To make use of this concept one needs to formulate rules for identifying such dispositions.

One can make a start on this by placing a person or animal in the situation which is alleged to evoke the disposition to operate and see what happens. One then identifies the disposition by the behaviour observed. If, for example, Mr. X is disposed to be irritable when faced with an income tax return, one identifies this one of Mr. X's dispositions by his particular form of swearing and snappiness in this situation. One can then check whether the name of the tax officer operates as a sign by seeing whether it arouses this disposition to be irritable, i.e. some of Mr. X's usual manifestations of irritation are elicited in the circumstances.

But there are obvious weaknesses in this position. Dispositions, in Osgood's view, seem rather like dressed-up versions of 'ideas'. Secondly, is there any reason for supposing that any obvious part of the behaviour pattern appropriate to the real object *is* always elicited by the sign? In Osgood's example, suppose the response to 'apple' is to free-associate the word 'peach', it is weak to argue that this is part of the 'behaviour family' elicited by an apple.

There are other objections that can be levelled against this view. For example, Osgood argues that it fails to differentiate sign-directed behaviour from many instinctive reactions. To my mind, it suffers, too, from the weakness of any theory that does not invoke the capacity to grasp similarities, recurrences and indeed relations of functional dependence boldly at the start. All these forms of recognition are in fact slipped in without scrutiny in such phrases as 'the observed behaviour'. This 'observation' is quite useless unless, for example, on different occasions one can say Mr. X's snappiness to the name 'Mr. Y' is just like, or rather like, that which he shows towards income tax returns.

Osgood's own theory involves a slight short-circuiting of Morris's view. Morris links sign and object via the partial identity of the object-produced and disposition-produced behaviour. Osgood argues, in effect, that the name becomes a sign virtually by eliciting some of the *same* behaviour as the object of which it is a sign. But he adds a rider that this bit of behaviour, presumably a partial revival of what occurred in the first instance, produces a distinctive self-stimulation. This in turn elicits a response that would not occur without previous association of the stimulus, which is acting as a sign, and the object signified.

Symbolically the view in its simplest form can be portrayed and exemplified thus:

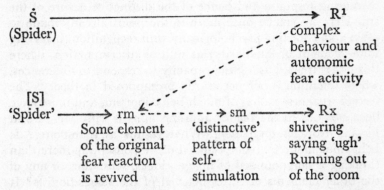

$\dot{S}$
(Spider) $\longrightarrow$ R¹
complex behaviour and autonomic fear activity

[S]
'Spider' $\longrightarrow$ rm $\dashleftarrow\dashrightarrow$ sm $\longrightarrow$ Rx

Some element of the original fear reaction is revived

'distinctive' pattern of self-stimulation

shivering saying 'ugh' Running out of the room

Osgood bases the distinctiveness of sm, the mediating stimulus, set off by rm the mediating response, on the fact that the latter is literally a revival of part of R¹. His theory does allow the end response, of shivering say, to be different from that originally evoked and to depend in the long run on the contiguous occurrence in time (or space) of $\dot{S}$ and [S]. And his schema can be complicated indefinitely to accommodate hierarchies of mediating responses, with end results remote from the overt or covert responses initially touched off by $\dot{S}$. To this extent it is a vast improvement on naïve behaviourism. It could perhaps be made to fit with *active* conceptions of thinking. As it stands, Osgood's approach fits more obviously with the current preference for a foreground rather than hinterland approach to signs. By this I mean that it focuses on the response which a sign elicits from the beholder or receiver. This contrasts with the approach whereby, given a sign, the theorist either inquires into its relation to the object signified or delves in search of that which is consciously, or more often unconsciously, 'expressed' by the user in employing the sign. The interesting bias of communications theory is towards the long-neglected question of the response elicited on the part of the *recipient*. As we shall see, however, in discussing Price, the relation of the user to the sign may be significantly different and too important to leave wholly out of account.

Would Osgood's theory survive the scrutinizing gaze of Binet? This I venture to doubt. It has two weaknesses. One is that there is no satisfactory account of the 'sameness' of the mediating response and hence of the distinctive nature of the sm. Here we return once more to the point already made so often about starting psychologically with recognition (involving some element of familiarity) as well as discrimination, where this last is treated as a basic capacity to respond to differences, whose retention is not necessarily presupposed in theory. The second weakness is that of much behaviourism, and must have been obvious to the reader amusing himself with Mr. X and his tax troubles on p. 272. What counts as a response? Is behaviour made up, compounded of, responses any more than thinking is compounded of images, ideas, sensations or any of the other elements or states beloved of the associationists? It was, and still is, the strength of methodological behaviourism to focus on that which can be observed and with considerable ingenuity quantified. But all the talk of 'responses' suggests these are already itemized by nature: whereas the first head-ache of a first-class experimentalist is often to distil from fluctuating and fluid activities that which he will count as a response of a certain kind. Osgood would be the first to agree with this in practice. But in theory, I am not so sure. For theory seems to need to start with all sorts of discriminating, recognizing, classifying, selecting processes, for which there is little room among behaviourist and semi-behaviourist assumptions.

This leads us to the Gestalt psychologists' approach to thinking, characterized as it is by three fundamental points. First, direct observation, discrimination, recognition, 'insight', are given the full psychological status one would expect from writers of profound social-psychological, experimental and philosophical sophistication, of which Professor Köhler is an outstanding example. In spite of this, the Gestalt notion of 'insight' has caused considerable perplexity. It remains some-what uncertain precisely what Gestalt psychologists claim in asserting that it exists and also whether a case for its existence is established. Without entering in detail into enormously controversial literature, it seems possible to identify broadly the problems on which controversy has centred.

At a simple level, 'insight' looks as though it involves the noticing, recognizing and grasping of relationships which amount to the processes intelligence theorists have defended. Gestalt psychologists, however, do not think in terms of items that are related. Instead, they stress the perceptual grasp of wholes in which, at most, relatively isolable elements and relations are embedded, these taking their character, in part at least, from the nature of the whole in question. For example, middle C takes on a slightly different character in the second inversion from that which it has in the common chord of C major. Gestalt psychologists have been specially interested in the perceptual conditions facilitating or hindering the grasp of the form or structure of a problem to be solved.

Thus, when Köhler[2] made his now famous study of apes in the animal colony in Tenerife, it seemed to him that, initially, an ape could seize on the relevance of two sticks, which if joined together would enable him to bring a banana within reach, only if they lay to hand in a perceptual configuration encouraging formation of a Gestalt, in which the distance between the ape and banana was bridged. In postulating insight as an explanatory process, Köhler stressed the suddenness with which an ape eventually grasped such a principle (after making 'good' as well as bad mistakes), together with 'smoothness' of subsequent performance and effective generalization to comparable situations.

Precisely the same phenomena of sudden drop in mistakes, smooth performance and generalization were noted by Yerkes* in his independent study of a rhesus and an irus male and a young orang-utan. Both investigators, as a result of their studies,

---

* Historically, it is interesting that just prior to the outbreak of World War One Yerkes had been in touch with Professor Rothman of Berlin, who founded the anthropoid station in Tenerife. He was invited to co-operate in studies undertaken there but was prevented from going. Köhler, aged then about twenty-six, went from Berlin to Tenerife in 1913, and was marooned there for the duration. Yerkes, meanwhile, spent part of a sabbatical year in 1915 investigating the problem-solving of a small group of apes in California, in ignorance of the work Köhler was doing.

thought that some of their apes showed insight, by these criteria, in their problem-solving; though there were marked and interesting individual differences in ability as well as in temperament and motivation. Later, when both of these studies were published, however, Yerkes stressed the contribution of previous learning and imitation to insightful behaviour, while Köhler laid more emphasis on immediate perceptual grasp of the problem's structure or form.

It would seem, on the surface, that further differences may have complicated the issue. For example, while Yerkes was probably right in insisting on the relevance of prior experience and imitation before recognition of a relationship difficult for a given species could come into play, Köhler was right in trying to study an ape's problem-solving in a medium more natural to it than that of some of the tasks that Yerkes had used. The contrast between Köhler's methods and those in Thorndike's studies of cats is sharper still. On the basis of these last, evidence only of trial-and-error learning had been claimed. One feels, moreover, that Köhler was defending not only the inherent possibility of noticing, recognizing, and appreciating structure, in effective problem-solving, but something more. In effect, while American investigators, in the empirical tradition, approached the issues in terms of responses evoked from their animals by elements and relations in the problem as presented, Köhler was tacitly guided by a different approach to thought, i.e. one that envisaged the ape as switching, from a relatively passive trial-and-error response, to active integration of data lending themselves inherently to spatio-temporal or causal organization. In Wertheimer's[7] studies of human productive thinking, these and also logical schemata play an important rôle, but it is very difficult to identify precisely what additional implications this active insight involves.

Later discussions have centred on a different issue, namely that between Gestalt psychologists still defending 'insight' and strict behaviourists, of which Yerkes was not one. The points here have been very usefully summarized by Osgood[4] in the light of experimental evidence from both sides. For example, in Tolman and Honzik's familiar experiment, 15 rats learned quickly to take the short route from the starting point to the

Thompson, with hinged cellophane doors replacing the blocks at A and B and sometimes left unlocked. This meant that instead of having to force the animals to explore the main runway initially, they seem to have done so naturally. The results, however, were less clear-cut. Of 11 rats only 2 chose path 3 on the first trial, nine on the second and three trials were needed for all 11 to reach the food.

In still another experiment, Dove and Thompson used blocks with heavily-painted lines which the rats could see from the choice point. The angle of entry from path 2 to path 1 was also changed from 90° to 45°, this entry still being via a hinged cellophane gate that did not permit re-entry of 2 after arrival in path 1. This time no animals chose path 3 on any of three trials. Discussion of these experiments tends to focus on the change introduced by altering the angle of entry from path 2, and not on the possible relevance of making the blocks clearly visible from afar. Conceivably, this may have meant that the rats did not explore path 1 (and so pass the entry point from 2) sufficiently often to grasp the spatial relations between it and the blocks. But whether or not this comment is justified, the issue remains undecided.

It remains to draw attention to two fundamental contributions, from the Gestalt studies of thinking, of particular significance in relation to Binet's evidence of interrelated trains of thought in different media and Price's view of concepts to be discussed in Chapter Ten. First, it is integral to the Gestalt approach that the concept of 'levels' of thinking, with its hierarchical overtones, be replaced by notions of dynamic functional interdependence, drawn from field theory in physics. Such an approach would seem to have the enormous advantage of flexibility. For the co-ordination of processes contributing to sustained thinking—such processes as discriminating, recognizing, imaging, intelligent relating, retaining, recalling and the interesting 'temporal integration' Professor Hearnshaw has suggested but not yet established experimentally to his own satisfaction—would not be imposed by still another thought-process which none of us can identify. Instead, co-ordination might be a function of varying degrees of dynamic relation between such processes as those listed. This is a change with far-reaching implications. Secondly, experimental psychology with a Gestalt orientation offers, as Köhler[3] once remarked, infinite possibilities for studying 'the facts of functional depenence which often lie outside the range of direct awareness'.

REFERENCES

Numbers in brackets indicate the pages in this book where
given references occur

1. Hearnshaw, L. S., 'Temporal Integration and Behaviour', Presidential Address, London: *British Psychological Society Bulletin*, No. 30, September 1956.
2. Köhler, W., *The Mentality of Apes*, translated by Ella Winter, London: Kegan Paul, 1925, Pelican Books, 1957.
3. —— *Dynamics in Psychology*, London: Faber and Faber, 1942.
4. Osgood, Charles E., *Method and Theory in Experimental Psychology*, New York: Oxford University Press, 1960, Chapters 14-16, pp. 605 ff. (276), 619 (277), 697 (273).
5. Yerkes, R. M., *The Mental Life of Monkeys and Apes: A Study of Ideational Behaviour*, Behaviour Monographs, Vol. 3, Number 1, Cambridge, Mass., Holt, 1916.
6. Yolton, J. W., *John Locke and the Way of Ideas*, London: Oxford University Press, 1956.
7. Wertheimer, Max, *Productive Thinking*, New York: Harper, revised edition, 1959.

CHAPTER TEN

CONCEPTS AND RECOGNITION

> . . . if there were no recurrent characteristics, *or* no resemblances between different objects—whichever way you choose to put it—there would be no conceptual cognition, and no use of general symbols either.
>
> H. H. PRICE

> Logic is the mirror of thought, and not vice versa
> JEAN PIAGET

THE PSYCHOLOGICAL controversy over imageless thinking that occurred in the first ten years of this century was never resolved. This is partly, I have implied, because underlying it was the conceptual problem of whether thinking should be treated as an active (or passive) form of awareness, fairly closely analogous to visual inspection, or whether it was more often a form of activity in which processes akin to moving, grasping, assimilation and re-ordering predominated over those of a scanning nature. To those committed to the inspectionist view, 'imageless thinking' may have seemed nonsense, partly because it was tantamount to inspection of nothing. Those moving, later, towards an action or behavioural approach to thought, did not always avoid the danger of throwing out the recognizing baby with its bath water, leaving a sponge reacting in its place.

Disagreements among those, in this controversy, who relied mainly on methods of introspection, contributed to the rise of methodological behaviourism; with its insistence on studying cats, rats and people from the outside, and its temptation to equate thinking with muscular and/or verbal responses, both of which lend themselves to relatively public scrutiny. Historically, Thorndike initiated the study of animals in puzzle boxes, this line of approach fusing shortly after with Pavlov's work on conditioning in dogs. Meanwhile, the inadequacies of a theory of perception, based on the impact of atomistic sensations, contributed, as is well known, to the gradual rise of the Gestalt approach to psychology, with its rejection of a purely associationist account of thinking.

In the previous chapter we briefly considered some points at issue in the later, but also prolonged and still unsettled, controversy between defenders of 'insight' in successful problem-solving and those seeking to trace the experimental findings to some form of conditioning. Though speculation in this complex field is extremely risky, it seems at least worth wondering whether unrecognized traditions and unstated assumptions have again confused the situation. For example, it has been clear for long that much of modern learning theory, so far as it rests on some form of conditioning, is none other than association, by contiguity in time and place, translated into physiological and experimental terms.[6] The noticing of similarities and differences is just silently assumed by the observers. It has long been realized, too, that the inborn, perceptual configurations, which Gestalt psychologists defend, are relics of the innate ideas, to which Locke objected, brought back for scrutiny from the tradition of Kant. But in their Kantian, and more modern, form these innate patternings are not items in the *content* of experience, so much as constitutional ways of structuring that which is the product of organized external stimulation and an embodied, perceiving, human being. Locke, were he still alive, would have little reason for rejecting the Gestalt evidence for innate structuring of the visual field in terms of figure and ground. Like many contemporary psychologists, for example Piaget, he might reserve judgment on the claims for more than this, e.g. for a whole range of perceptual constancies. But Locke, as a doctor, would hardly doubt that the physiological constitution possessed by species or by individuals sets limits to the perceptual capacities that they have. The relevance of this platitude will be more apparent later.

In relation, more specifically, to insight versus conditioning, it is possible to wonder whether *all* forms of insight, as defended by Köhler[7] and Wertheimer, must consist of the all or none process sometimes implied. Does insight cease to be insight if it is sometimes the outcome of learning? Spinoza[16] half-implied that the third degree of knowledge might arise from the second, though between the first and third the difference was irreducible. Have the Gestalt psychologists, in stressing the difference between the first and second level, overlooked the possible contribution of learning in moving from the second to the third? We may summarize the relevant questions in the following way: Are the Gestalt psychologists right in treating some sudden, smoothly operating and generalizable problem-solving processes as different in principle from 'conditioned' responses or habits, because without assuming certain forms of noticing, discriminating, recognizing and grasping relationships no experimentation is meaningful? Like Spinoza, do Köhler and Wertheimer, when writing of insight, sometimes have in mind the intelligence in action beyond which we cannot go? Are they right, too, in supposing that such processes are also involved in high-grade symbolic thought? But are they misleading, or perhaps mistaken, in so far as they seem to imply that learning is irrelevant to the emergence of such processes at a higher level? Could the Kantian tradition have too strong a hold and would a different philosophical approach to concepts clarify any of the issues involved? With these questions in mind, let us turn to a subtle, and psychologically-minded, living philosopher writing in the English empirical tradition, to see what illumination we can extract.

Professor H. H. Price's *Thinking and Experience*[12] was first published in 1953. It was reviewed appreciatively by Professor C. D. Broad.[2] Its second edition appeared in 1962. For light on current thinking of thinking in its historical context, we need to extract three main themes from Price's rich store: his elucidation of rival philosophical treatments of concepts; his own wide conception of thinking, rooted, as he believes it to be, in the process of recognition; and, finally, his version of a dispositional treatment of concepts, differing as it does from Osgood's, sketched in Chapter Nine.

Price sets the stage for us historically, by contrasting the view he designates 'classical' with that emerging, broadly between 1910 and 1920, when a shift towards dispositional treatments of concepts began to take place. Something of the background to this change we have seen. On the earlier viewpoint Price comments:

> By classical I do not just mean Greek or Graeco-Roman. It is true that this conception of thinking did originate in Greek times, and Plato, or perhaps Socrates, was the first exponent of it. But it continued to be accepted in one form or another until the second decade of the twentieth century. Its essential tenet is that thinking is differentiated from other forms of cognition not only by being a special sort of activity, but also by having a special sort of *objects*, which are variously called universals, concepts, or abstract ideas. Thinking is conceived to be the inspection of such 'intelligible objects' and of the relationships between them. Those who hold this view would not of course deny that symbols, e.g. words or images, are very often used in thinking. But it would be said that we *can* think without them, and sometimes do. Moreover, it is held that their function, when we do use them, is a merely auxiliary or ancillary one. . . . When symbols are used in communication it is held that they direct the hearer's or reader's attention upon the same intelligible objects to which the producer of the symbols is attending or was attending at the time when he produced them.[12]

I believe it is fair to amplify this statement of Price's by adding that writers in the empirical tradition, such as Locke, whom we have discussed, tended to suppose that such abstract ideas were acquired by a process of abstraction (or subtraction) from particular sensations or corresponding images, whether simple or complex. Rationalists tended not to inquire very closely into how such concepts were formed, because their interest was epistemological and not in developmental psychology. Hence they tended simply to exemplify abstract ideas, often by reference to those involved in mathematics, which offered the best illustrations of 'clarity' and 'distinctness'.

The restriction of thinking to either 'concept discovery' or concept formation has been, until very recently, a characteristic slant of experimental psychologists of all persuasions.[14] This was illustrated in Bruner's[3] *A Study of Thinking*, though his latest studies are taking a different turn. It was also assumed in Hull's[5] famous study of written Chinese characters. In this experiment, 144 Chinese characters were made from twelve different groups, each member of which shared a common feature, presented with varying complications. With each of the twelve common features was paired a nonsense syllable on initial exposure. The subjects' acquisition of such 'concepts' was assessed by means of (a) their ability to name them as they were shown in different contexts; (b) their drawing these common features; (c) the amount of prompting needed during the learning process. One result was the quantitative demonstration that such learning is gradual. Since Hull was endeavouring to be a strict behaviourist, no use of introspection was made in this study, though it is patent that Hull himself must have been able to judge his examples of 'common feature' to be similar in order to use them at all. This comment returns us to Price, showing the two very different philosophical approaches to what is involved in grouping items together as alike.

On the first theory, that of universals, there is indeed a 'common feature' shared by all members of the class that possess it. One form of this approach is traceable to Plato's doctrine of *universalia ante rem*. Price refrains from discussing this in detail in view of its remoteness from current common sense. The other classical form of the theory goes back to Aristotle's *universalia in rebus*, which treated recurrent characteristics as somehow *in* the objects exemplifying them, without commitment to the unpalatable Platonic belief in these universals as theoretically inspectable entities of a different logical (and ontological) type from the particular objects characterized.

The second theory, equally possible in principle on purely philosophical grounds, depends less obviously on the notion of 'common characteristics', and the so-called process of abstraction whereby they are filtered out. Instead, it involves that of taking a specific perceptual item and deriving the notion of a class of similar objects in terms of their resemblance in a certain respect to the item chosen. The emphasis thus lies not on identifying common predicable qualities but on assessing degrees of resemblance to (and differences from) an exemplar, or very closely resembling group of exemplars, taken as a norm. Assimilation in virtue of perceived similarity plays a more obvious rôle than identification of an inherent quality.

As Price points out, a weakness of the first theory, designated the philosophy of universals, is that it gives no obviously satisfactory account of the different degrees in which members of acceptable classes resemble each other. Its strength lies in the ease of handling it linguistically; an ease, one ventures to add, which may well be related to the grammatical structure of languages influenced by Greek. The second approach, that of resemblances, can more easily accommodate practical conventional agreement on the degree of dissimilarity that calls for a change of grouping. Its weakness lies in explaining what is a 'specific respect'. It is true, in fact, that anything perceived is complex. The simplest patch of colour, for example, is not without some shape. All distinguishable sounds have some degree of duration, pitch and intensity. So to the process of qualitative identifying, presupposed by the first theory, there must correspond those of numerical identification, recognition, discrimination and assimilation, presupposed by the second.

Psychologically, the significant fact is that the philosophy of resemblances lends itself much more easily to the treatment of concepts on dispositional lines. There is less temptation to treat the likeness of a dozen wild daffodils in terms of an 'abstract idea' that must somehow be 'before the mind', or capable of inspection, when one thinks of them in the winter. The theory does not exclude, in principle, any of the kinds of imaging psychologists freely admit to exist, whatever the experimental difficulties of studying them. Many psychological experiments on concept formation *seem* to have been limited by the tacit assumption that the 'common feature' view is the only one, even though the language of 'ideas' has been avoided.

The possible advantage to the psychologist of the 'philosophy of resemblances' leads us on to consider our second main theme from Price's book. This is his broadening of the notion of thinking (and of concepts) so that at one extreme simple sign-guided behaviour would exemplify an element of both, and at the other extreme there may be as complex a set of operations in symbols as anyone likes to suggest. In fact, Price is so concerned with arguing that sign cognition, within many animals' capacity, is elementary thinking, and with the intricacies of differentiating symbols from signs, that he omits detailed consideration of high-grade thought. Such thinking, happily, is exemplified in his book. One can but hope that he will one day reflect in print on the exercise of his skill. At the root of thinking, thus broadly described, Price insists that there lies the process of recognition. Here we must try to show more specifically what appears to be involved.

Price is at pains to distinguish two kinds of recognition. First, there is that of something as a member of a species, e.g. a given car as a Jaguar. Secondly, there is recognition of a recurrent object, illustrated in noting the same car (or its owner) once more ahead in a traffic jam. Of these two modes of recognition, which Broad conveniently dubs 'specific' and 'numerical', the specific seems the simpler, as the numerical tends to involve some sort of belief about the object's continuation. What Price would do with recurrent flashes, as from a lighthouse, I am not sure; though common sense would suggest belief in a continuant, human or mechanical, producing these illuminations.

Price then makes a further and fundamental distinction between primary and secondary recognition, getting into trouble from Broad, who doubts if numerical recognition could ever be primary. To discuss this point would take us too far afield. Suffice it that, for Price, primary recognition is a compound of noticing and retention. It is a little unfortunate that he does not elaborate on 'noticing', for he seems to need to build in, at this level, the possibility of primitive responsiveness to similarities and differences, when these occur simultaneously in a sensory field, a situation he does not fully consider. It is hard to see that retention is involved when one inspects the likenesses and differences among the petals of a small yellow chrysanthemum, well in the centre of the visual field, during a momentary gleam of winter sunlight. Indeed, Price comes near to admitting this still more primitive responsiveness when he writes:

We shall have to suppose, I believe, that the human mind has an innate (unacquired, unlearned) tendency to notice

and remember—to be 'struck by' and 'impressed by'—
this special sort of likeness situation, where there is one
likeness in the midst of many unlikenesses.[12]

To check whether noticing or responding to likeness and
difference either does or can occur without an element of
retention, seems to defeat all possibilities of experimentation,
retention being presupposed in any study that could be devised.

Later on Price goes further in implying that embedded in
primary recognition is a noticing too primitive for the distinction of veridical or non-veridical to apply. In this implication
Broad senses either thin ice or a tautology; while the psychologist diagnoses epistemological worries over which he is not
concerned—having become inured professionally to the possibility of being wrong at any level of response, however
primitive, if it is taken to inform about the external world.
There is no difficulty in granting, however, that retention plays
a fundamental rôle in any recognition (or discrimination) that
involves a time interval, however short. Provisionally, we may
further grant Price's claim that primary recognition, involving
the minimal level of abstraction (or stimulus generalization),
may relate to simple or very complex combinations of characteristics (including qualities and relations) and usually, if not
always, antedates our powers of considering these in the absence
of their perceptual presentation. Such recognition could, as
Price suggests, have different degrees of vagueness, and amount to
a mere hint of familiarity or to an awareness of having experienced x before without being able to recall when or where. In
Price's view, primary recognition and feelings of strangeness are
complementary opposites. He adds the insightful psychological
point, that a process of recognition involving selective or
distorted noticing and/or failure of accurate retention, and
therefore faulty if taken as a source of information about the
past, could still be the starting point of an elaborate piece of
conceptualization. One may comment that this state of affairs,
far from uncommon in daily life, is often involved in prejudice
or the illusions, delusions and hallucinations of mental illness.

Price's secondary recognition is *one species* of sign cognition,
which, in turn, is responding to x as a sign of y, when y is not

sensorily present and the conjunction of x and y has had to be learnt. 'Sign cognition is the characteristic mode of mental operation at a level of mental development where cognition and action are not yet sharply differentiated'.[12] Price is emphatic that simple forms of sign cognition are within the power of animals. In this he has ample support from animal ethology and learning theory, though the latter would regard the phrases 'sign cognition' and 'secondary recognition' as much too reminiscent of 'conscious cognizing' to be acceptable. I hazard the guess that though Price refers respectfully to 'releasers', he is not treating the secondary recognition of mice and men as rooted in discriminations open to a clinical thermometer. He implies that noticing, primary and secondary recognition need not be conscious but also that they very often are.

Broad underlines four features of note in Price's discussion of sign cognition: (1) it involves two aspects, an immediate sense perception of some sort and a conceptual element; (2) it is in principle independent of words or images, though it could involve either or both; (3) it is closely bound with relevant practical behaviour *with reference to* the significate; (4) the ensuing reaction, whether overt or private, remains closely tied to sensory or quasi-sensory experience. Broad also stresses the learning presupposed and then gazes with deadly clarity at the crucial question implied by (1), namely: what is the nature of the 'conceptual' element? Having noted this problem, and left it unsolved, he moves on to agree with Price that three other features of sign cognition are such that the relations of an individual to the significate resemble those in what we should 'unhesitatingly call thinking'. These features are: (1) liability to error; (2) any reaction elicited is directed to something *absent*, i.e. not sensorily present at the moment; (3) some degree of abstraction is involved, e.g. a cat responds to a *range* of mouselike smells or movements, though it is granted that the smells or movements are precise in a given case. Finally, Broad lends guarded support to Price's supposition that, psychologically, something analogous to logical concepts such as negation, alternation (either—or) and condition (that will occur if . . .) can be detected in some sign-guided responses. It is worth adding the comment that when Price hazards that 'disappointed expectation' is the origin of notions of negation, he is in a far stronger position, having clearly accepted recognition of similarities and differences at the start, than was Freud when trying, as we saw in Chapter Five, to tackle a closely analogous problem.

We must now try to come to grips with that suspicious-looking 'conceptual element'. To do this we must scrutinize Price's condensed and not entirely clear discussion of the conditions under which the significate is effective though absent. The reader will have noted that this is consonant with Thurstone's treatment of thought as arising when overt action is blocked, i.e. the response is not entirely evoked by immediate stimulation. Secondly, in scrutinizing Price's views, we are approaching Osgood's[10] problem from the opposite end and with a rather more generous allowance of basic processes.

To do justice to Price we must invoke some more of his distinctions, namely those between short- and long-range signs and between strong and weak signs, emphasizing, as he does, that the distinctions are themselves different and by no means always correlated. We also need his differentiation of predictive, postdictive and juxtadictive signs, dependent on whether the significate is in the future, the past or the present. The distinction of short- and long-range then refers to the time interval in predictive and postdictive signs, while strength and weakness refer to the objective reliability of the signs in question (rosy-fingered dawn implies strongly that the sun is about to rise), and/or to the extent of the perceiver's learning what is correlated and/or to his credulity. Strictly, Price should also include the objective intensity of the stimulus and the state of the perceiver's sensory functioning. The drowsy observer may miss the first pale streak in the sky. This brings into focus the fact that Price is restricting his discussion to stimuli that succeed in impinging, though not necessarily to those doing so at a conscious level.

Given this equipment of distinctions, Price then argues that the conditions under which a person's responses, overt or otherwise, cease to be immediately stimulus-bound, and become directed by the non-presented significate, are a function of the interest of the percipient in that significate, and the temporal range and relative strength of the sign in question (whether that strength is objective or subjectively assessed we can now leave aside, for convenience). If the sign is strong and the significate impinges immediately there is 'no time to think'. Lengthen the time interval and weaken the sign or the interest, and the situation alters. Price's exposition nevertheless is difficult, partly because it is not, here, well-exemplified and partly because, in a psychologist, it arouses ruminations on the conditions in which the perceiver would probably forget all about the significate and his responses would become bound by other signs or stimuli. Although in his book as a whole Price gives due weight to retention, in this particular context his little word 'interest' covers the whole psychology of motivation, while straight retention, dependent as it probably is on necessary if not sufficient physiological conditions, does not get adequate stress. Let us work out an example in order to show some of the points at issue.

A motorist drives along a route where there is an awkwardly small and dangerous roundabout at the intersection of two main roads. The initial warning sign of a roundabout is small and stationed a very long way in advance of its significate. On Price's theory, a set of processes relevant to the roundabout would be initiated by the sign, (a) if it is seen, (b) if it is strong, in virtue of the highway code, which normally it is, (c) if the motorist is experienced. These processes would develop, the sign being no longer in view, if the motorist also had a strong interest in avoiding the dangers of that particularly awkward junction, which he knows. They might develop thanks to a strong habitual interest in safety. They could include moving one foot towards the clutch, lightening pressure on the accelerator, visual imaging of the roundabout in question, verbalizing about 'that nasty junction', etc. In virtue of the unobtrusive long-range sign, however, the motorist with little training, habitual or immediate interest, and/or poor retention might abandon these preparations. He then comes to deal with the roundabout in a thoroughly 'stimulus-bound' emergency manner and may, very rightly, be branded as 'thoughtless'.

What has Price's theory got that is not covered by Osgood's?

Frank admission of discrimination and recognition of similarities so that expectation makes sense; possibly more than this, which we will see in discussing signs and symbols. Meanwhile, this point leads us directly to Price's treatment of concepts as systems of recognitional capacities, whose operation may be revealed in ways quite other than the classical inspection of 'common features', abstract ideas or images, though imaging* as a process is far from excluded by Price. This conception of thinking is also quite other than that which restricts it to operations on words or symbols obedient to rules and without an obvious means of cashing these operations in images or percepts. While Price is emphatic on the rôle of symbols in highly-developed thought, he is equally insistent that ostensive definition is a prerequisite of an intelligible symbolism. To these considerations we will also return later.

In what ways is the existence of these non-inspectional concepts manifested? Price refers to at least eight which it is convenient to extract and illustrate. I have ventured occasionally to substitute others for Price's examples.

The operation of concepts as systems of recognitional capacities may be seen in:

(1) *States of sensitization, vigilance or expectation*
   Exemplified in: the mountain walker's sensitization to signs confirming or negating the likelihood of a storm, if he has seen a flash; the motorist's vigilant watching for a child, cat or dog, on alert by a low movement beyond a parked van; the housewife's expectancy at the click of her gate at the time when her husband usually returns.

* I have adopted this Ryle[13]–Price form of reference in order to avoid all discussion of the status of these supposed entities. Imaging corresponds nicely to Armande's brilliant phrase *pensée imagée* (p. 309). It carries no alarming metaphysical implications, and allows us to indulge in this process in all modalities, as richly as is convenient—without being hag-ridden by hallucinations. Broad[2] remarks that 'visual images do resemble pictures enough to make the description of them as "mental pictures" far more illuminating than misleading to anyone who is not either woefully silly or wilfully naughty'. Psychologically, however, the analogy does encourage forgetfulness of other *kinds* of imagery, e.g. auditory, olfactory, tactile or kinaesthetic.

(2) *Recognition of instances to which the capacity is linked*

Exemplified in: the child's successful rummaging for his teddy or a biscuit, though he may not yet know the words for either.

(3) *Natural and other sign cognition and the actions or incipient actions characteristic of sign-guided behaviour*

Exemplified in: the recognition that black clouds mean rain, that is revealed in fumbling for or fishing a mackintosh out of a rucksack. It is possible, as in the example given, for the person's response to be unwitting.*

(4) *Production and recognition of 'quasi-instantiative' particulars, whether images or physical replicas (including dumb show and other mimetic behaviour)*

Exemplified in: a small child pointing to a cat in a story book, bringing his toy cat when asked what he saw in a house or saying 'miaow' to some cat-like object.

The concept of 'cat', or whatever it is, need not of course be the one generally accepted by the public. A toddler of twenty-two months passionately insists that a particular fluffy dog presented at Christmas is in fact a *pussy*. This is on the basis, it would seem, of primary recognition of specially furry experiences closely resembling those evoked by an unusual toy cat in her possession. Adult intervention and explanation quell the cries of 'pussy', but the child toddles off insistently miaowing under her breath. From the psychologist's point of view the facts suggest responses already systematized by virtue of earlier experiences. But the systematization is not yet on the lines fully shared by adults. What is *not* implied is face-to-face inspection of the 'abstract idea' of a cat.

(5) *Detection of inadequacies in exemplars produced under* (4) *and substitution of others more adequate*

Exemplified in: a small child rejecting a Playbox biscuit on which the legs of a horse are missing and choosing a biscuit with an animal better designed.

* The distinction between (1) and (3) is at most only one of degree.

(6) *Production of generic images, both of the Galtonian variety and the particular which is incomplete*

The first of these is difficult to exemplify and there is some considerable doubt about Galton's finding. Presumably, however, we can allow under this heading images such as Freud discusses, roughly corresponding to Galton's composite photographs, also vague schemata capable of determination in various ways. Some people may experience an ill-defined sketch of Trafalgar Square, accompanied or followed by a series of much more precise 'shots' of it from different angles, when this place is mentioned.

(7) *Production of real-life instances and the detection and correction of their inadequacies*

Price remarks that however complete one's concept of a cat or an earthquake one may not be able to produce one. But suppose one asks a golfer what a mashie shot is, he may do more than answer in words or imitate. 'Without a word, he goes into his bedroom, fetches a mashie and a golf ball, places the ball on the lawn, and lofts it gracefully over the College Chapel.'

(8) *Production and understanding of words and other non-instantiative symbolic particulars (e.g. gesture symbols) through associative linkages established initially by ostensive definition*

Exemplified in: a five-year-old child's cautious identification of x (not seen for some time) as 'the lady who looked after us when we played with toys'.

The incomplete description cited shows the amount of shared experience that may be necessary to ensure common reference on the part of speaker and hearer. Price's insistence on ostensive definition as being a prerequisite of an intelligible symbolism gains ample support from those studying children's acquisition of language. He is right also to stress that an understanding of pointing is presupposed, and, virtually, that mistakes can creep in all along the line. A child actually surveying an antlered stag in a park may cry out excitedly 'A big hat!' and momentarily fox the slow-witted adult on what is the focus of attention. But as Price says: 'it is the capacity for making mistakes, not the incapacity of it, which is the mark of the higher stages of intelligence'.

Is such an approach psychologically viable? Only the fool-hardy would venture agreement or disagreement in view of the complexity of the issues involved. While granting its initial attraction let us bring into focus some of these complexities. A question raised by Mundle,[9] also reviewing Price, plunges us *in medias res*: how, in his view, are the different manifestations of a concept related to each other? For convenience of exposition, I will deal with this problem from two different angles, according to whether the concept is, as it were, discovered because 'grounded in nature' (Locke's[8] 'real essence'), and according to whether it is a concept invented for social or scientific con-venience (Locke's 'nominal essence'). In the second case, we are dealing with concepts which are constituted in the process of thinking and whose relation to perceptual phenomena may be very indirect indeed.

Approaching from the first angle, many people's spontaneous answer to Mundle's query would be at the level of rough and ready realism. There are more things in heaven and earth than are dreamed of in philosophy, and some of these lend them-selves to the recognizing, discriminating, classifying processes Price explicitly allows us. The similarities (and dissimilarities) of dandelions amongst themselves, and their broad differences from the sparrows in a neighbouring bush, are not merely the result of man imposing his perceptual schemata upon nature. Such common sense is doubted only by philosophers and pheno-menologists whose incipient megalomania tempts them to suggest that man creates, *unaided*, his conceptual world. This is not to deny the active, structuring, nature of perception, on which current psychologists lay much stress. It is only to say that nature facilitates this activity, and without this aid we should get nowhere conceptually. Price, on such a view, *could* reply to Mundle that the different manifestations of a child's particular concept are earthed, as it were, in the dandelions on the lawn. If making this answer at all, he would word it in a far more elegant form, because of the philosophical puzzles about the concept of 'physical object'.

Aside from this philosophical issue, certain aspects of the psychological controversy over insight and learning are relevant here. While psychologists do not question, still less doubt, the existence of external objects (one can imagine them certifying each other for this), there are at least two different approaches to the perceptual constancies, which provide in part the basis for our belief in these entities. Gestalt psychologists argue for an inborn hierarchy of potential calibrations, or states of neuro-psychic equilibrium, between the perceiving organism and the organized system of impinging stimuli constituting, as it were, the *Ding an sich*. Here we see the extension of the Kantian tradition, mentioned earlier, with a kind of cognitive homoeostatic principle superimposed. 'Insight', at a perceptual level, is thus the sudden re-structuring of a dynamic perceptual field, such that a state of equilibrium is attained between perceiver and perceived. Insight at a higher level is *in principle* the same.

Opposed to this is the approach of Piaget,[11] suspicious alike of Kantian principles extended so far, and, indeed, also of the evidence that the perceptual constancies are as constant as the Gestalt psychologists maintain. In these doubts, Piaget would be supported by many psychologists less aware of the inherent oddity of the Gestalt epistemology, which, like Spinoza's, seems to leave no effective room for error. Piaget, and many others with him in rejecting a naïve sensationism or reflexology, would lay much more stress on the rôle of learning in acquiring the concepts needed for operating in the external world. Such learning would be rooted for Piaget in processes alike in many ways to those invoked by Price. For example, recognition as we saw in Chapter Eight, forms part of Piaget's 'assimilation'. Piaget, more than Price, considers the modification of an established system of responses (Price's 'concept') under his heading of 'accommodation'. Piaget's restriction of 'conceptual thought' to what Price regards as full-dress, symbolic, logical thinking seems less happy. It suggests that Piaget might still be guided by the 'philosophy of universals', whereas that of resemblances would stand his developmental approach in better stead.

But if a theory invoking old-fashioned public physical objects is inadequate, and one relying on perceptual constancies is disallowed, Price's answer to Mundle's question seems to need a fuller account of 'pointing'. This, indeed, he begins to develop in terms of an unlearned tendency to curiosity about the spatial context of that which catches our attention. On the other hand, he does not discuss what appear to be the social psychological prerequisites of two different people's concepts ('systematized recognition capacities') having a common reference. Nor, so it seems, does Piaget fully meet this theoretical point, in spite of his concentration on the processes whereby children acquire their conceptual grasp of the external world.

Approaching Mundle's query in terms of concepts avowedly constitutive, i.e. created to coordinate data, we are led into Price's intricate discussion of the relation of signs and symbols. These last can be identified, for the moment, as sounds, shapes or marks, whether types or tokens, used in a systematic fashion in communication. If I have understood Price correctly, he is attacking an approach very familiar to psychologists. It is the argument that because symbols (e.g. words) are learnt, in part at least, by a prolonged process of association and/or conditioning, their function is analogous to that of any learned sign, e.g. that black clouds mean rain. The problem of treating symbolic thinking as a high-grade version of sign cognition, so it is argued, presents no special difficulty in principle, and a pseudo question is raised in supposing otherwise. Humphrey has maintained a position such as this. Price's criticism rests on the inference that this is to treat all thinking as analogous to interpreting natural signs and the relation of the *user* to the sign is left out.* It is not denied that some of our thinking, publicly performed in actions or words, or privately in these and other media, falls into the category of natural sign interpretation. One might feel, indeed, that it is the besetting sin (and the virtue) of psychologists to treat everything they themselves dream, imagine, say or do as a form of natural sign, the significance of which needs divining by delving—a virtue in so far as a saving scepticism may creep in when the signs seem unusually oracular.† However, the nub, as I see it, of Price's difficult discussion

* That the relation may be different is also implied in some of the odd phenomena found in aphasia.

† But the mental set may have slanted interest away from 'active thinking' for a long time.

is: what is the function of signs (?symbols) in the difficult process of concept *creation*?

This introduces us to more complexity still. There is a sense in which Price, too good a philosopher to be wholly consistent at the expense of a possible truth, is committed to saying that while all sign cognition* exemplifies thinking, in some sign *usage* there is a process more thoughtful.

> Sign cognition is a form of thinking . . .; it is one of the ways in which concepts manifest themselves. But what sort of thinking is it? One hesitates to appear to use the distinction between 'passive' and 'active', because these terms have been so heavily charged with emotion. . . . But if we can treat the distinction between passive and active as a distinction of degree, and disinfect it of its emotional aura, then we have to say that sign cognition is a *relatively* passive attitude, less active than other forms of thinking. A being who could understand signs, but could get no further, would certainly be thinking. But yet we should hesitate to call him a 'thinker'. This is because his thinking is something imposed on him from without, dependent on perceptual cues. He thinks, but he does not think for himself. The initiative is not in his hands. . . . And all this is still true when the signs happen to be the sounds, gestures, marks on paper, diagrams, etc., produced by other human organisms.[12]

Price skilfully avoids the vexed question of 'intention', though here and there one suspects its relevance is implied. One wonders, too, how low in the biological scale he would allow that *thinkers* can occur. What of the bird emitting a warning note while the cat lurks in the tulips, and stopping when a human being goes out to collar the cat? Would Price maintain, and would Thorpe[15] agree, that the bird thus protecting the area nestlings is very nearly a *thinker*?

It would seem, psychologically, that for describing the creation of concepts rather than the acquisition of those already culturally formed, recognition, discrimination and acquired

---

* This is in cases where recognition lies at the root. The clinical thermometer is not capable of 'sign cognition'—that is, if I interpret Price correctly.

verbal or allied skills do not suffice. However useful a rôle these, and even the habit of syntactical rule-following may play, the essence of Price's thinking, he clearly believes, is not habitual. Indeed, the original thinker is the one who effectively challenges the linguistic rules, without breaking them so far as to be incomprehensible.[4]

Again, only the foolhardy would hazard what else is involved besides the processes Price specifically mentions. Just in the last few years, psychologists have begun to turn once more to consider creative thinking and the literature already grows apace. Meanwhile, irrespective of accepting his theoretical assumptions, we may start by invoking some of the processes Freud distilled and described—projection, displacement, condensation and the like, together with those which Binet's writers and chess players revealed. We have, in short, to consider all the means we use to sift and analyse a problem and to crystallize complex attitudes and emotions, including personally-valid comparison and the physical changes that may form part of this total process. Professor Harding,[4] by use of analogy, has hinted at what may be involved. Historically, we may detect the wheel that Binet[1] re-started to spin showing some sign of coming full circle. It may well be the whole man who is the thinker.

Like that of Price, Harding's subtle discussion cannot possibly be summarized. We can, however, extract three points of special relevance. The hint that physical processes are not irrelevant to thought is implied in the following. Harding, contrasting other types of thinking with the thought involved in solving a problem already defined or presented in cognitive terms, remarks:

> Much of our thinking is not of this [latter] kind. It consists rather in the recognition of our own motives, the exploring of our interests, the formulation of desires and intentions, the definition and re-definition of attitudes and preferences. Bodily states of need and of conflict between needs, states of contentment, satiety, discomfort, gradually make their way into awareness, where they appear as more or less specific desires and attitudes. On their way towards formulation all these impulses are brought into some

degree of relation, tangential or intimate, with possibilities revealed by present perception, with memories of past occasions and premonitions of consequences, with conceptual systems, sentiments, moral codes, rules of logical thought and so on.

Both the emergent impulses and the processes that modify them may exist in modes far different from words or imagery; these latter forming a late stage of their definition.[4]

Under these different modes he includes, among other things, expressive movements, widely illustrated and defined so as to cover the intimate gesturing of the body and even the blenching and blushing of the gut.

Such an approach is compatible with Price's dispositional treatment of concepts as involving recognition; at least in so far as, for both writers, concepts cease to be entities 'lodged in the head' and become systems to whose manifestation physical changes may be integral and of which overt movements may be part. That a concept may be created in the original handling of a common medium, with its own rich implications and laws, is further implied in Harding's discussion of Eliot's *Burnt Norton*.

One could say, perhaps, that the poem takes the place of the ideas of 'regret' and 'eternity'. Where in ordinary speech we should have to use those words, and hope by conversational trial-and-error to obviate the grosser misunderstandings, this poem is a newly created concept, equally abstract and vastly more exact and rich in meaning. It makes no statement, it is no more 'about' anything than an abstract term like 'love' is about anything: it is a linguistic creation. And the creation of a new concept, with all the assimilation and communication of experience that that involves, is perhaps the greatest of linguistic achievements.[4]

Finally, referring to Freud's confusing tendency to include, as 'unconscious', processes constitutionally uninspectable by their owner, as well as those dissociated or repressed because of threat, Harding employs an illuminating metaphor involving distance as well as depth. In Harding's writing the watcher is still perhaps too prominent wholly to please a philosophical critic with more time to think of also identifying, in turn, with the bed of the sea, the troubled or peaceful waters, the ships, or the active sailors supposedly there, or even to remember von Schubert's little boat, riding at anchor while the pilot sleeps. But given this slight shift of emphasis, the metaphor clearly leads us where we want to go:

> We stand at the harbour of our mind and watch flotillas of ideas far out at sea coming up over the horizon, already in formation of a sort; and though we can re-order them to a great extent on their closer approach, we cannot disregard the organization they had before they came in sight. They are all submarines, partly under water the whole time and capable of submerging entirely at any point and being lost to sight until analytic techniques undo the repression. But it constitutes a fundamental difference whether an idea is out of mind because it has been forced to dive or because it has not yet come up over the horizon. Sometimes repressed ideas may be close in-shore, forming the co-conscious that interested Morton Prince. Others may be both under water and at a great distance; they find expression in some sorts of dreaming, especially the sorts that have most interested the Jungians. And in creative work great numbers of ideas, more or less organized, are simply out of sight beyond the horizon and can be brought into view only through the redisposition we make amongst the in-shore mental shipping that we *can* see and control.[4]

It is time to close this long discussion with four summary comments. The first is that Price's dispositional approach to conceptual thinking in terms of (i) a philosophy of resemblances, (ii) processes of noticing similarities and differences in qualities and relations, recognition and retention, *might* encompass all that the Gestalt psychologists wish to defend by 'insight', without so elaborate a Kantian superstructure. Secondly, this approach would seem to be compatible with considerable experience and learning being required before recognition of relations, and their transfer to other conditions, can occur at a high level of complexity. This is specially apparent in the *creation* of concepts, in which other basic processes beyond those discussed by Price are almost certainly involved. Thirdly, Price's insistence on the differences in the relation between signs and their users on the one hand, and signs and recipients on the other, is very important and lends itself to development. But, finally, there is need to ask what social psychological assumptions would seem essential before the understanding of 'pointing', and the communication Price takes for granted, are theoretically possible. If, indeed, it is the whole man who is the thinker, what must be assumed to underlie the evolution of a symbolism that he shares with his fellows, symbols whose usage may have a simple referential function or which may become the targets of deep and shared projection? Speculation on this other unsolved problem leads us to Chapter Eleven.

REFERENCES

Numbers in brackets indicate the pages in this book where
given references occur

1. Binet, Alfred, see Chapter Seven.
2. Broad, C. D., Review of Price's *Thinking and Experience*, *Mind*, 1954, pp. 390-403.
3. Bruner, J. S. and others, *A Study of Thinking*, New York: Wiley, 1956.
4. Harding, D. W., *Experience into Words*, London: Chatto and Windus, 1963, pp. 108 (299), 176-7 (298-9), 192 (300).
5. Hull, C. L., *Psychological Monographs*, Vol. 28, No. 1, p. 123.
6. Humphrey, George, *Thinking: An Introduction to its Experimental Psychology*, London: Methuen, 1953.
7. Köhler, W., see Chapter Nine.
8. Locke, John, see Chapter Two.
9. Mundle, C. W. K., Review of Price's *Thinking and Experience*, *Philosophical Quarterly*, 1954, pp. 156-65.
10. Osgood, C. E., see Chapter Nine.
11. Piaget, Jean, *The Psychology of Intelligence*, London: Routledge & Kegan Paul, 1951.

CHAPTER ELEVEN

LANGUAGE, EXPLORATION AND INTERACTION

'So I wasn't dreaming, after all,' she said to herself, 'unless—unless we're all part of the same dream. Only I do hope it's *my* dream, and not the Red King's. I don't like belonging to another person's dream'.

Alice through the Looking Glass

Grün ist die Flur, der Himmel blau,
Doch tausend Farben spielt der Tau;
Es hofft die Erde bis zum Grabe,
Gewährung fiel dem Himmel zu;
Und sprich, was ist denn deine Gabe,
Gemüt, der Seele Iris du?

ANNETTE VON DROSTE-HÜLSHOFF*

CLASSICAL GREECE, as represented by Plato and Aristotle, related rational and irrational thought in ways, if not wholly different, yet varying in emphasis and implying in the long run a difference more profound.

For Plato,[17] rational thought was the activity of the immortal soul. At the core of rational thinking, at least when this was viewed as the route to infallible knowledge, lay the capacity to recognize in the sensorily presented, the $\epsilon \hat{\iota} \delta o s$, or abstract idea, which was there exemplified. For the Plato of the Socratic dialogues such recognition involved reference to another world. Knowledge was in fact recognition, and this belief underpinned arguments both for the pre-existence of the soul and for its

---

* Annette von Droste-Hülshoff is by common consent the greatest of Germany's woman poets. The citation is from a complex and mysterious poem in which she treats psychological responsiveness on analogy with the dew that, earthly and heavenly alike, reflects and transmutes the external world as does the imaginative wondering of a child. See Annette von Droste-Hülshoff, *Poems*, edited by Margaret E. Atkinson, Oxford University Press, 1964, pp. 155, 184.

immortality. The animal passions, and the more praiseworthy traits such as courage, had to come under the guidance of the rational soul before a man achieved the all-round integrated activity which classical Greece regarded, and applauded, as rational in a broader sense. Colouring Plato's approach was the asceticism that filtered into Christian theology, and the assumption that it is only part of the man, for Plato his immortal soul, that truly *thinks*, in the sense of attaining true concepts by means of recognition.

For Aristotle,[2] less attracted by the ascetic, and with a biological rather than Pythagorean and mathematical orientation, the slant was different, in spite of clear traces of Plato's earlier teaching. For the Aristotle of the *De Anima*, it was the whole man who thought; and the capacity for rational thinking, that distinguished man, presupposed the feeding, growth and reproductive capacities of living things and the sentience, desire and movement shared with animals below man in the biological scale. For Aristotle, this all-round capacity to think died with the man. It is true, of course, that Aristotle, perhaps still under Plato's influence, tried to combine this wider conception of thinking with the power to reflect logically that is involved in his doctrine of *nous*. Over the ages there has been a division of scholarly opinion on whether this last implied a personal, immortal soul that thought, or whether, in some obscure way, Aristotle was trying to treat the living and dying thinker as capable of exemplifying an impersonal rationality but not as in himself possessor of an immortal rational spark.

This historical controversy need not concern us. What is of interest is the difference between treating thinking as the activity of *part* of a man, and about which it makes sense to ask which part is functioning, and approaching thought as an activity of the whole man. In the second instance, questions about which part (or faculty) is functioning drop out, to be replaced by those of the criteria by which it may be convenient to distinguish thinking from any other activity in which the whole man may be involved.

Modern psychology has tried for long to get rid of faculties, which keep on popping up again disguised as abilities. It is still bedevilled by the temptation to section the personality, witness the stereotyped psycho-analytic view with a three-fold division as implausible as Plato's if taken literally. In general, psychologists have failed to face the whole-part problem, with two unfortunate results.

On the one hand, the strong position of the methodological behaviourist, endeavouring to approach the whole man and devise concepts and methods for describing what he does, has often been undermined by naïve behaviourism, with its atomism of reflexes, as bad as that of the associationists, and its temptation to identify psychological processes with the action of some section of the body. Hence, to take the more ludicrous and familiar examples, thinking, supposedly, *is* the movement of the larynx and imagining *is* the muscle tension in the arm, simply because experiment has suggested that these physical changes are involved when the whole man (poor fellow) tries to formulate the answer to a question or imagine moving his arm. The experimental findings are still of interest. But to *identify* any psychological process with a physical change, whether or not it is in some sense underlying, correlative or even integral to the process, is not merely to make a category mistake. It throws away the initial advantage of approaching the behaviour and experience of the whole person, so as to explore the means of describing it more systematically than the conceptual framework of soul, mind or faculties readily allows.

Failure to come to grips with the whole-part problem has led on the other hand to a curious position. Recognition, in one form, has been accepted without much question by many psychologists in their studies of remembering, whether or not these studies have emanated from behaviouristically-oriented laboratories. But it has been viewed with dark suspicion if brought forward as an important concept in describing perception, learning or thought. In that context its use is supposed to re-introduce 'mentalism' and mystery. Why? Partly for veridical reasons. Possibly its use does imply possession by mice and men of a capacity that we deny to sticks, stones and stars. This on the face of it is not dangerously heretical. Large stones in their turn have that extraordinary ability to stay in one place for centuries which we deny to men and even more to mice. There seems no *a priori* reason for being afraid of differences as such. There is more than this involved. In the context of perception and thinking, mention of recognition is tacitly supposed to imply that some *part* of the person must exercise this function. For vague historical reasons it is also often assumed that the user is smuggling back a distinct entity, the mind or soul, as the part in question. With Plato's approach a modern psychologist, rightly in my opinion, feels he is ill-fitted to cope. His reasons may be sound methodologically and philosophically. They were brilliantly outlined by William James[13] some seventy years ago. The reasons may be qualified by humility or by something far less commendable. One may ask, however, if the sensible experimentalist would be so chary of invoking recognition if it were filtered out of this historical, theological and metaphysical context. Might it not then come to be treated, *for scientific psychological purposes*, as one basic concept required among others for describing what a whole person (or animal) does when he perceives or thinks? This remains to be seen.

Assuming Aristotle was right, however, to say that it is the whole man who thinks, we are still left with the vast problem of the convenient criteria for distinguishing thought from action, and thought concerned with a world that is potentially share-able from that involving the private experiencing 'whereof one must be silent'—because an intelligible way of discussing it has not been forged. Let us glance at the first of these problems once more.

I have said and implied much in earlier chapters about the switch from a primarily inspectionist view of thinking to an approach that approximates thought to action. But I have also tried to show that psychologists having an interest in intelli-gence have generally avoided the radical step of equating action and thought, though this last is treated as a form of activity. Among the defenders of intelligence, and those of insight, there are echoes of the inspectionist viewpoint, in so far as processes such as recognition are retained. As used by Binet,[3] recognition of similarities was almost an epistemological prerequisite of any account of thought. For Piaget[16] it is one fundamental form of assimilation. Spearman's[24] perception of relations seems superficially in a rather different category at first, especially as he treated similarity as one relation to be perceived. There is a sense, however, in which Spearman's treatment both of perception of relations and eduction of correlates involves, among other processes, a sort of second-order recognition of similarities between relations. Among the other processes obviously involved are not only elementary retention, but also discrimination and comparison, i.e. some of the active operations to which Locke drew attention at the start of his *Essay*. Throughout this book I have implied that without some such remnants of the inspectionist viewpoint no account of either appropriate and effective or of logical thinking seems possible. So far as they go, such processes can be fairly classed as basic to thinking as an activity which also calls for greater retention to be effective. Are any other criteria of use?

For writers on intelligence, so far as they consider this problem, if thinking is a form of activity it is still sensible and desirable to distinguish it broadly from movement that is overt; witness Thurstone's[27] approach to intelligence as arising most characteristically when overt action is blocked. But this is a rough and ready distinction, which, if unsupported, breaks down when one is faced with highly *thoughtful* actions, for example, those of a surgeon on the one hand and an executant artist on the other. It is obvious that, say, a first-class operation (or the performance of a concerto) exemplifies thought formulated in an activity that is partly overt and of an extremely skilled and difficult kind. Simpler actions may also be formulations of thought. Hence one is driven to make another distinction, that between stimulus-bound, sign-directed and symbol-* directed activities, much high-grade skilled performance being a mixture of all three. Other activities exemplify these modes of response in varying proportions. Thus we class habits of any sort, whether verbal, muscular or motivational, as stimulus-bound and to that extent limited, even very limited, so far as they are classed as thinking at all. Skilled performance in any medium seems to be ranked as great, partly in terms of its symbolic content as well as the performer's technical command of the medium involved. Symbolic thought like the queen in chess has the greatest potential freedom of movement.

* In the user's sense of symbol implied by Harding[11] and Price.[18]

But if thought and action were psychologically distinguished partly by the degree and type of retention required, and the rôles of recognition, discrimination, comparison and the like, and partly by the incidence of stimulus, sign and symbolically-directed response, we have still to give some account of how such signs and symbols arise. This is to approach from a different angle the second central problem of a holistic approach to thought: that of differentiating the objective, i.e. potentially shareable, activity of thinking from that which is not, in so far as its direction involves private and personal responses apparently incapable of communicable formulation. Even verbalized associative thinking soon gets into this last class. The first few steps may be intelligible to someone of closely similar background. But there usually comes a point when identifying the reference or the governing theme is anybody's guess (or the psychotherapists' divination) unless the thinker is willing to earth his musings in some point of common reference, however surprising. There *can* be a swan sitting on the sun-dial or a parcel on a platform that spontaneously moves. So the speaker's verbalizations may be cashable in unusual or usual shared experience, but without some such earthing communication is lost. Thought processes hardly yet formulated at all put the thinker himself in the state of doubt epitomized in the famous comment: 'How can I know what I think until I have thought it?'

We have already encountered forms of this second major problem in Chapter Three on Spinoza, in Freud's[9] struggles to account for the rise of reality-oriented thinking and in Price's treatment of symbols and signs. It is worth attacking it again, but from the linguistic angle, in view of the great changes in approach to language, born of this century's work.

One corollary of the primarily visual approach to thinking was not merely the thorough-going inspectionism recently under philosophical fire. Intimately involved with it was belief in an unsubstantial pageant of sensations, images and ideas, the drop curtain between each of us and external reality and sometimes an iron curtain dropped between ourselves. It gave rise to curious problems, such as that of the existence of other minds. I would not wish to despise pageants or fail to give curtains, iron or imaginary, their appalling due. But it is one thing to speak, as little Armande[3] could do, of *pensée imagée* and even of a thinking about objects in which imagery plays no rôle. It is quite another to speak as if a crowd of individual and independent entities, sensations, images and derived ideas jostled around in a private container which both is and is not 'the mind'.

Until the 1920's, linguists in their turn tended to treat language as 'expressing' such images and ideas. It is true that fifteen years or so earlier, Russell, on logical grounds, had dispelled the notion that to every meaningful word there must correspond some *thing*, with the implied host of fictitious problems raised by significant statements about chimeras and round squares. It remains the case that as late as de Laguna's book, published in a different tradition in 1927, it was possible to cite numerous contemporary linguists all seeing language as *expressing* ideas. In an illuminating article appearing eight years later, Esper[7] drew attention to an assumption characteristic of this approach, namely that a one-one correspondence could exist between the inward emotion, idea or image, allegedly prior and then expressed, and the individual movements or words by which this last was achieved. He also highlighted important directions of change, in particular those derived from Dewey, from Ogden[15] and Richards, and from Malinowski's[14] important supplement to *The Meaning of Meaning*.

Viewed from an even longer distance, we can see some of these changes, for example, the linguist's challenge to the existence of 'ideas', as reflecting the impact of behaviouristic psychology. And after Freud's insistence on displacement, condensation and allied processes, few reflective writers can have continued to treat a verbal expression as always directly mirroring a feeling or thought. So far as Freud himself continued to talk about ideas, but lodged these fictitious entities in the unconscious, one may infer that either he did not fully realize the implications of his own insight or that his approach was too coloured by linguistic fashion to be clear.

In contrast to the influence of these broad developments, the impact of Dewey, Ogden and Richards, and Malinowski was more specific, in manifesting a shift of interest from language as expressing the speaker's point of view to language as evoking response in hearer or reader. This change of interest is apparent from the following. Dewey, quoted by Esper, was writing in 1926:

> The heart of language is not 'expression' of something antecedent, much less expression of antecedent thought. It is communication; the establishment of co-operation in an activity in which there are partners and in which the activity of each is modified and regulated by the partnership.

It is possible to sympathize with this change in approach to language without going so far as to accept Dewey's allied pragmatic theory of truth, of which Russell[21] legitimately and wittily made mincemeat. In the opening sections of *The Meaning of Meaning*, published in 1923, Ogden and Richards had maintained:

> We should develop our theory of signs from observations of other people, and only admit evidence drawn from introspection when we know how to appraise it. The adoption of the other method, on the ground that all our knowledge of others is inferred from knowledge of our own states, can only lead to the *impasse* of solipsism. . . . Those who allow beyond question that there are people like themselves also interpreting signs and open to study should not find it difficult to admit that their observation of the behaviour of others may provide at least a framework within which their own introspection, that special and deceptive case, may be fitted.

In fact, they implied, exclusive preoccupation with 'ideas' which are held to be expressed by speech, leads to neglect of the behaviour and concrete environment to which the speech is related.

In his brilliant supplementary essay to *The Meaning of Meaning*, Malinowski supported the move from focus on 'ideas expressed' to focus on the social function of language, bringing in arguments from social anthropology. Esper, I think rightly, contended that four main principles could be inferred from what Malinowski said; they can be summarized thus:

(1) The language of a group needs to be studied against the background of its general culture, mode of life and customs, and each utterance needs interpretation in its linguistic context and that of the whole situation in which it occurs.

(2) In their primitive forms, language and speech are modes of action, and indispensable links in concerted action. Their function as instruments of reflection is derivative.

(3) In so far as speech utterances are modes of *action*, meaning is definable primarily by the effects produced, both practical and social.

A word, signifying an important utensil, is used in action not to comment on its nature or reflect on its properties, but to make it appear to be handed over to the speaker, or to direct another man to its proper use.

(4) Basic grammatical structure and categories are an expression of categories corresponding to men's modes of behaviour, their practical ways of dealing with their environment, rather than a reflection of 'logical' categories.

It would be out of place here to attempt either to do justice to Ogden and Richards and to Malinowski or to comment on the fairly obvious weaknesses of their position if it is pushed too far. By implication I shall have more to say on this in a moment. Suffice it now that the move away from interest in 'expression of ideas' towards that of evoking response in others was a momentous step. Not least important was its lifting of the problem of linguistic reference, or 'meaning', out of a mysterious region inside the speaker's (or hearer's) head and into a species of shareable social space.

Following Sapir, and indirectly influenced by Russell, Whorf[29] appeared in the late 1920's, approaching in the opposite direction from Malinowski. Where the latter had argued, as against *a priori* logic, that grammatical structure and categories reflected men's modes of behaviour, Whorf was concerned to show that lexical and structural aspects of the language within which they had grown up could and did affect men's practical categorising of their worlds. Still later, experimentalists, for example, Roger Brown[5] and his associates, have shown that *lexical* differences can affect the categorising of apparently neutral sensory stimuli and the ease of recognizing those previously presented. Such lexical differences are exemplified in the range of expressions the Eskimos have for states of snow, or the Arabs have for those of a camel, compared with the relevant simple verbal resources in English. Brown and his colleagues reserve judgment on the effects of structural differences in languages.

Provided they are seen to be dealing with two different levels in a given language's usage, Malinowski and Whorf provide useful correctives to each other. For Malinowski may deter one from generalizing as far as Whorf in supposing that all the categories we employ are *merely* a matter of linguistic usage and in no way directed by natural fact. Conversely, Whorf draws attention to the genuine risk of promoting linguistic habits into laws of nature or of thought.

On Whorf's deduction of linguistic relativity one may comment that its plausibility rested on a tacit restriction of thinking to operations within some common, if geographically restricted, symbolic medium. While 'language is not a cloak following the contours of thought', it may still be true, as we saw in Chapter Ten, that *some* early stages of a process of thinking may develop outside such a common symbolism. This is consistent with sustained developed thinking needing a systematic symbolism for its maintenance,* and a common one if it is ever to be understood. In the nineteenth century, the Académie Française, driven to desperation by debate on the origins of language, issued its famous edict forbidding this question to raise its head again. One can sympathize fully with such desperation. But Whorf's tacit restriction of thinking to operation in a common symbolism makes it *a priori* impossible to see how any such symbolic medium ever could arise, whether it be Chinese, Hopi, Navaho or any of those languages classed by Whorf as 'standard average European'.

Supposing the rôle of language is at least as much evocative of overt response (and of thought) as it is a speaker's or writer's mode of formulating both, unless, like Ogden and Richards, one simply by-passes solipsism, the genesis of common reference

---

* Because of the need to lighten the load on retention, as Locke realized.

remains to be explained. How comes it that an *appropriate* response is evoked and by what criteria do we judge that it is so? When, for example, Malinowski's[14] fishermen ejaculated 'technical expressions completely untranslatable except by minute descriptions of the instruments used, and of the mode of action', how did their hearers know what to do? The current conventional answer is 'conditioning in early childhood', or whenever they learnt to fish. Will this do? Logically, we reach here the same position as in Chapter Six when an experimenter is studying a mouse's responses to presented soap and cheese. Can we say anything more interesting *psychologically*? What follows is no more than tentative speculation, suggested, in part, by the many recent studies of children (and monkeys) who are deprived. In view of the existence of autistic children, however, a skilled experimenter may perhaps distil from it a more precise hypothesis that is susceptible of check.

We argued in Chapter Five that, in developing reality-oriented thought, Freud was in danger of either going round in a circle, i.e. invoking discrimination and recognition in order to prove these can occur, or needing a wider range of motives than his theory could accommodate. Suttie in 1935 launched a different attack on Freud's position, the relevant contrast between his view and Freud's being shown in the following way.

Freud, as is well known, attempted to derive tender socialized responses from re-directed 'object love' of a sexual nature. This in its turn presupposed, developmentally, a primary narcissism which is theoretically consonant with the Freudian position, outlined in Chapter Five, whereby internally-originating stimuli are the most intense. Whereas many psycho-analysts have doubted the existence of primary narcissism, to my knowledge the possibility of direct social response has not been generally substituted for the *re*-directed primarily sexual response Freud posited. It would, indeed, be a major heresy to take such a step.

Suttie,[25] originally psycho-analytic in sympathy, started with a solipsism he believed similar to Freud's, in so far as he thought that in early life there is no initial discrimination of 'other' and 'self'. At the time of Suttie's writing, however, Freud's[9] *Project*, so revealing of the roots of his later views, was not yet published;

so the fundamental problems underlying the development of reality-oriented thinking had not fully declared themselves. Suttie thus developed an account of social, tender responses, not, I think, fully appreciating that it implied a total rejection of the epistemological solipsism, from which it is hard to rescue Freud without landing him with the other unpalatable alternatives sketched above. Let us look at Suttie's view in a little more detail, summarizing the relevant points under eight main headings.

1. For Suttie, the human infant is born with a primary biological need to attach itself to the mother, without whom, under natural conditions, it would in fact die.

2. The psychological aspect of this self-preservative attachment is probably reflected in the child's experience as a need for company and discomfort in isolation.

3. In the primary 'solipsistic' state there is no discrimination of 'other' from 'self'.

4. In contrast to Freud's view, for Suttie this undifferentiated condition gives place directly to one in which love and anger are both directed to others.

5. Love of others comes into being simultaneously with *recognition of their existence*. [Suttie's italics].

6. Hate is not a primal independent instinct but a development or intensification of separation anxiety aroused in turn by threat to love.

7. This primal love or attachment (and its obverse, anger) while it subserves self-preservation by maintaining the nurtural relation to the mother, is something more than the sum total of organic needs and gratifications and has a quality of tenderness from the start.

8. The original mother-child bond is vaguely and intuitively appreciated by the latter as one of mutual absorption, which as the baby develops interest in its own body and immediate surroundings, gradually gives way to a companionship of interest. Suttie adds:

> It is of course arbitrary to say at what point the *companionship of love* becomes the *companionship of interest*, but there is no doubt that the feeling-relationship of the companions

does change *as attention ceases to be absorbed wholly and reciprocally each in the other and becomes directed convergently to the same things*. Co-operative activities, identical or complementary attitudes to outside happenings, build up a world of *common meanings* which marks a differentiation from simple love, wherein 'the world' of each is the other person. The simple direct bond has become a triangular relationship wherein external objects form the *medium of play*.[25]

In this position of Suttie's, two points are worth especial note. First, while we may reasonably believe that the so-called solipsism of proposition 3 describes a probable state of affairs, propositions 4 and 5 imply a straight denial of epistemological solipsism. In fact they suggest the possibility of some direct, *potentially social*, response normally focused on, or elicited by, the biological mother. It might or might not turn out to be confined to her, species specific or elicited to the full only by living things or those initially appearing to respond as such. But to raise these qualifying questions is to approach Suttie in the light of what came after.

Our second point relates to the rather curious history of Suttie's viewpoint. On first publication, in 1935, *The Origins of Love and Hate* was well reviewed but seems to have constituted too overt an attack on Freud for its wider implications to be fully appreciated by many people. Furthermore, in Suttie's exposition his theory was not tightly related to hard-boiled empirical observations. Though this comment may perhaps exemplify the 'taboo on tenderness' on which he laid stress, Suttie's writing is still apt to strike both the ordinary and the psychologically-sophisticated reader, at ease in the company of very small children, as verging on the sentimental. One is fobbed off, in effect, with Malinowski's 'phatic communion' when one asks for far more precise indications of the kind of observation which would lead one to place some relationships clearly within Suttie's first class, and others as exemplifying shared awareness and exploration of surroundings. This is granting the existence of borderline situations in which distinctions are arbitrary.

Suttie died on the day of his book's publication. So elaboration of his views in response to critical comment was out of the question. The book remained in print until 1959. In 1960 it was re-issued as a Pelican. In the meantime, three lines of research had got well under way, which now show some signs of converging at a point wherein Suttie's obscure realization of the function of *shared* awareness and interest, in stabilizing and partly creating a common perceptual (and referential) world, might prove of value. But it is rare to find Suttie cited in the most relevant publications. Bowlby[4] provides an exception.

Of these three lines of research, by far the most obviously important is that into maternal deprivation and its effects. Many investigations in this direction were stimulated not by Suttie, who seems to have first used the phrase 'separation anxiety' in this context, but by Bowlby's insistence, since the early 1940's, on the adverse outcome of separation from mother or mother substitute in early childhood. But, as Professor Ainsworth[1] implies in her admirably balanced conclusion to the W.H.O.[30] report of 1962, the sometimes conflicting evidence from these inquiries needs to be flanked with that from learning theory on the one hand and animal ethology on the other (and supplemented by more studies of *normal* human interaction) before its precise *theoretical* significance can be assessed. This is notwithstanding the fact that enough evidence exists of the harmful effects, at certain stages of a child's development, of deprivation (with or without separation from a permanent mothering personality), for its practical import to be taken very seriously. From a theoretical standpoint, Bowlby's grasp of the relevance of ethological concepts and methods for the study of human social development is seen by Ainsworth as his most significant contribution in the past ten years.

From the vast literature on learning theory, animal ethology and on these human effects of maternal deprivation, I propose to highlight only certain implications which bear on the problem of linguistic reference with which we are here concerned. I then want to suggest where a more carefully formulated version of Suttie's view might be brought back into currency in guiding further controlled observations of normal infant-adult interaction, and that between an infant and friendly older children.

From developments in learning theory we need to extract

two main considerations. First, the evidence of latent learning in animals (i.e. of learning when no obvious biological deficit, such as hunger, thirst or sex, is removed) has led many investigators to widen their list of basic drives by reintroducing some such concept as exploration, curiosity or 'effort after meaning', even when it is the humble rat who is supposedly seeking knowledge for its own sake. It is just possible to cram such an exploratory concept into the currently fashionable homeostatic model by assuming that for a given organism a certain level of cognitive confusion (or dissonance) induces a conflict, tension or fear that needs to be reduced.

Secondly, there is the evidence, perplexing particularly for the more rigid Hullian type of behaviourist, that skills learnt under partial reinforcement are more resistant to extinction than those learnt by full reinforcement. That is to say, a skill learnt under conditions of intermittent reward, and failure to find a reward, are retained longer when no further reward is forthcoming than those originally learnt under conditions of regular reward. There is no current agreement on how these facts are to be explained. But the existence both of the experimental findings and of controversy lends some support to rising doubts on the adequacy of the need-reduction model of motivation for explaining *all* kinds of activity. Is it remotely possible that, in the experiments resulting in this finding, the animals had no tension 'reduced' by exploration, or by intermittent finding of peanuts or food pellets, but derived a certain amount of enjoyment in just doing something skilled or in having a look round? Why does a woman revel in knitting or shop-gazing when she neither needs the garments nor attempts to buy? It is very hard to say on any of the homeostatic theories of motivation and much easier to account for in Aristotelian terms, wherein the acquisition and exercise of a skill is intrinsically pleasant—including, one must add, the skill of domestic discrimination!

In short, two great strands of evidence from learning theory point on the one hand to the existence of an 'exploratory' drive and on the other to the possibility that 'need reduction' or 'removal of deficit', though fundamental, may not suffice as a motive for *all* kinds of activity.

Two main contributions from animal ethology also have to be stressed. First is the evidence produced for an optimum period in the acquisition of certain responses. For example, a budgerigar will learn human speech only up to a certain age and not if it lives in the company of one of its own species. This notion of an optimum period for imprinting remains of interest, whether further research succeeds in showing that the difficulty of acquiring a new response after a certain stage of development is due to loss of an inherent receptivity or to the intervention of other processes. For example, if a hand-reared gosling adopts its human caretaker, does it fail to respond later to its own mother goose because the peak of receptivity is past or is it because she has taken on the status of something strange and alarming? And is this process reversible and, if so, how?

The second main contribution from the animal ethologists lies in their ingenious experimental methods for studying the type of sensory patterning or stimulus that evokes specific responses in members of different species. Tinbergen's[28] studies of the beak-opening of the herring chick and von Frisch's[10] studies in *The Dancing Bees* are well-known classics in this field. For authoritative discussion of all this evidence the reader is referred to the second edition of Thorpe's[26] *Learning and Instinct in Animals*.

Turning now to the literature on maternal deprivation, we find three specially relevant points to be stressed. In the first place, it is of historical interest to realize how the initially somewhat vague notion that separation from mother or mother substitute is of importance, has become so sharpened by controversy and careful investigation, that, as Ainsworth has clearly argued, three distinct conditions need to be distinguished. These are: (a) insufficiency of interaction between infant and ministering adult; (b) 'distortion in the character of the interaction, without respect to its quantity'; and (c) 'the discontinuity of relations brought about through separation'. Distortion would be illustrated by hostility, over-indulgence or repressive control.

Our second point relates to the effects of deprivation. Ainsworth[1b], summarizing most of the available research findings up to 1961, comments as follows:

Maternal deprivation has a differential effect on different processes: most vulnerable seem to be certain intellectual processes, especially language and abstraction, and certain aspects of personality, most especially the ability to establish and maintain deep and meaningful interpersonal relations, but also the ability to control impulse in the interest of long-range goals. There is some reason to believe that the age of the child—more accurately, the state of development of the child—has an influence on the processes affected; thus, for example, it seems reasonable to conclude from present evidence that deprivation during the first year of life affects language and abstract functioning (and indirectly the I.Q. or D.Q.) more than does deprivation later on. It seems likely that discontinuity of relations has its chief effect on the capacity for affectional ties, especially in instances where separation from mother-figures is important.

It is tempting, on theoretical grounds, to speculate on the possibility that these two upshots are interrelated. On the one hand, without a caretaker who patiently and affectionately responds to the infant and shares the environment with him, the child is retarded in learning to categorize at all, or to categorize the world of experience in the same or approximately the same way as the adult. But without some acquired skill in such categorization the difficulty of sharing the experienced world is automatically enhanced. This adds its own quota of trouble in future social relations. Even with the normal adult equipment of well-established categories, it is notoriously hard to maintain a relationship that has much significance with large numbers of people, those who come but go, or those who return only after an interval of time beyond one's grasp. For an adult it is also extremely difficult to establish or maintain significant social rapport with those whose atrocious memories prevent their picking up conversations where they were left before interruption. Small wonder if the infant with multiple caretakers (of whom he has no clear concepts) or caretakers with multiple infants, whose transmitted signals of recognition (if any) are pre-linguistic, encounter insoluble and disheartening problems. This is not to say that only one person should ever care for a new-born child. On present evidence this extreme would seem to bring other drawbacks in its train. But the findings do suggest that a small constellation of recurrent figures, round a central permanent one, gives the best chance of all parties being able to integrate cognitively and socially in the processes of exploring potentially structurable experience, and of building a sustaining system of social and linguistic links by that experience being shared.

But what can we possibly mean by experience that is *shared*? This is the point where perhaps a more specific version of Suttie's view would carry us on into the field of careful observation and experiment in *normal* circumstances, of which Ainsworth stresses the need and which is just opening up in work such as that reported in *Determinants of Infant Behaviour*.[8]

To suggest that adult and infant can experience 'the same thing' would be to beg the whole question with which we are here concerned, namely that of the basis of the *referential* use of language in which any common systematic symbolism is rooted. To take a simple example, what is merely warm bath water to the hardened hand of an adult is blazing hot to the infant, as judged by his immediate cringing or crying. Moreover, the sensory content of adult experience is enmeshed in a system of acquired interpretations. Assuming that the infant can slowly come to recognize that which recurs in its experience and is broadly 'similar', whether it be in fact the taste and smell of warm milk or the kinaesthetic or tactile experiences of being handled in recurrently similar ways, we have got to shift the emphasis away from content to response before we can make any sense of the notion of recognition *shared*. Such a shift would be consistent with the current emphasis on the activity of perception in contrast to the stress of former theory on its presented sensory content. Possibly, as part and parcel of the 'effort after meaning', 'dislike of cognitive dissonance', or any of the other current concepts theoretically linked with the reinstated 'exploratory drives', we may have to inquire for evidence of attempts on the part of human infants to calibrate their selective attention with that of the adult, just as, in an ordinarily good nursery, adults and children spend considerable time calibrating theirs with that of the baby. His wandering attention or gurgles are often focused on something, and by a process of trial and error surrounding onlookers seek to find out what this is. Is this a process that he is either born to reciprocate or with a little encouragement acquires very early in life? And is it this which, biologically, subserves the constitutive symbolizing tendency which Cassirer[6] thought characteristic of human beings?

Ainsworth has laid stress on the 'inadequate interaction' that is involved in deprivation. Some experimenters, e.g. Joyce Robertson,[20] have already started to focus their observation on what this 'interaction' involves. Schaffer,[23] on the basis of studying hospitalized children, and at first excluding the evidence from those for whom fever, pain or the like might be clearly relevant, found two major patterns of response according to whether separation and deprivation took place before or after about 7 months of age. Later follow-up, including those too ill to have been studied initially, suggested that those deprived of sustained interaction before 7 months of age were characterized by 'inactive, quiet preoccupation with the environment, by a scanning of surroundings without particular focus, and by a lack of responsiveness to social advances'. This suggests that focusing, interaction and social response sometimes go together.

So far as I know, however, the theoretical modification of Suttie I am suggesting has not been fully considered. It is to hypothesize that, in the human infant, part of the so-called clinging or following response, so beautifully shown by Harlow[12] to exist in infant monkeys, and on which Bowlby has laid stress as existing in human beings, involves in their case an obscure attempt to calibrate observation with that of another member of the species (primarily the mother) and to seek for evidence that that calibration has occurred. At a simple level, the adult dealing with a pre-linguistic child looks and points towards something, the child follows the adult movements or set and not infrequently looks back at the adult to see if his discrimination and recognition tally.* Note, however, the object becomes

* Conversely, Ainsworth has noted as specially striking 'the extent to which the infant himself takes the initiative in seeking an interaction'. 'At least from two months of age onwards, and increasingly through the first year of life,' the infants she observed 'were not so much passive and recipient as active in seeking interaction.'[8]

common by virtue, in part at least, of shared response and not exclusively the other way round; though Suttie was right, of course, in thinking that, at a later stage, shared observation and interest in things and activities, now accepted as 'objective', can itself act as social cement. But, as in the case of social contact between adults, an infant's proffered sharing needs reciprocation. Before he can really talk, a baby may hand an adult its empty bottle, making a noise remarkably like 'ished'. The adult takes the bottle, enunciating 'finished' very slowly, and an equally slow smile spreads across the baby's face. What happens when such social acts are persistently overlooked or snubbed?* Such anecdotal evidence requires far more systematic check, for we have at present no knowledge of the precise nature of the cognitive/social process apparently involved or the stage at which it can reliably be seen to occur. Could it, for example, possibly, if obscurely, antedate visual focusing? Is the latter preceded in any sense by some sort of tactile or kinaesthetic equivalent?

Some such shared categorizing seems to precede the acquisition of language. And no doubt some recurrent roughly similar sounds are linked with established categories by a simple conditioning process. Thereafter, however, categorizing and the acquisition of language are bound, in part at least, to go hand in hand. But this is to give the Whorf hypothesis only a limited validity. For it remains theoretically (and we hope practically) possible for the original child or adult thinker to experience freshly and perhaps contribute his own quota to the conceptualizations embedded in his mother tongue.

Such emphasis on the exploratory, conceptually-constitutive aspects of infant-adult interaction is dictated in part by need to stress the relevance of this literature on maternal deprivation to our question about the referential use of language. Some readers may feel that it is unduly academic and intellectual to underline the cognitive implications of this research, with less than usual emphasis on the emotional and therapeutic. But as I have

---

* I have deliberately omitted: (i) the problem of the over-stimulated child, and the exhausted parent without skill in diverting interest to other people, (ii) elaborating on the rôle of other children in helping to satisfy an infant's structuring needs.

already suggested, the cognitive and social cannot really be divorced. Moreover, such an objection would seem itself to be coloured by an out-of-date Platonic assumption that thought and emotion are of necessity opposed. We saw in Chapter Ten that Piaget had successfully avoided this pitfall. And it is refreshing to find recent investigators, for example Rheingold,[19] once more referring naturally to the normal child's *glee* in the exercise of a simple cognitive skill. In the current advance towards careful controlled observation of the normal, mobilizing the experimental methods of ethology, and with the intent to treat 'interaction' with greater freshness and precision, we have the third contribution to our topic from studies of maternal deprivation.

Plato somewhat bedevilled 'recognition' by denying it a sensory basis, and making it the activity of the immortal soul. As Russell[21] comments, he forgot about the cortex. In now stressing recognition and suggesting, moreover, that the process can be shared, there is no need to make any mystical assumptions and much need to experiment, in order both to make the notion more precise and to specify the conditions in which sharing seems to occur. These should include studies of the recognizer's bodily state and stage of neurological and allied development.* In so doing we imply with Aristotle (and Binet) that it is the whole man who thinks (and recognizes). We add to this the suggestion that on occasion he can guess, with a high degree of probability, that one or more of his fellow creatures is actively doing the same.

The Parthenon, sunlit, remains a lovely thing, capable of catching the stranger unawares, and even those who have been nurtured in its sight. It has indeed a profound austerity. But to a modern psychologist there would appear a vein of intellectualist sentimentality in implying that it is either the product or the symbol of 'pure abstract thought'. True that historically it has deeply tragic associations, as well as those of victories bought at untold cost, in the lives of ancient and modern believers in freedom to think. In all its shining stillness, however, it is also a

---

* It is arguable, for example, that recognition requires an intact feedback mechanism operating between the hypothalamus, the pituitary and thyroid glands and the central nervous system, as well as intact receptors.

symbol of intensely hard and effective activity. How did the architectural plans get drawn? How did men and animals get those stones into place? The Parthenon, whether sunlit, floodlit as a modern building, or lit by a full moon as becomes the very old, evokes not thought *or* emotion but the two inextricably mixed, in the state of 'arousal' that physiologists and psychologists now seek to describe and of which the normal outcome is also some sort of activity. What form this takes will depend on the person, his past, present and future and the skills and circumstances of his individual life.

A polyglot bunch of tourists clambering round the place in the dark, and emitting 'Gee!', 'Whew!', '*Schön!*', and all their international equivalents, do not doubt that a roughly similar something has caught their varying eyes. Nor do they doubt, on occasion, that variously jagged stones are catching internationally-varying feet. The path up the Acropolis remains just sufficiently hazardous to remind one of the more serious perils of ever trying to think. The smile arising from recognition of shared awareness may be obvious in the sunlight and cut across linguistic failure to understand. Some degree of such shared awareness is not impossible in the dark. It can, indeed, be intensified in seriously adverse conditions, when a task reveals its potentiality for really grave risk. Under any conditions, however, recognition is far from infallible, and precise veridical shared recognition may be very rare indeed, a fact of which Greek drama made great play. Only approximate in its daily use, except perhaps among those who have loved and thought together for years, it probably remains the best cognitive link that we have. As I have tried to argue, shared recognition that recognition is occurring lies at the root of our use of symbols, whether logically systematized or projective, and for complex thinking some symbolic system is needed.

As moderns, most of us cannot subscribe to the lofty additions with which classical Greece, in the form of Plato, surrounded simple recognition as a psychological process. We do not take kindly to Pythagorean mysticism, reincarnation or a supernatural world of archetypal ideas. But in returning to Aristotle's whole man who thinks, I do not see why we should reject the element of psychological truth that Plato perceived. For us this straightforward and simple process may be given a humbler setting for its early development. Platonic loftiness and asceticism never convinced Héloise. Freud's insistence on disappointment as the tragic teacher, while true to the tone of the Oedipus myth, omits all consideration of the outlook of Antigone, dying like her lover, to keep affiliation alive. Nor, curiously, did Freud ever come to grips, theoretically, with laughter, so often the nursery product of recognition shared and by no means the same sort of phenomenon as wit. Greek recognition, without its contextual overtones, seems needed as a corrective to the Freudian over-insistence on blind biological drive to the exclusion of a little child's social and exploratory delight.

But if thinking as a total and motivated activity needs to be rooted in recognition for its formulation to begin (whether the early stages of formulation lie in incipient actions, in images or in words), for complex thought a symbol system is required, to ease the load on our power to retain and develop the data and relationships which such thought involves. And for communicable thinking to occur, that symbol system must be one that is shared. Following Binet, Piaget, Suttie, the ethologists, the current workers on maternal deprivation and, indeed, something near to pedestrian common-sense, I have stressed the early setting in which this sharing makes its start. Only more research can show how much later progress can be made if this early start is lost. With or without the early setting that makes a delight of some symbolic concept formation, the later stages of this process, as Piaget has shown, are only gradually acquired. Each of the potentially symbolic media that we use as adults, whether these be plastic, visual, musical, mathematical, or the more generally familiar linguistic, has its long history of overtones and implications. Part, of course, of learning to think lies in learning to handle a medium with its own laws and with what the Italians call *le sfumatore della lingua*.

It is one of the ironies of history that in the nineteenth century man saw himself humiliated by his relation to the apes, while in the twentieth it is evidence from animals and children that may convince us we can think. It would be tragic, not ironic, to disregard these clues. For making a friendly and interesting nursery is partly within our control and some nursery skills come not amiss in sophisticated life. These include, of course, the handling of hunger and thirst, of sex and aggression and of attempts to explore and structure the physical world in which we live. A wise nursery also assumes and encourages interest in social response and it throws in for good measure the skilled sharing of a joke.

REFERENCES

1. Ainsworth, Mary D., (a) see Foss, B. M., (b) see World Health Organization, pp. 97-159.
2. Aristotle, *De Anima*, translated by J. A. Smith in *The Works of Aristotle*, edited by W. D. Ross, Oxford: Clarendon Press, Vol. III, 1931. *Ethica Nicomachea*, translated by W. D. Ross, London: Oxford University Press, 1931.
3. Binet, Alfred, see Chapter Seven.
4. Bowlby, John, 'The Nature of the Child's Tie to his Mother', *International Journal of Psycho-analysis*, Vol. XXXIX, 1958; see also Foss, B. M., Vols. I and II.
5. Brown, Roger, see Saporta, Sol.
6. Cassirer, Ernst, *An Essay on Man*, New Haven: Yale University Press, 1944.
7. Esper, E. A., 'Language' in *Handbook of Social Psychology*, edited by Carl Murchison, London: Oxford University Press, 1935, pp. 417-60.
8. Foss, B. M., editor, *Determinants of Infant Behaviour*, London: Methuen, Vol. I, 1961; Vol. II, 1963, p. 101.
9. Freud, Sigmund, see Chapter Five.
10. Frisch, Karl von, *The Dancing Bees*, translated by Dora Ilse, London: Methuen, 1954.
11. Harding, D. W., see Chapter Ten.
12. Harlow, H., see Foss, B. M., Vols. I and II.
13. James, William, *Principles of Psychology*, London: Macmillan, 2 Vols., 1890, Vol. I, Chap. 10.
14. Malinowski, B., 'Supplementary Essay' in *The Meaning of Meaning*, see Ogden, C. K., and Richards, I. A.
15. Ogden, C. K., and Richards, I.A., *The Meaning of Meaning*, London: Kegan Paul, 1923.
16. Piaget, Jean, see Chapter Eight.

17. Plato, *The Dialogues of Plato*, translated by Benjamin Jowett, London: Oxford University Press.
18. Price, H. H., see Chapter Ten.
19. Rheingold, H. L., see Foss, B. M., Vol. I.
20. Robertson, Joyce, see World Health Organization, pp. 121, 164.
21. Russell, Bertrand, *A History of Western Philosophy*, London: Allen & Unwin, 1946, pp. 176, 850 ff.
22. Saporta, Sol., and Bastian, J. P., *Psycholinguistics: a book of readings*, New York: Holt, 1961.
23. Schaffer, H. R., see World Health Organization, pp. 138 ff., 164.
24. Spearman, C., see Chapter Eight.
25. Suttie, Ian, *The Origins of Love and Hate*, London: Penguin Books, 1960.
26. Thorpe, W. H., *Learning and Instinct in Animals*, London: Methuen, 2nd edition, 1963.
27. Thurstone, L. L., see Chapter Eight.
28. Tinbergen, N., (a) *Social Behaviour in Animals*, London: Methuen, 1953; (b) *The Study of Instinct*, Oxford: Clarendon Press, 1951.
29. Whorf, Benjamin Lee, *Language, Thought and Reality: selected writings of B. L. Whorf*, edited by J. B. Carroll, New York: Wiley, 1956.
30. World Health Organization, *Deprivation of Maternal Care*, Public Health Papers 14, Geneva: 1962.

INDEX